SURVIVING POVERTY

Surviving Poverty

Creating Sustainable Ties among the Poor

Joan Maya Mazelis

NEW YORK UNIVERSITY PRESS

New York

NEW YORK UNIVERSITY PRESS
New York
www.nyupress.org

© 2017 by New York University
All rights reserved

ISBN: 978-1-4798-7359-3 (hardback)
ISBN: 978-1-4798-7008-0 (paperback)

For Library of Congress Cataloging-in-Publication data, please contact the Library of Congress.

New York University Press books are printed on acid-free paper, and their binding materials are chosen for strength and durability. We strive to use environmentally responsible suppliers and materials to the greatest extent possible in publishing our books.

Manufactured in the United States of America

10 9 8 7 6 5 4 3 2 1

Also available as an ebook

Dr. Steven Shapiro, my English teacher during my senior year of high school, once told me, "Whatever you decide to do in life, make sure that it matters, and that it matters to you." I dedicate this book to Nancy Brook (Jacobs) LaFrenz (1974–2005) and to Joe Cytrynbaum (1972–2009), for reminding me what matters.

And to Amelia and Sam, and to all the children of the study participants whose stories appear in this book: may the world grow kinder, and may we all work together to make it so.

CONTENTS

On December 16, 2003, activists from the Kensington Welfare Rights Union (KWRU) stage a protest outside the mayor's office in Philadelphia's City Hall to demand "Homes for the Holidays." People gather at 4 p.m. and stay for several hours. Singing Christmas carols, the activists share food one of them has made and brought for dinner—they scoop the bean stew into small plastic bowls and pass them throughout the crowd, making sure the many children present eat first. Someone passes out bread. A leader calls on people individually to tell their stories. Each one of them says she is a homeless member of the Kensington Welfare Rights Union. The leader tells them never to be ashamed of their homelessness. The group sings more Christmas carols, and then someone brings out a cake; it is one of the children's birthdays. Another leader begins to sing a song:

> I went down to the rich man's house, I took back what he stole from me. . . . I took my humanity, took back my dignity . . .

The children and activists join in and the group begins to sing the verse again, with a slight variation:

> I went down to the mayor's house, I took back what he stole from me. . . .
> I took my humanity, took back my dignity . . .

Soon administrators agree to meet with the homeless individuals, one at a time, and ask them questions. One member tells me they ask her things like, "How long have you been homeless?" "Where are you staying now?" "How many kids do you have? "Why are you homeless?" Eventually administrators offer to put people, for that night, into shelters, but KWRU leaders say that is unacceptable, that their numbers include some domestic violence victims who can't be safe in shelters, and that these shelters themselves say that they are not set up to deal with victims of domestic violence.

As KWRU activists argue and administrators stand their ground, a Civil Affairs officer announces to the crowd, "It's 7:08 p.m. This is your first warning. The building is closed, so you'll need to exit. You will get another warning—in five minutes I will say 'it's 7:13. It's time to go.' And five minutes after that anyone who's still here will be arrested."

The crowd begins to disperse, with many of the adults herding all the children downstairs and outside. A few minutes after everyone regroups outside, a police van drives off with five KWRU activists inside, five women who decide they are willing to be arrested to prove their point. A news camera follows the ones who remain, and one woman shouts, "How can you arrest people for being homeless?!" The city hall officials begin to walk back through the city hall gate, and close it behind them.

A few weeks after the protest, I learn KWRU has secured five housing vouchers for members, many believe as a result of their protest. As Walter says of the group, "Our strength is in our unity, is in our coming together." It was that way that night.

I conducted the research for this book from 2003 through 2006, with some follow-up in 2014–2016. I attended this protest and a number of others, and spent a good deal of time at KWRU's office. This book is based in part on observations from these field experiences, but mostly on semi-structured interviews with twenty-five KWRU members and twenty-five people unaffiliated with KWRU who are also extremely poor Philadelphians. Many of the participants have lived their entire lives in poverty, often in the same or nearby neighborhoods they live in when I meet them. A few participants had slightly more economically secure childhoods on the lowest rungs of the middle class ladder, but have lost their footholds because of a disruption such as a parent's drug addiction or death.

The majority of participants in this study have experienced homelessness, and some were homeless at the time of the interviews. This book addresses social support, social capital, and isolation—emotional subjects with significant economic effects for these desperately poor people. As KWRU member Walter tells me, to describe why members need the community KWRU provides, "you show me a poor person, or a homeless person, I'll show you somebody that's isolated." The weakening of the public safety net accompanying widening inequality in the United States has increased the significance of such isolation.

This book illustrates some of the problems that make the drastic reduction of state aid disastrous for the nation's poorest. It describes problems no private safety net can solve, in spite of a growing rhetoric that refuses to provide state support. Yet KWRU is a non–kin-based private safety net, uncommonly strong, that has flourished among the poor in Philadelphia. I argue that this private safety net significantly lessens members' struggles. I conclude this book with proposals based on my findings, such as funding organizations built on the most effective aspects of KWRU, that are achievable even in the current policy environment.

ACKNOWLEDGMENTS

I am grateful to many people and institutions that helped make this study possible. I wholeheartedly thank Ilene Kalish, Caelyn Cobb, and NYU Press for believing in this project, and for their expert assistance. I thank production editor Alexia Traganas, copy editor Usha Sanyal, and the entire NYU Press team for their careful attention and hard work. I am deeply grateful to four anonymous reviewers for their constructive and supportive advice, which I have no doubt made the book better than it would have been without their guidance. Errors and omissions that remain are my own. A University of Pennsylvania School of Arts and Sciences Dissertation Fellowship Award in 2003–2004, two grants from the Otto and Gertrude K. Pollak Summer Research Fellowship fund from the University of Pennsylvania Sociology Department, in 2002 and 2003, and a National Science Foundation Doctoral Dissertation Improvement Grant Award in 2004–2005 enabled the research phase. In the writing phase, I benefited from an NSF/RU FAIR ADVANCE Mini-Grant and a Research Council Grant at Rutgers University.

My graduate school mentors, Kathryn Edin, Douglas Massey, and David Grazian, showed me unending patience and shared insightful advice and unwavering support over the years. Dave stepped up to fill a role on my committee without even knowing much about my work and offered valuable advice. Doug was always prompt with constructive criticism, and has demonstrated incredible flexibility, loyalty, and encouragement. Over the years, he's taken every opportunity to let me know he'll always be in my corner. Kathy has been advisor, mentor, friend, and cheerleader. She pushed me to work beyond limits I perceived, always having faith that I could do more. She believed in my strengths and forgave my weaknesses, and I feel lucky to say we've been in a mutual admiration society for nearly eighteen years. She continues to always make time for me at conferences, so we can discuss my work over an early breakfast or an afternoon coffee. I would not be the sociologist I am today without her.

Also at the University of Pennsylvania, Kristen Harknett and Elaine Simon both offered support and advice. The late Michael Katz provided guidance in the early stages of this project and his work continues to be a source of inspiration. Amy Hillier was a classmate in an Urban Studies seminar Michael Katz taught in 1998–1999, and now is at the Cartographic Modeling Laboratory and a professor in the Department of City Planning in the School of Design at the University of Pennsylvania. Amy sat down with me to create multiple maps for my first write-up of this research. A decade later she created the revised, consolidated map that appears in this book. Her expertise is evident, and I am lucky to have her as a friend.

Xavier de Souza Briggs was exceedingly generous with guidance, moral support, and research opportunities on the Three-City Study of Moving to Opportunity when he was at Harvard University and MIT that allowed me to think about my own research in new ways; Xav is an intellectual role model as well as a friend. And working on the MTO project gave me the opportunity to meet and become friends with several others who've offered support and advice as well: Carla Barrett, Maria Rendon, Cynthia Velazquez Duarte, and Silvia Domínguez.

Friends and colleagues have helped more than they realize. As this book demonstrates, social ties really do matter. Matthew Desmond, Judith Levine, Mario Luis Small, Sandra Susan Smith, and Celeste Watkins-Hayes are all scholars I've been fortunate to meet at conferences who have given me deeply valued advice and encouragement, as have editors Naomi Schneider, Suzanne Nichols, and Peter Mickulas. At Yeshiva University I was lucky to find so much support among my colleagues, especially Silke Aisenbrey, Lauren Fitzgerald, and Stephen Pimpare. At Rutgers University, student Brendan Gaughan provided helpful research assistance. The invaluable secretary of the Department of Sociology, Anthropology, and Criminal Justice, Sherry Pisacano, has consistently gone above and beyond to offer moral as well as practical support. My departmental colleague Stacia Gilliard-Matthews and former Associate Chancellor for Civic Engagement Andrew Seligsohn, now moved on from his role at Rutgers-Camden to be president of Campus Compact, have been there for me without fail, with open arms and open ears. Their support, along with that of Marie Chevrier, Mary Beth Daisey, Tyler Hoffman, Natasha Fletcher, Howard Marchitello, Lori Minnite, and Melissa Yates has made Rutgers an environment conducive to this book's publication. I thank Lauren Silver, a friend since graduate school and now a colleague at Rutgers, for an early read-through of a draft of the reciprocity chapter. Paul Jargowsky has consistently helped me move forward and encouraged me in numerous ways. I am lucky to have him as a mentor and supporter at Rutgers. Dean Kriste Lindenmeyer is the kind of Dean assistant professors wish for: endlessly supportive, positive, and with boundless faith in my work and my ability to do it.

While mentioning some would surely mean omitting many, friends from graduate school have alternately listened, offered advice, and lent an ear or a shoulder. Friends old and new offered their encouragement online and in person. Helen Lee read an early version of a book proposal and offered sound advice to strengthen my policy recommendations. Monica Flory and Caroline Tiger, friends and fellow writers in my neighborhood, provided much-needed company many days at our local coffee shop. That coffee shop, Philadelphia Java Company (Java), and its owners and baristas, allowed me to sit for hours and work. My neighborhood is a reminder of the beauty of what social ties can offer. I am incredibly fortunate to have too many social ties in this little community to name, who've cheered me on as I wrote this book—and Java served as a common meeting place.

Keith Brown, David Cohen, Silvia Domínguez, Jamie Fader, Tanya Golash-Boza, Joanna Kempner, and Susan Markens offered help as I navigated the book process, with humor and insight, as did departmental colleagues Cindy Dell Clark and Cati Coe. Bridget Costello's friendship and support are unmatched, and over the years she has become the kind of friend some people only dream of. The members of my online writing support group, Daily Writing Updates, are largely strangers to me, but I've greatly appreciated the comfort and help these fellow writers and academics provide.

Jamie Fader and Joanna Kempner both suggested I look into securing a developmental editor when I was early in the book-writing process. It might be the best advice I've ever gotten. Showing the value of ties that last, I asked my childhood friend, Kate Epstein, who had worked as an editor, if she knew of anyone who could serve this role. Kate said she could, and so began a period in which I have received the best editorial help any academic writer ever could. Kate helped me think through big ideas to come up with the story arc for the book, gently suggested additions and changes to make my argument clearer and stronger, and was at times alternatingly friend, coach, therapist, and editor.

My family has been exceedingly patient. My mother-in-law, Dee Auclair, has been supportive throughout the process. My late father-in-law Mike Auclair passed away too soon to see this book in print, but his certainty it would be published boosted my ego at an important juncture. My sister, brother-in-law, niece, and nephew—Lorraine, Brian, Shaina, and Cooper Flaherty—have been incredibly encouraging, and the arrival of my infant nephew Benen provided a welcome distraction in summer 2015. My parents, Anne and Jack Mazelis, have provided emotional—and financial—sustenance that made this all possible. My mother was my first editor and is my biggest fan, and has caught minor errors countless times over the years. My father sees the applicability of my work to everything he reads, and is always eager to share his discoveries with me to show me the relevance of this project. They both listened as I planned and conducted the research and thought through ideas aloud. They had faith I could do this, and do it well, even when I didn't trust myself. Thank you to them for everything they've done for me, for always being proud, and for always believing in me.

My husband, Steve Eau Claire, has never known a time when I was not working on this project in some form. Steve has comforted me when I've wept and reveled with me when I've celebrated. He's cooked, cleaned, cared for our kids while I wrote, made me laugh, calmed my worries, and listened to me think aloud. Our dog, Wilbur, patiently suffered from loneliness as I ignored him more than I wanted to. Our children, Amelia and Sam, at times had to compete for my attention with this project, but their gleeful pride at its publication has been a source of energy and comfort when I've been at my busiest.

The employees and directors at the agencies where I recruited respondents provided valuable referrals and facilitated completion of data collection. They offered introductions, contact information, and private space to conduct interviews. The members of the Kensington Welfare Rights Union allowed me to infiltrate their lives and world and welcomed me into the fold with warmth, humor, understanding, and patience. In particular I thank Cheri Honkala, Galen Tyler, Willie Baptist, Tara Colon, Liz Ortiz, and photographer Harvey Finkle, for their continued interest and support of this project and patience in providing me additional information and perspective. Of course this work would not have been possible had the forty-eight women and two men discussed within these pages not agreed to speak with me at such length and with such candor. I am very grateful for their openness and willingness to participate. I hope this product of the research does justice to their beliefs and experiences.

Introduction

Social Ties among the Poor in an Era of Unprecedented Inequality

The only solution is not a Rambo, Superman, or Bionic Woman solution. It's not an individual solution. The only solution is a collective solution. We should unite together, and figure out creatively how we should survive, survive today, and how we can fight for tomorrow, where we're not simply surviving, but we're thriving. . . . Our strength is in our unity, is in our coming together, and not in some kind of exaggerated, individual effort to try to deal with it. I mean, you've got to do the best you can, but as an individual you should seek to unite with others.

—Walter, 55, Kensington Welfare Rights Union member

A married thirty-one-year-old Latina mother of one young child, struggling to get by, Betty is intensely alone. Long dark hair pulled back into a loose ponytail, large pink-tinted glasses frame her sad eyes during our interview; she lifts her glasses to wipe away tears as she tells me in a quiet voice how overwhelmed she is with managing household responsibilities and her perceptions of what she might be doing wrong as a wife and mother. Betty speaks freely and openly with me, although she is soft-spoken and at times seems self-conscious. She is friendly and outwardly positive even in the face of her palpable sadness.

A high school graduate and a current welfare recipient, Betty has extensive work experience in retail customer service. She is currently enrolled in a welfare-mandated customer service job training program. Her two-year-old daughter attends a day care paid for with a child care subsidy, but Betty finds it substandard and feels her daughter doesn't like it there. She yearns for a job and wants to be a better wife and mother than she feels she is. In our interview, she seems to blame herself for every problem in her life. She sees herself as inadequate.

Betty grew up with her mother, father, and four younger brothers in New York, just outside the city. Her father had other children from a prior relationship as well; all her siblings and half-siblings were boys. She's been married for two and a half years. Betty's family members do not form a private safety net for her—instead they are a source of stress. As a child, she was a victim of sexual abuse by an older male relative, and when she told her parents about it, they didn't believe her. Her mother didn't approve of Betty's husband; for an entire year she and her daughter lived with Betty's mother while her husband, not permitted in the house, slept in his van outside their home; they could not afford a home of their own at the time. Meanwhile, her relationship with her mother-in-law was no better, and they fled New York for Philadelphia in part to get away from these relatives. She and her husband argue frequently: He doesn't understand her depression, and he spends his earnings as a construction worker on food and entertainment for himself without including his wife and daughter in his expenditures. She pays the rent out of her welfare check, which she gets by telling the welfare office she and her husband are separated, and in some ways they are: he sleeps downstairs and she upstairs. They are having problems and likely would be physically separated if their financial situation allowed, but she tells me, "Right now he's staying in the house because I don't want him sleeping in the car." She takes care of their daughter alone, and she doesn't always have enough food to eat.

Betty rarely speaks to her neighbors. She tells me, "I don't get into that." She seems not to have friends in Philadelphia, and while she has some extended family in the city, she can't count on family for help. "They stay to themselves," she says. She feels they do not to want to associate with her. In our interview, she focuses on what she as an individual can do to better her situation. She holds out hope that the job training she's enrolled in will lead to stable employment with adequate pay, and she clings to the notion of an imagined future as an art gallery owner, but with no clear notion of how she might achieve that goal. She admits to suffering depression worsened by deep loneliness. But when I ask her, "What should people who are struggling do?" she tells me they should have a positive attitude.

Betty's situation might be substantially improved had she the comfort of friends around her for emotional support as well as practical assistance; people sometimes pool resources to eat meals together or watch one another's children. Without others to whom she can turn in moments of need and crisis, she's left feeling bereft of the kindness and care that could prop her up from the depths of lonely despair. But she also lacks the sort of private safety net the poor require to survive in the context of the post–welfare reform era's disappearing public safety net. As Robert Putnam has noted, social networks comprised of family have gotten smaller, but nonkin social networks even more so.[1] He also notes that the general collapse of social networks disproportionately affects people in lower social classes; Betty's case, his work suggests, may be typical.

* * *

Paloma is three years younger than Betty, and Latina as well. She also struggles to survive. I meet Paloma through KWRU, and through the organization she's come to know and trust a network of people. Like Betty, Paloma graduated high school and had a series of jobs—as varied as cashier, restaurant hostess, file clerk, lifeguard—she credits to being "articulate" and knowing "how to dress for an interview," but she describes the salaries as inadequate for survival. In our interview, she's energetic, vivacious, and passionate about poverty alleviation. Paloma speaks rapidly to me. Her enthusiasm is infectious at KWRU rallies and meetings; other members smile and laugh at her quick wit and she freely gives hugs to all those she comes across.

Her father died when Paloma was only fifteen. That rite of passage was difficult for her and for her mother, who turned to alcohol. Mother and daughter grew apart. Paloma moved out of her mother's home, and when she was nineteen she and her boyfriend became homeless when they were evicted from their apartment for not being able to pay their rent. They slept one night in a public park, and the next day she found members of KWRU distributing food from a van. The organization gave the couple a place to stay; she is still an active member today.

Paloma and her boyfriend had three children together and remained a couple for ten years. He was a drug user and ultimately they broke up because of it. Now she has a Section 8 housing voucher,[2] secured with

KWRU's help, which provides her and her eight-, five-, and two-year-old a measure of stability and security. Food stamps, but not cash assistance, help to sustain her and her family, and she has received donated clothing and furniture through KWRU, leaving her with few expenses compared to those without a housing subsidy or such donations. She has opened her home to new members of KWRU who need a place to stay. Paloma believes those struggling to get by should join others to work for survival together.

Paloma tells me that many people travel to social service agency after social service agency to get resources; just surviving can be a full-time job. So she has sympathy for those who are struggling and sell drugs in order to survive, but tells me they should join an organization to work for their survival. She describes staying to herself in her neighborhood out of a concern for safety, but longs for a neighborhood where everyone knows each other and helps one another. KWRU provides Paloma with the community she desires—a safe space where she doesn't have to stay to herself. The group expects members to help one another and to attend rallies it organizes to protest conditions faced by the poor. Paloma tells me through KWRU she's learned her poverty couldn't possibly be all her fault because there were so many others facing the same situation. She sees people in KWRU as her family and plans to continue working with the organization to combat poverty.

* * *

As the public safety net has eroded, society places increasing pressure on individuals and private safety nets. This is turn encourages the language and perspective of individualism, in a vicious cycle. We need to pull ourselves up by our bootstraps because there really is no alternative, no understanding of the collectivity of society taking care of those in need. As risk is privatized, individualism as a philosophy is bolstered and social ties seem counter to prevailing ideology; people resist others' aid, enacting an individualistic focus in everyday life.

Betty and Paloma illustrate a crucial distinction in the lives of the desperately poor, one at the center of the analysis in this book. Desperate poverty looks significantly different with social ties than without, and in spite of their many similarities and their shared experience of poverty, these two women have very different lives. Betty's life reflects the problems of living without an alternative to self-reliance; Paloma's reflects an alternative to which few poor people have access.

Inequality and Poverty in the United States

As I write this in 2016, it seems that everyone is talking about inequality. As Jill Lepore argues, "What's new about the chasm between the rich and the poor in the United States . . . isn't that it's growing or that scholars are studying it or that people are worried about it . . . [but that] American politicians of all spots and stripes are talking about it, if feebly: inequality this, inequality that."[3] Lepore is correct: while the richest of the rich have been amassing greater and greater amounts of wealth, deep poverty has been increasing and the American Dream is further out of reach for more people than it ever has been before. While the Great Recession and Occupy Wall Street helped shine new light on the issue, the gap was vast a decade ago.[4]

Nonetheless, many prominent figures, including Pope Francis, have drawn increasing attention to the injustice of the prevailing economic system and growing inequality,[5] and many politicians have responded, at least in their rhetoric. This has included a number of candidates for both the Republican and Democratic nominations for the 2016 presidential race,[6] suggesting growing concern about the issue. Hillary Clinton has called attention to policies that have exacerbated inequality by increasing the wealth of the rich through tax cuts and corporate loopholes.[7] Bernie Sanders has noted, "income and wealth inequality has reached obscene and astronomical levels," stating, "inequality is worse now than at any other time in American history since the 1920s."[8] While in Sanders's case, this constitutes a continuation of the political rhetoric he's voiced for decades, his prominence suggests the political resonance of this discourse. Many in America acknowledge that inequality robs people of good lives while privileging a few. Even politicians who believe America can sustain the present state of inequality recognize their constituents' concern over the issue, particularly as the Great Recession has made downward mobility, and the deep poverty participants in this study have experienced, more apparent.

Inequality and poverty are of course different, but they are inextricably intertwined, and worsening inequality exacerbates poverty.[9] Elise Gould and Alyssa Davis find that

> growing inequality is the primary reason the poverty rate has remained elevated over the last several decades. . . . Since 1979, increasing inequality has been the largest poverty-boosting factor. . . . Despite our growing economy and the fact that poor workers are now more educated than ever, rising inequality has worked to keep low-income people in poverty.[10]

As inequality widens, deep poverty is more apparent: in a society where the wealthiest have so much, the fact that those at the bottom have *nothing* is all the more striking, which may explain the growing attention to these issues. And deep poverty has been increasing since the mid-1970s, following an almost three-decade period of shared prosperity.[11] President Richard Nixon advocated in 1969 that the government pay a guaranteed minimum income to families who could not provide for themselves.[12] Instead, beginning in the 1970s the United States began to embrace neoliberalism, a theory that a free market can best solve social problems.

As Joseph Stiglitz argues, "Our skyrocketing inequality—so contrary to our meritocratic ideal of America as a place where anyone with hard work and talent can 'make it'—means that those who are born to parents of limited means are likely never to live up to their potential."[13] Jennifer Silva identifies a counterintuitive effect of this change: the abandonment of systems that support upward mobility seems to support American faith in individualism. She argues that people "are left with a worldview that conceives of rights in terms of 'I's' rather than 'we's,' with economic justice dropped out of their collective vocabulary. Rooted in everyday instances of disappointment and betrayal within the family and institutions, the cultural logic of neoliberalism resonates at the deepest level of self."[14] She describes a "therapeutic discourse" made ubiquitous through self-help literature, Oprah Winfrey's ideas, and Alcoholics Anonymous that strengthens a "culture of self-reliance fostered by neoliberalism in the economic sphere by teaching young people that they are responsible for their own emotional well-being in the private sphere."[15] She notes,

"Happiness comes to be understood as the by-product of individual will, rather than structural circumstances."[16]

Silva argues that the self-blame she documents in her participants has its roots in an economic shift, even as the therapeutic ethos feeds it: "As power shifted from labor to big business, industrial work grew less and less secure and valued. This decline in the economic sphere was accompanied by a shift in working-class consciousness, leaving its members to believe that they had no right to demand equal opportunities because their own shortcomings were blamed for their lack of success."[17] People explain inequality by focusing on their own failings rather that seeing wider structural explanations, attributing success to character or innate power rather than being born advantaged. Richard Sennett and Jonathan Cobb identified a similar dynamic four decades earlier, writing that society requires people to "understand what happens to them in life in terms of what they make of themselves."[18] Individualism has long been a part of American society, but it began to drive U.S. policy in a new way in the mid-1970s.

Neoliberalism, the Privatization of Risk, and Social Ties

The rhetoric of reducing the size of government and the dependence of people upon government pushes society toward what social scientists call the privatization of risk. And in the context of the privatization of risk, Jacob Hacker argues that Americans have heard the message "loud and clear . . . that they alone are the ones responsible for their successes and their failures, that they alone are the ones who need to invest in education, take on a mortgage, ensure that they have health coverage, put away enough for their retirement—and bail themselves out . . . if things go bad.[19]

Neoliberalism supports deregulation, tax cuts, and the privatization of public services. The institutions created after the Great Depression to shelter the most vulnerable in society have worn away to almost nothing under its sway. For example, federal housing initiatives have dismantled public housing, privatizing housing options for the poor in programs such as market-based housing and voucher programs. The end result is a considerably shrunken pool of affordable housing options for the poor.[20] Dependence on food banks has risen as funding for WIC (vouchers or checks through the Women, Infants, and Children program to purchase specific foods)[21] has shrunk.[22] These policies privatize risk and contribute to inequality, insecurity, and poverty.[23]

In the past, people had security through long-term employment at one place, a good pension, and health care benefits. As these conditions changed, the state declined to take a large role in funding higher education, health care, or retirement for everyone. A college degree became necessary but not sufficient to establish a stable career, health care costs skyrocketed, and employers abandoned pension programs. Individuals now assume nearly every risk involved in obtaining education, coping with illness and injury, and growing old. Congress insistently requires citizens to take on this risk.[24] Government programs would effectively require all taxpayers to share these risks, and pension programs used to distribute them, at least, among a large group; privatization and individualization impose the risk on each individual.

The consequences of the privatization of risk are severe. Losing a job or having a health crisis can trigger insolvency. Personal debt has skyrocketed as people use debt to pay for necessities such as medical care and housing. Parents pay growing portions of their income for housing to get their children into high-performing public school districts, taking on risk to better prepare their children to take on their own risks when they become adults. Even areas of growth in federal funding signify the neoliberal shift: college loans, rather than grants, grow, in a further shift of financial burden to individuals. Crippling college debt has ripple effects in adulthood and for the next generation.

As Jacob Hacker outlines, "The notion that certain risks can be effectively dealt with only through institutions that spread their costs across rich and poor, healthy and sick, able-bodied and disabled, young and old"[25] has been largely abandoned. Under the influence of what he calls the "Great Risk Shift,"[26] "winner-take-all has become the defining feature of American economic life."[27] As to everyone else, a lack of knowledge, skills, credentials, and money makes it impossible to protect themselves from crises, be it unemployment, disability, family dissolution, rising health costs, housing instability, and in some cases food insecurity.

In a cruel twist, neoliberalism makes social ties far more important than they used to be *and* urges people to protect themselves from poverty alone. As Marianne Cooper writes, "If today's families want a safety net to catch them when they fall, they need to weave their own."[28] As responsibilities for and burdens of economic risk shift from government and business to families,[29] private safety nets become crucial for survival. But at the same time, the privatization of risk is both cause and consequence of an individualistic perspective, which in turn breeds social isolation, hindering the ties between people that are the foundation of private safety nets.

The corollaries to neoliberalism privilege individualism and personal responsibility—theories that deny the structural causes of inequality even as they support policies that worsen them.[30] This rhetoric nonetheless makes neoliberalism sound appealing—as if it's not about abandonment, but freedom: it promises efficiency and escape from governmental control while stealing state aid and a reliable social insurance system.[31] Neoliberalism teaches people they must solve their problems alone, because they, not a rigged system, caused their problems. Deep poverty signifies that you've done something wrong, and you alone can and should fix it. These moral lessons further bolster neoliberal policies to reduce the government's role in addressing poverty and inequality. This may explain why Americans still have confidence in their own chances and continue to want equal opportunities rather than equal outcomes, in spite of evidence that policies that appear to privilege equal opportunities actually do not provide them.[32]

Neoliberalism thus encourages people to avoid social ties—that is, people with the potential to offer them social support and social capital. The types of support are limitless, but in this study included information exchanged regarding social services; emotional support and validation; help with day-to-day needs like food, transportation, housing, clothing, and child care; help with finding a job; and help with money.

Social capital consists of resources gained through social ties with others, but it's more than support. Social capital consists of "assets gained through membership in networks"[33] or "the set of resources that inhere in relationships of trust and cooperation between people."[34] These definitions highlight the importance of trust, cooperation, mutuality, and continuity of relationships. Social capital allows individuals to alternately draw on and invest in continued support. The more you use your social capital, the more of it you have, for it is predicated on investment.[35] Social capital is multifaceted support arising from ties built on reciprocity, trust, and continuity.[36]

Neoliberalism has to a great extent robbed participants in this study of the option to pursue social capital. The non-KWRU participants in this study exemplify Silva's statement that "The rise of neoliberalism in the economic sphere has prompted a radical re-envisioning of social relationships at the deepest level of the self."[37] KWRU members, on the other hand, have built social ties, ones that sustain for years and even decades, creating a safety net of relatively strong fabric. In this, they challenge the individualism that neoliberal rhetoric has encouraged. This building of ties does not, by itself, challenge privatization. It also does not mean that KWRU members have ceased to blame the poor, including themselves, for their poverty. But they have rejected to some degree the implication of this blame, which is that they are better off alone. KWRU's core values reject poverty stigma, and its broader mission—to demand public funding to address poverty's consequences through protest—challenges neoliberalism's policy prescriptions, even if not every member fully subscribes to these ideas. This study contrasts KWRU members with a group that eschews nonkin social ties—not because they are able to survive alone in neoliberal society, but because they rely on kin ties, which, as this book will explain, they find compatible with the logic of individualism. This book contrasts a group who take the neoliberal cue to focus on individualism with a group who—to degrees that vary among individuals—reject it, and this book interrogates the causes and consequences of these differences.

Study Design and Comparison

Betty and Paloma represent the two groups of participants I interviewed for this book. Betty avoids social ties and Paloma relishes them. Betty focuses on what she feels she has done wrong and how she might make better decisions in the future that would lead to a future out of poverty. Neoliberalism has set the stage for her life: exacerbating poverty and dissolving the public safety net, it makes a private safety net of social ties all the more important to survival. But by convincing people that they as individuals are alone responsible for their place in the socioeconomic system and seeking to obscure the structural causes of poverty, it encourages avoidance of social ties and hindrance of collective approaches to poverty reduction. Paloma rejects neoliberalism in that she welcomes the social network that envelops her and uses it to survive. Many KWRU members do not share her wholesale rejection of neoliberalism in that they do not embrace the perspective that they are not to blame for their poverty, or believe that KWRU's aim of building a collective response to poverty and demanding greater state aid for the poor broadly is achievable, but Paloma is not alone in her perspective. In addition, most KWRU participants recognize the positive power of social ties in their lives, because even ties with people whose resources are as limited as those of KWRU members become productive in the context of its model.

This study relies mainly on qualitative, in-depth interviews with twenty-five members of KWRU, including Paloma, and twenty-five individuals, like Betty, who are not members of the organization. I also conducted participant observation with KWRU members. Both groups are poor. There are similarities but not equivalencies in their economic situations: for example, participants from both have histories of low-wage work and welfare receipt. Participants from both groups live in varied Philadelphia neighborhoods: Kensington, West Kensington, West Philadelphia, and the Northeast; there are also non-KWRU participants who live in South Philadelphia and Germantown. KWRU participants have more experience with homelessness and KWRU participants are less likely to have kin ties that meaningfully contribute to their ability to survive. They are also older and have more children on average. The appendix provides more details on the study design and provides both summary and specific information on the participants. Other research has found that poor people without kin to turn to make do with available social services and with help from others with whom they form sometimes fleeting ties. This book identifies an unusual circumstance between KWRU members: they formed *sustainable* ties with one another, without kin relationships, unlike anything nonmembers described and generally absent from recent research on poor people.

The KWRU members who participated in this study are generally more disadvantaged than the non-KWRU participants; their extreme disadvantage is what led them to KWRU for help. Thus, my findings likely understate the benefits of KWRU membership, because I am comparing them to people with more advantages than they had when they joined. Without KWRU membership, KWRU participants would be in deep poverty with virtually no aid from anywhere. While most study participants had been homeless at some point, all of them had some sort of shelter—however tenuous—when we spoke. My methods did not involve seeking participants at homeless shelters or who were panhandling on the streets of Philadelphia, but KWRU participants would have been reduced to such measures without the organization.

In this book, I take a sociological theoretical perspective. This means I recognize that human beings have agency, or the ability to make choices, but the choices they have are limited. As Robert Putnam notes, "Researchers have steadily piled up evidence of how important social context, social institutions, and social networks—in short, our communities— remain for our well-being."[38] The communities that surround individuals matter. And the conditions that surround those communities matter as well. People are not masters of their own fates, although their decisions affect their lives in important ways. Like all Americans, poor people have choices, but poverty circumscribes those choices.

A Distinctive Organization in the Poorest U.S. City

Cheri Honkala was a welfare recipient in Minneapolis in the 1980s. When she decided to apply for public assistance and for a Pell Grant to further her education, the state charged her with welfare fraud due to rules prohibiting simultaneous grant and assistance receipt. She pled not guilty and the trial caught the attention of the National Welfare Rights Union (NWRU).[39] Honkala became interested in NWRU's work taking over abandoned properties for homeless families. She started a group called Up and Out of Poverty Now and another called Women, Work, and Welfare.[40] As she tells me, "One concentrated on welfare recipients and the other on homelessness, and we were taking upwards of 75 houses at any given time. Then I began to win hundreds of houses for families in Minneapolis." Honkala relocated to Philadelphia, and the city has been her home ever since. She founded KWRU in April 1991. The Kensington name has symbolic significance, and the organization's office is based in the neighborhood, but its target membership and mission are not bound to the neighborhood. It is a statewide organization, and Kensington is a North Philadelphia neighborhood that was once a manufacturing center but is now among the poorest areas in Pennsylvania, in the poorest big city in the United States. Whereas 15 percent of the U.S. population was poor in 2014, including 27 percent of children, nearly a third of Philadelphia's population lives in poverty. It has the highest rate of deep poverty—defined as 50 percent of the official poverty line—among all big cities in the United States, at 13 percent.[41]

While gentrification has witnessed some recent increases in Philadelphia's population, it's apparent to anyone walking through Bella Vista one day and West Kensington the next, just a few miles directly to the north, to see how "renewal" is confined to particular spaces while others remain isolated, neglected, and devastated. Kensington is emblematic of late-twentieth-century deepening poverty and widening inequality in the United States. It was also the site, in 1903, of a historic strike by 100,000 textile workers—at least 10,000 of whom were children—to demand mill owners reduce their work week from sixty to fifty-five hours, and, later that same year, the origination point of a march by children organized by Mary Harris "Mother" Jones to demand better child labor laws.[42] Many KWRU members do not live in Kensington itself, but they live with its legacy and its struggles.

Philadelphia is one of the largest cities in the United States, even as it lost population in the twentieth century as both cause and consequence of economic decline and crime. The city is ethnically diverse,[43] owing in part to successive groups of immigrants that have moved into some neighborhoods as more affluent residents have moved out. Historians note that these patterns started a long time ago: "The great Industrial Revolution of the 19th and 20th centuries came to Philadelphia early . . . . and left Philadelphia early."[44] Philadelphia lost 75 percent of its manufacturing jobs between 1955 and 1980, and the population declined from 2.1 million in 1950 to fewer than 1.5 million in 1999, only coming back up to a bit over 1.5 million as of 2014.[45]

Kensington reflects these trends. It was historically a white working-class area of the city, but over time it's become poorer and more racially diverse.[46] Many of the manufacturing jobs Philadelphia lost came from Kensington, which was a mill town from the 1860s to the 1930s.[47] In the twentieth century, Kensington experienced industrial growth and working-class prosperity, but a decline occasioned by deindustrialization followed. Kensington is now home to the city's poorest whites as well as the most desperately poor of the Puerto Rican migrants.[48]

Deindustrialization took a toll on much of Philadelphia, as did a lack of investment in the city's public schools and services, but the disappearance of textile manufacturing ravaged communities like Kensington. In his ethnographic study of Philadelphia after deindustrialization, Robert Fairbanks II describes Kensington as "one of the most heavily blighted pockets of spatially concentrated poverty in the United States," noting that over half the Kensington population lives in poverty and nearly half of the area's properties are vacant.[49]

Patricia Stern Smallacombe describes the neighborhood's industry in the twenty-first century as "a surviving though greatly diminished manufacturing, distribution, and retail sector; nonprofit institutions serving an increasingly impoverished and hard-living population, many of whom receive government assistance or other forms of disability insurance; and a thriving underground economy of drugs, prostitution, and other legal and illegal activities."[50] Weakened social institutions have made things worse, lowering trust and collective efficacy.[51]

KWRU defines itself as "a multi-racial organization of, by and for poor and homeless people. We believe that we have a right to thrive—not just barely survive. KWRU is dedicated to organizing of welfare recipients, the homeless, the working poor and all people concerned with economic justice." KWRU has three main stated goals. The first is to "speak to the issues which directly affect our lives: poor people have been excluded from debates, such as welfare reform, which have huge impact on our families. We are committed to tell the stories of what is really happening in our lives and in poor communities across the country." The second goal is to "help each other, and all poor people get what we need to survive: We are committed to seeing that all people have the basic necessities of life—food, clothing, utilities, medical care and housing. We have assisted over 500 families in obtaining housing and utilities." This includes temporary shelter in Takeover Houses and Human Rights Houses—the former being an extralegal response to lack of housing, in abandoned buildings, and the latter being homes they rent with foundation funding. The final goal is to "organize a broad-based movement to end poverty: We know that there is enough to go around in this, the richest country in the world. We believe that the American people are a just and loving people and that we can build a movement, led by poor people, to end poverty once and for all."[52]

KWRU is an organization founded by and run by the poor. There are no paid staff members.[53] The organization relies on the commitment of a few key members, poor people themselves, who've been involved for years and run the group's activities on a daily basis: plan protests, apply for grants, and put together educational materials. Those who go to colleges and universities to speak about poverty and the organization's work put much of their stipends back into the organization and keep the rest, but leaders have no other source of income through the organization. KWRU relies a great deal on the free labor of student interns, idealistic college students who want to help the organization with their antipoverty efforts.

During my research, KWRU maintains an office in West Kensington where people in need can come by for help. They provide aid with navigating available social programs, like helping people fill out paperwork for the welfare office and calling caseworkers. They call utility companies to request payment plans or bill reductions for both members and people who walk in looking for help. They distribute donated food in poor neighborhoods. KWRU offers shelter for homeless families in three forms: Takeover Houses, Human Rights Houses, and the homes of members. Takeover Houses are squats in abandoned properties. KWRU legally rents or owns the Human Rights Houses, which foundation funding makes possible. It should be noted that Human Rights Houses have cost as little to purchase outright as a few thousand dollars in the poorest parts of Philadelphia. Members who get help from KWRU are expected to give help in return, a topic discussed in chapter 4. They volunteer in the office and on food distributions, and attend rallies. As they become more economically stable, usually through securing permanent housing with the group's assistance, they frequently allow new homeless families to stay with them, continuing the cycle of support.

At the time I began my research with KWRU in late 2003, members and activists had a busy daily schedule and the office on North 5th Street was always abuzz with activity, typically focused on local protests as well as providing practical assistance to members and walk-ins, as I'll describe below. In 2009, three years after the conclusion of my research, KWRU lost its major foundation funding, which reduced its ability to provide temporary housing for homeless families. Over the next few years KWRU effectively merged with the Poor People's Economic Human Rights Campaign (PPEHRC),[54] an umbrella organization encompassing dozens of groups, spearheaded by KWRU leaders in 1998.[55] In addition, in 2012 KWRU founder Cheri Honkala ran for vice president of the United States on the Green Party ticket with Jill Stein. As of 2016 PPEHRC continues to maintain a local office where members assist people who call or walk in needing assistance.

In June 2015 PPEHRC cosponsored a U.S. Social Forum in Philadelphia (USSF), during which members of various organizations came from throughout the country as well as several international locations to discuss issues such as mass incarceration and climate change.[56] I heard one attendee refer to the four-day conference as "Occupy but organized," referring to Occupy Wall Street. PPEHRC was one of two "anchor organizations" (along with Disabled in Action) for the USSF. The website and the conference program listed over twenty partner organizations.

As KWRU did in 2003–2006, PPEHRC in 2016 engages in what they call "projects of survival" to "reclaim vacant government owned homes to house homeless families and individuals that are often turned away from city shelters or are victims of fire, domestic violence, and/or foreclosure" through housing takeovers; they also distribute food to those experiencing hunger and food insecurity and recently, are engaging in urban gardening efforts as well.[57] PPEHRC has an educational arm, similar to KWRU's, to cultivate the skills and capacity among members to lead campaigns to effect change[58] and the organization has run bus tours around the country.[59] The group's protests, like the 2003 event I described in the Preface, are focused on getting needed assistance.[60] PPEHRC confronts the push toward neoliberalism directly and consciously, through the practice of working with others instead of as individuals, and by using what public resources there are and demanding more of them.

Perspectives on Social Ties

The contrast between study participants like Betty and study participants like Paloma is at the heart of *Surviving Poverty*. Betty is struggling to survive virtually alone, in job training as part of an effort to improve her lot through human capital investment, but with little hope of improving a life of subsistence. Paloma has found a measure of security through KWRU. Poor people tend to avoid social ties, as Betty does, but my observations suggest that, in spite of the cost of building them, social ties offer the poor benefits, both emotionally and in terms of their ability to survive. The benefits are even stronger when the ties are sustainable—that is, when circumstances enable them to last. I define sustainable ties as ties between nonkin that provide deep, meaningful support and have the potential to last over time. The situations that brought study participants to join KWRU open up the possibility for people who might otherwise "stay to themselves" to build such ties. While they are still very poor, they value these ties and use them to make their lives better.

Falling Without a Net

Like the poor generally in America, study participants face a tattered public safety net and a structural context that provides only the most limited of opportunities. A number of scholars contend that policy makers presume the existence of a private safety net, comprised of kin, to justify the ongoing dismantling of the public safety net.[61] As Judith Levine[62] argues, welfare reform also included rhetoric about transferring responsibility for poor families from the government to the community. She states, "One of the underlying philosophies of reform was that it was not government's job to permanently support those in need. Instead, reformers believed, it was the job of communities—of friends, of family, of neighbors—to support each other. By removing the entitlement to cash assistance benefits and creating time limits on those benefits, government was giving the message that it was time for social networks to step in to fill the void."[63]

Many, including many of the poor themselves, praise welfare reform and the ideas it represents, that families and community should help the poor in lieu of government programs.[64] However, this study demonstrates a reason that welfare reform has failed: the private safety net cannot fully compensate for the lost support. Kin support may be weak even when it is available—the family members of poor people do not have many resources either.[65] But it is often absent, and individuals like Betty who lose that support are at risk of homelessness—as are their children.

The assumption that all poor women leaving welfare have families willing and able to fill the void is faulty. Low-income people struggle in the United States; they struggle to survive and to get ahead, to hold on to hope and hold on to self-worth, and to find voice and find community. As a large body of recent research demonstrates, those with the greatest need for support are the least likely to have it available to them.[66] Private safety nets are simply not always available to people to fall back on in times of need.

Given their limited opportunities, the participants in this study consider the options they do have and they make choices about how to live their lives and how to survive; many dream of a future out of poverty. Factors beyond their control structure the ways in which they seek out assistance. For participants like Paloma who choose to join organizations, the actions of those organizations—which also reflect structural constraints—matter as well.[67] As Mario Luis Small and Scott Allard note, "The fewer the resources to which people have access, the more their circumstances will depend on the organizations in which they participate, the systems in which these organizations operate, and the institutions governing the behavior of both."[68]

Even though I would assert that Betty might benefit from KWRU membership, this is not a story about how poor people's choices structure their circumstances; rather, it takes the structural reality of systemic disadvantage as a starting point. Betty would still be poor, and KWRU membership might not work for her, although it did benefit most members. Critics of studies of social ties, networks, and capital assert that such studies blame the poor for their plights; I have no intention of placing blame on the poor for their poverty.[69] Larger structural forces cannot be ignored. This book asks, given the structure, what do people do? How does the structure shape and limit their agentic decisions?

The poor are not a monolithic group, so their choices and strategies vary within the confines of the possibilities available to them. The attitudes and actions of the poor do not only reflect structural determinants.[70] Even faced with virtually identical material conditions, people respond to their situations differently, and this difference does not reflect deviant values but the use of different strategies to cope with their material situations, all typically combined with mainstream cultural norms and values.[71] The structure shapes the context in which people make decisions, and insufficient resources shape poor people's lives in countless ways.[72] My research reveals many details of the challenges study participants face, and this book recounts those insights; I acknowledge agency without blaming people for their poverty, recognizing they are actors who make choices within a realm of *constrained* possibilities.[73] Participants who isolate themselves seek a leg up and out of poverty by avoiding ties with others they perceive as potentially dangerous or resource-draining. Those who work together with others to survive seek a private safety net to help them avoid the worst consequences of the direst poverty. As I document in this book, all these people want to avoid welfare and to be self-sufficient and independent, rendering efforts at attitudinal change misplaced and misguided; blame for poverty does not rest on the shoulders of the poor. Unfortunately, this fact contradicts the prevailing opinion of the American people, as Jacob Hacker and Paul Pierson write: "More than most societies, Americans believe that people rise or fall as a result of their own efforts, and therefore get what they deserve. . . . We distribute blame and praise to individuals because we believe that it is their individual actions, for better or worse, that matter. *People get what they deserve.*"[74]

This book's discussion of the varied strategies of the poor presupposes the fact that poverty is structurally created; responses to it are structured as well; those responses and their consequences are the focus of this book, joining other studies of how low-income people develop and maintain support networks.[75] Margaret Nelson, in her 2005 study of single mothers in poverty, notes:

> The more closely I looked at the choices single mothers made in every realm of their lives (and perhaps especially in their negotiations for material and emotional support), the more it seemed that those choices were shaped by ideological constraints that single women neither invented nor chose. . . . Public morality matters to single mothers, and it especially matters because of the sharp awareness that their family form is subject to denigration. The lives of the single mothers I studied thus provide evidence of both the effects of structure on decision making and of opportunities to exercise agency.[76]

Ties are not a cure for what ails the poor.[77] Only a massive revival of the public safety net, reversing the state's neoliberal neglect, and systemic changes in the organization of the labor market can offer such a panacea, but the reality of the experiences of those I interviewed and spent time with suggests the importance of social ties in their lives. This book describes the tension between social isolation and social ties among the poor and the consequences of each for a set of participants in a major urban area; its findings inform our understandings of what shapes the attitudes and decisions of the poor, how they survive, and the benefits they may gather by being tied to one another. My findings suggest that social service agencies might use social ties to alleviate, but not end, poverty.

In spite of the enormous gains poor people in America could gather from social ties, they are at great risk of social isolation. An individualistic ideology tends to pervade their views about survival, poverty, and mobility. Although America's structural context prevents poor people, by and large, from ascending the class ranks, a tradition of individualism and striving for a better life reveals itself in the outlook of most poor people. Poor people typically expend a great deal of energy just surviving, and consequently only a subset of the poor actively engages in strategies to achieve mobility out of poverty; even these strivers can only accomplish so much in the context of formidable structural barriers.[78] They imagine dreams fulfilled by personal effort and sound decision making, even though structural realities circumscribe the potential impact of their individual actions.

Like most Americans, most of the fifty people I interviewed in my research prioritize individualism and consequently wish to refrain from relying on others. Individualism leads them not only to hopes of more education and a better job but also to avoid social ties; development of and reliance on ties contradicts their perspective on the importance of going it alone. But great need sometimes overwhelms pride and an individualistic focus and people can begin to build, lean on, and develop social ties that can provide significant support and lasting relationships. By recruiting half of the participants through KWRU, I was able to identify poor people who did create social ties and build social capital.

Social ties between the poor formed in desperation are sometimes short-lived, such as the disposable ties Matthew Desmond documented.[79] But KWRU creates the possibility for poor people, often on the brink of homelessness and with no one to rely on, to build lasting social ties with one another—ties that last far longer than the ones Desmond identified.

Participants exhibited a range of beliefs about the strategies best for poor people to pursue, centering on varied levels of faith in human capital investment and a tension between avoidance of and reliance on social ties. While the stretched resources of the poor mean that investing in human capital can make it impossible to invest in social ties, I found that the strongest connection to avoidance of social ties lay in a strongly held belief in individualism. My data suggest that intense need, rather than a changing view, leads to investment in social ties, but that the investment itself tends to overwhelm individualism. In fact, KWRU members often espouse perspectives prioritizing individual agency, but their need for immediate aid leads them to invest in ties in spite of this.

Researchers have long documented that survival strategies among the poor typically include reliance on social support, frequently from people in their social networks, who may have scarce resources themselves. While scholars have found extensive kin ties in poor communities,[80] others have documented a lack of kin ties for some.[81] Those unable to rely on family use what exists of the threadbare public safety net and piece together help from social service and philanthropic organizations. When these sources fail, some develop disposable ties with virtual strangers in order to gather needed resources, but this response is unreliable and fraught with problems.[82] KWRU, on the other hand, provides an opportunity for poor people to build sustainable ties with one another and with the organization in an ongoing support relationship, one in which they can invest and on which they can draw. While the relationship can be burdensome, most study participants from KWRU recognize its value.

The Aims of This Book

Surviving Poverty examines how people develop and avoid social ties, and the consequences of those actions. I conducted in-depth ethnographic interviews with twenty-five members of KWRU, mostly women, and twenty-five women who were using social services targeted to the poor, between late 2003 and mid-2006 in Philadelphia, Pennsylvania.

I also conducted participant observation of KWRU participants and obtained follow-up information in the year and a half before this book went to press, between mid-2014 and early 2016. Approximately one-third of each group identify as white, a third as Latina, and a third as African American. All sixteen whites and eighteen African Americans are native-born. Of the sixteen Latinas, three were born in Puerto Rico; only two others were born outside Philadelphia, in other cities in the United States. Consequently, this book does not portray the immigrant experience or immigrant social networks.

I establish that participants, like most Americans, subscribe to individualism, which causes them to cling tightly to the belief that they should manage their struggles independently; that they avoid social ties, considering them dangerous, in part because they stigmatize other poor people; that great need can bring people to overcome these obstacles and seek help at an organization that promises help; that reciprocity requirements make the cost of social ties very high; and that ultimately the sustainable ties KWRU provides make members' lives better. As I'll explain, KWRU membership is demanding. Lacking paid employees, KWRU depends on members to staff their food vans and attend their rallies; it runs on reciprocal demands, the way another organization would run on dues. Yet many members maintain their membership for years.

KWRU's model offers important insights for agencies that seek to improve the lot of poor people in the United States. Study participants and others like them would have a better chance of surviving—and thriving—if they could pursue human capital investment, build sustainable ties, and if the services available to them provided the broad and deep support necessary to address varied aspects of their struggles. While most programs they can access consist of singular attempts at change (welfare-mandated job training, GED test preparation, parenting classes), there are programs that provide a variety of services as a bundle, in one location and with useful coordination. Such programs could also create community; if such programs required reciprocity from the clients they serve, those clients would feel the power of their personal investment and overcome their shame at asking for help, instead viewing it as a draw on their own investment. As the KWRU model suggests, keeping such reciprocal demands manageable is key; if the burden is too great, it will hinder rather than foster sustainable ties.

Beyond what personal ties can offer lies the need for other macro-economic policy changes. KWRU describes safe, affordable housing as a human right; it is also the foundation on which the poor build stable lives. The expansion of housing subsidies and child care subsidies would go a long way to giving the poor the possibility for socioeconomic mobility. Human capital investments should yield returns as well, especially given their emphasis in neoliberal rhetoric: education and training obtained by the poor should be linked to available jobs, and those jobs should pay a living wage. *Surviving Poverty* concludes with some proposals for how to begin to remake the reality of social ties, human capital, and the poor's access to them both.

Overview of Chapters

Chapter 1 focuses on a key obstacle to changing the poor's access to social ties. It describes the widespread perspective among study participants that through individual effort and persistence they can achieve a better life. They believe in the achievement ideology—the belief that effort will always lead to success—and that personal failings rather than structural barriers ensure that poor people stay poor. They blame the poor, including themselves, for being poor, and believe that hard work, persistence, and additional education and training will be the ticket out of poverty. They seek to be independent; doing things on their own bolsters their notion of being in control and their faith in the power of their own agentic decisions. A key part of their recommended strategies rests on avoiding social ties, in part because such ties represent a failure of independence.

Chapter 2 describes many participants' avoidance of social ties. In general participants avoid contact with neighbors, considering their neighborhoods places of fear, stress, crime, and violence. The chapter examines reasons for keeping to oneself, including the individualistic ideology I describe in chapter 1, and the fear that neighbors will gossip about one's problems, which individualistic ideology makes unthinkable. I argue that individualistic ideology also supports pervasive stigma about poverty, which causes participants to avoid associating with others who are in many ways like them. It makes them comfortable avoiding social ties that might require reciprocity that they might not be able to provide—or that will be a drain on their precious resources. The findings in chapter 2 relate most strongly to participants who are not members of KWRU. But most KWRU members exhibit these beliefs and avoidances as well, making it all the more remarkable that they overcome fear, judgment, and pride to enter a situation of reliance on others.

Chapter 3 describes the great need that leads people to join KWRU. Homeless, recently escaped from domestic violence, or at risk of losing welfare benefits, food stamps, or other crucial forms of support, they seek support from an organization that could assist them to secure benefits or temporary housing. Chapter 3 describes the public face of KWRU, the difficult circumstances people confront that lead them to KWRU, how the organization addresses their practical needs, and the decision to initiate social ties with strangers to aid survival in a society that exerts considerable pressure to pursue stability and success as individuals. While some KWRU members still have stigmatized views of poor people and at times espouse individualistic ideology, the group's mission specifically seeks to dismantle that stigma; a number of members begin to recognize that personal failings alone cannot cause all poverty. However, this change generally seems to be the result of time as a KWRU member; people do not initiate contact with KWRU because of a change of opinions from those described in chapter 2, or as a consequence of a reasoned decision to build social ties for survival.

Chapter 4 explores KWRU's reciprocity norms, which substitute for the membership dues that members could never pay. KWRU requires a great deal from people in exchange for the help provided, reflecting the fact that KWRU leaders do not see it as a social service organization. Rather, they aim to build a network on a foundation of support exchange. They provide assistance to those who seek help, but they require members to attend rallies and protests, to visit and help out at the office, and to provide help as possible to other members. This help may extend as far as opening one's home to a fellow member. The chapter also discusses the fact that these reciprocity requirements can be onerous and members who take them lightly may be pushed out for failing to fulfill the obligations of reciprocity in the group.

Chapter 5 discusses the sustainable ties KWRU members build through the organization. These ties are not based on kinship, but, reflecting the supportive and lasting nature of these ties, members speak of

KWRU members as the family they never had or the one they wish they had. I discuss how KWRU supports these ties, including the fact that rifts between members—even between members and a leader—do not dissolve the member's tie to the organization, unless the member refuses to obey reciprocity norms. The relationships fostered within KWRU provide emotional support and give members a community, and a sense that they are neither alone in their struggles nor alone in the world. The homelessness that brings so many to KWRU's doors demonstrates a lack of family support; KWRU begins to serve as a substitute family.

Building sustainable ties exacts a high cost for KWRU members. However, this very cost brings benefits: unlike the one-way support offered by social service agencies, the reciprocal exchange of help within KWRU fosters trusting relationships among members and between members and activists. The social capital those relationships provide yields instrumental support that proves key for survival. While escaping poverty is not achievable with a simple recipe of either avoiding or developing social ties, the social ties such as those available to KWRU members bring more rewards than costs.

In the book's conclusion I propose that social service agencies would benefit from taking KWRU as a model, that this would allow them to make it possible for the poor to simultaneously invest in human capital and social capital through sustainable ties. Such agencies could require a reasonable number of volunteer hours in ways that work with clients' education, employment, and child care needs. If such volunteering could fulfill TANF work requirements, agencies could allow recipients to meet multiple needs simultaneously. Through requiring reciprocity, agencies could foster relationships and lessen their burden. Agencies could require clients to provide services that fit well with their skills, interests, and abilities. An exchange of services could offer the benefits of social capital that KWRU can only offer in isolation from and opposition to human capital. Social capital might enable agencies to serve a greater number of people, offsetting some of their costs by creating a social network that facilitates child care or housing assistance and lessens the need for subsidies.

I also suggest a number of more general policy changes based on my findings. A lack of affordable housing and affordable and accessible child care remain the most substantial daily hurdles most poor people face. The private safety net of social ties has historically helped fill the gap left by an inadequate welfare system, a system made more inadequate by welfare reform. But the private safety net is often frayed, not up to the task. Even as neoliberalization outsources the safety net from the public to the private realm, it weakens the threads that weave the private safety net. Agencies that strengthen the private safety net could confer real benefits, and KWRU represents a distinctive model that would make such a task possible.

1

Keep Working to Be What You Want

The Power of Individualism

If you work and you work and you work hard . . . you can get . . . . anybody can have anything they want if you work hard for it. That's how I look at it. I mean, life is only the way you make it. If you chose not to make nothing out of it, then that's on you.
—Kim, 44, GED student

I meet Kim at an agency in South Philadelphia where she is enrolled in a course to help her prepare for the GED exam. A high school dropout with extensive work experience but currently unemployed, Kim is in her forties and ready for a future brighter than the past she laments. Tall and thin, wearing jeans, hair pulled taut in a neat, high ponytail, her skin a medium brown free of lines and wrinkles, Kim looks younger than the age she reports, even though two of her three daughters are in their twenties, married and living independently. Kim herself has never been married. Throughout our interview she speaks to me confidently and energetically of the rewards of hard work and personal responsibility. When I ask if she thinks it's fair that some people have a lot and some people have very little, she doesn't directly respond to the question, but references the idea that you can have what you want if you try, implying that it's poor people's fault if they're poor.

Kim's recommendations for people who are struggling center on personal actions: "Get up and get a job. Or try to get a training or something like that there to better themselves. You know what I'm saying? You got to do . . . it starts within you. It starts with you. Everything starts with you. You have to . . . you have to want it or get up and get it. It's not gonna come to you. It starts with you. You can't get nothing if you don't go for it." Her manner of presenting herself has likely been an asset when she's sought a job, so it's not surprising she's had such relative success in employment in the past, even with her lack of educational credentials. At the same time, the experience she describes in high school belies her suggestion that effort is the only crucial factor. She tells me she was forced to restart the ninth grade twice after she passed it due to paperwork errors as she transferred schools. This situation would discourage any young person from completing high school, but a wealthier teenager at a better-resourced school would be unlikely to experience it.

Kim's thoughts about the American Dream and its unlimited potential mirror those of the wider public as well as those of most study participants. They likely share few of the life experiences of Republican Paul Ryan, who is, as of this writing, Speaker of the House and was the vice presidential candidate on Mitt Romney's 2012 GOP ticket, and yet they might agree with his statement that the safety net is a "hammock which lulls able-bodied people into lives of complacency and dependency."[1] In this chapter I describe this common perspective, its roots, and some of its consequences. The very fact that participants hold this perspective reflects the hollowness of the stereotype—they do not approach social programs with a sense of entitlement, but rather with a sense of individual responsibility and a revulsion for dependency. Many other studies with more broadly generalizable findings reveal that these participants are typical, and the lazy dependents they revile a fiction. For example, most poor people have strong work ethics, link work to morality, and have strong ties to the labor market.[2] Yet the myth remains that the poor are lazy. And it is likewise common for poor people to describe other poor people this way.[3]

This chapter relies on interviews with both KWRU members (noted within as members) and nonmembers. As it shows, participants frequently espouse the ideas neoliberalism encourages. It describes the prevalence of individualistic ideology among participants, then discusses their faith in a related notion: that investing in human capital through education is a means to mobility. The next section describes participants' views on the choices and decisions that lead to mobility or continued poverty, highlighting the pervasive idea that people control their own futures. Finally, it documents the recognition by some participants—many of whom contradict themselves as they express this recognition—that individualism has its limits.

The Achievement Ideology

The people who shared their stories with me generally describe education and work experience as a sure route to success and a necessary piece of any path out of poverty. I examined whether people like Kim, whose classes toward the GED represented a current investment in human capital, differed from those not currently making such investments, but found they did not. The latter group *aspires* to invest in human capital like the former group. For example, Karen, an African American woman in her forties, is staying at home with her three-year-old but is sure the certificate in computer literacy she is determined to seek in the coming years would lead to her "moving on, moving up in someone's company" within five years. Her husband currently supports her from his earnings as a bricklayer, which are uneven, especially in the winter. Should that marriage break up or he lose his income, she will be very vulnerable, as she used to be addicted to crack and has a criminal record, which, while she's been in recovery for seven years, affects her employment prospects.

The American Dream[4] presents a powerful mythology: work hard, play by the rules, achieve success. It is central in American ideology and its effects are broad and deep. As Jennifer Hochschild describes, it is "the promise that all Americans have a reasonable chance to achieve success as they define it—material or otherwise—through their own efforts, and to attain virtue and fulfillment through success."[5] While intergenerational mobility is lower in the United States than in other affluent countries, the American Dream, as Hacker and Pierson state, "portrays the United States as a classless society where anyone can rise to the top, regardless of family background."[6] The myth is grounded in the notion of a straight line between hard work and success. It calls for individuals to embrace self-reliance and exert effort; it represents faith in the reach of human agency, or free will, to accomplish personal goals.[7] As Hochschild notes, "Not all Americans can achieve their dreams no matter how hard they try. But the American Dream obscures those structural facts under a cloak of individual agency, thus giving people unjustified hopes and unwarranted feelings of failure."[8]

Americans focus on the individual responsibility that accompanies such a worldview.[9] Silva points out that growing inequality seems to increase some people's commitment to the achievement ideology. She describes her working-class research participants as "the young people who would benefit most from social safety nets and solidarity with similarly disadvantaged others," and yet they "cling so fiercely to ideals and practices of untrammeled individualism and self-reliance, not only as the way things are but also as the way they should be."[10] While this clinging of course reifies the existing power structure, she argues that her participants' "everyday experiences of humiliation and betrayal, their recognition that the social contract they depended on has been severed—or simply never existed in the first place," are the crucial drivers:

> Over and over again, working-class youth learn that they can depend on others only at great cost. In turn, they numb the ache of betrayal and the hunger for connection by seizing upon cultural scripts of self-reliance, individualism, and personal responsibility. . . . They become acquiescing neoliberal subjects. . . . In this way, potential communities of solidarity are broken apart by the strain of insecurity and risk.[11]

Silva's participants, like mine and many others',[12] consider opportunity for economic mobility to be widely available and inequality to be expected and just. Putnam concurs that "historically . . . most Americans have not been greatly worried about . . . inequality: we tend not to begrudge others their success or care how high the socioeconomic ladder is, assuming that everyone has an equal chance to climb it, given equal merit and energy."[13] An oft-quoted passage from a speech Bill Clinton gave early in his presidency supports this: "The American dream that we were all raised on is a simple but powerful one—if you work hard and play by the rules, you should be given a chance to go as far as your God-given ability will take you. This American ideology that each individual is responsible for his or her life outcomes is the expressed belief of the vast majority of Americans, rich and poor."[14] Barack Obama noted the centrality of this as well, grouping the American Dream with "our way of life, and what we stand for around the globe" in a speech addressing the threats inequality and immobility pose.[15] The myth suggests the existence of an unfettered meritocracy in which people rely on their own skills, talents, and intelligence and apply them persistently and with dedication; their reward is occupational success, financial comfort, and the esteem of others. When Americans succeed, we take credit for our successes and pride ourselves on these accomplishments. When we fail, we blame ourselves.[16] And we observe others through that lens as well; we look upon the rich and successful with admiration, congratulate them for their hard work, and seek to emulate them, while we look upon the poor and homeless with contempt and disdain, attribute their failings to personal inadequacies and irresponsibility, and seek to distance ourselves from them.[17] We exhort them to work harder, to take responsibility, to believe in themselves. Many of us blame ourselves for any poor outcomes in our own lives as well; we see these as our failures, and we strive to do better in the future.

Bebe cares for children at the home of a KWRU participant in exchange for shelter; she is not a member but I meet her in the member's home and decide to interview her. When I interview Bebe shortly after her eighteenth birthday, she tells me as she folds the children's laundry:

> I can't say it's their fault for being poor, because nobody wants to be poor, nobody wants to be living on the street, but it might have somethin' . . . like I feel like if you're poor . . . you know how you're poor and these ladies they be poor and they keep having more and more kids. Like if you know you're poor you shouldn't be having kids. You shouldn't keep bringing more kids to this world, because that's just putting yourself in a bigger hole than what you are in. So sometimes I think it's their fault for doing stuff like that. I understand sometimes they want to have kids, some people don't know that they're having kids, like and sometimes it might be a mistake, but still like people bring kids to this world, and I know a lot of people that bring kids to this world and don't have money but want to keep having kids. And sometimes I think it's their fault for doing that.

Bebe is patient and positive with the children she cares for, even as she unhesitatingly shares concerns with me about her economic situation: "There's a lot of things that I want to do that I can't have. Sometimes I have no money at all." She condemns people with children she thinks they cannot afford, though she seems to make an exception for her host, reflecting both her gratitude and her admiration for the woman's strength and constant effort to survive and care for others. Without a high school diploma or clear options for a future out of poverty, Bebe also tells me she plans on delaying having her own children until she is well into her twenties, perhaps as a measure to avoid the condemnation she attaches to others.[18]

Sometimes, study participants begin to see faults and fractures appearing in the ideology; they remember they *have* worked hard and done everything they ought to, and confront a reality lesser than they dreamed. Yet as Putnam writes, "on balance most Americans have believed (at least until recently) that equality of opportunity characterizes our society—that the American Dream, in other words, endures."[19]

Participants wonder about the role of luck, or God's will; rarely do they note the possibility that the reach of our agency may have limits. Denise, for example, describes herself as a Christian and tells me that she thought her situation would improve through "my own hard work and my faith in God, and my faith in myself." The external factor of God's will is not a barrier, according to religious study participants who subscribe to the achievement ideology; rather, through faith in God and prayer for good results, those who proffer such actions as strategies believe they can engage in action to accomplish their goals through God.

The notion that personal effort and persistence lead to success, at the heart of the American Dream, is the crux of the achievement ideology, "the reigning social perspective that sees American society as open and fair and full of opportunity. . . . Success is based on merit, and economic inequality is due to differences in ambition and ability. . . . The American Dream is held out as a genuine prospect for anyone with the drive to achieve it."[20] This important component of quintessential American individualism goes back as far as the writings of Benjamin Franklin.[21] It's similar to the Protestant Ethic, which Max Weber, drawing on Franklin's work, wrote about so influentially: hard work leading to material success is a sign that the successful worker is destined for heaven and eternal salvation. Weber argued that this Protestant Ethic was the foundation of the spirit of capitalism in the United States.[22]

Believing in the achievement ideology has powerful effects, some of which are positive: people are motivated to work hard, even in the face of evidence of structural and discriminatory barriers that could be paralyzing. It can give us a reason to get up in the morning, to live to fight another day, to have hope. In addition, individualistic beliefs that support building human capital and general industriousness foster a sense of personal empowerment and control. These effects can also lessen depression, increase hope, and improve happiness and health—though other research suggests that poor people who act on individualism suffer negative health consequences.[23] And although many of those most successful in American society were born with incredible advantages, it remains true that for many others, hard work is a necessary, if not sufficient, component of success. Similarly, those who reject the achievement ideology may be dooming themselves to failure: the old axiom applies that you cannot succeed if you don't try.[24]

Of course, people like Kim and Karen can avoid failure by refusing to try. Fear of failure stops many from attempting to reach goals for which they feel unprepared or unqualified. Opting out of studying for an exam allows a student to comfort herself by saying, "I would have done better if I had studied." Rejecting the achievement ideology can protect a sense of self in this way. Meanwhile, if Kim works diligently at her course and scores well on the exam but, like many unemployed holders of GEDs, doesn't get a job or a better job than the one she most recently lost, she may blame herself when she fails, leading to the hopelessness that belief in the achievement ideology is supposed to help her avoid. Although the achievement ideology confers optimism, for the many poor people who do not succeed, it compounds their difficulties by causing them to blame themselves.[25]

We exhort the poor in the United States to work hard, to make better choices, to lift themselves up by their bootstraps. Savannah is a thirty-two-year-old Latina participant who dropped out of high school. Chin-length curly brown hair and glasses frame her face, and she is friendly but professional with me. She opens the door to her small and beautifully decorated home on a block marked by a number of boarded-up houses and welcomes me in. She has a back injury that she says may prevent her from working (most jobs she might get require prolonged standing) and she lives in a poor North Philadelphia neighborhood with her father and her young child. She evokes the popular bootstrap notion when she says of wealthier people, "Their parents, their grandparents worked, worked hard for their kids to have what they have now, [but] they got up there and they started from the bottom. . . . They worked theirself up. If they really want to, they want to get ahead in life. . . . You know, you can get up there, you know?" Most participants do not overtly object to the unequal distribution of wealth and deep poverty, partially because wealth serves as an inspiration to them. Savannah says, "Well, they worked hard for that. And if they did it, why can't I? I can have the same thing as they, you know," even as she tells me she isn't sure if her back injury will ever allow her to work consistently.

In the United States, we as a society tell the poor to accept the personal responsibility and moral obligation they have to labor and to persist. And for the most part they accept this ideology; Denise's attitude is common among participants: "But there is one thing I know, you know, you can come from any background and it doesn't set you back a lot. It may set you back, but . . . you're gonna always come back to have the strength to pull yourself back up. So like I pulled myself back up." Denise is proud of the fact that she graduated high school even though she had a child at age sixteen and was raised by a single mother who relied on a combination of public assistance and working nights.

Polly is in a customer service job training program through welfare, where I interview her first during a supervisor-approved break and then complete the interview another day after her classes, using an empty conference room the agency provided us. She says welfare gave her a choice as to whether to enter a training program or to find a job, and she says she chose training because she thinks it will improve her life. A high school graduate and mother of one small child, Polly matter-of-factly says, "Some people, they really work hard for their money and some people don't. You really work hard for what you get. You got to work hard for what you want." She lives with her mother, and may have the opportunity to pull herself up with that support, though it's difficult to imagine her doing so without it.

As Martin Luther King, Jr. said, "It's all right to tell a man to lift himself by his own bootstraps, but it is cruel jest to say to a bootless man that he ought to lift himself by his own bootstraps."[26] Paloma, the KWRU member we met in the Introduction, is unusual among study participants when she echoes King's themes, telling me:

> Some people do struggle and get out of [poverty], but I think that people help them along the way. I don't think anybody does anything by themselves in this world. I don't give a fuck who they think they are. If they really analyze their life, somebody helped them, opened some door to get

somewhere. And other people are just born lucky. I think the majority of the people who are well off are born lucky. It's very few that actually like pull themselves up by their bootstraps and become rich overnight.

Many of those most disadvantaged have the same values, goals, and hopes as members of the wider society.[27] Poor people in inner city neighborhoods share the basic American values of individual hard work; William Julius Wilson found that his study participants "over-whelmingly endorsed the dominant American belief system concerning poverty . . . [and] agreed that America is a land of opportunity where anybody can get ahead, and that individuals get pretty much what they deserve."[28] People think the homeless are lazy and don't want to work, yet as Snow and Anderson state, "like other Americans supposedly im-bued with a strong work ethic, many of the recently dislocated believe that if they only look hard enough, they too will find work that provides a living wage."[29]

Katherine Newman[30] also found a strong work ethic among poor people. The crack dealers Philippe Bourgois studied "like most people in the United States, firmly believe in individual responsibility" and articu-late a value of work over welfare.[31] Mitchell Duneier[32] found that many poor men believe strongly in personal responsibility and hard work, and believe that others take advantage of welfare. Michèle Lamont[33] also found that hard work and responsibility were important to the working-class men she studied, and that they associated poverty with laziness. It was rare among participants in my study to reject the achievement ideology. Like most Americans, they view the story of aspirations and goal-oriented behavior with optimism and hope.[34]

KWRU member Tina exemplifies the believer in the American Dream. A military veteran discharged when she became pregnant with her youngest child, she lives with her infant daughter in a single room in a rooming house, sharing a bathroom down the hall with other tenants she doesn't know. Their fathers have custody of her two older children, an artifact of her time away in military training camp and now neces-sitated by her lack of funds and space. Tina's toned biceps evidence the push-ups she does every day to keep fit and strong. At twenty-nine, Tina imagines her future, gazing out the window while bouncing her daugh-ter gently on her knee to quiet her, telling me she hopes she and her current boyfriend stay together, "And that we can have a life together someday and raise the kids, you know, the right way. And maybe when [the baby] gets a little older, maybe I'll be able to go to college. And be a chef and get that job that I want and own that restaurant that I want and have everything that I feel like I deserve, you know. I think that I deserve it. I think that I worked hard enough to where I think I deserve, I think I should have what I want."

Politicians and members of the public have always divided the poor into those who are "deserving" and those who are "undeserving."[35] However, the "deserving" poor is now a virtually empty category. If people are solely responsible for their skills and educational attainment, there are few or no socially acceptable and legitimate reasons to be poor in America.[36] The moral hierarchy of deservingness is connected to the ideology of individualism. Tina does not speak of deserving assistance by virtue of misfortune or even military service. She describes herself as deserving of a future of independence by virtue of her hard work. In one year she imagines working and being in school; in five years she would like to be married, and in twenty years she wants to own her own restaurant. Due to her hard work and positive attitude and persistence, she believes she deserves to have what she wants in life and sees it as a realistic possibility.

Human Capital

If we focus on individual responsibility to achieve our goals, likewise the mechanisms we recommend as the means to attain them are specific actions we can take as individuals. Policy makers, the public, and the poor alike value human capital, the skills and credentials from formal education and training and employment experience. We hold human capital up as the route to success, the good life. Participants in this study are no different. They often extol the virtues of investing in human capital; some are actively doing so through education or work, but even among those who are not, the view that education and work experience will lead to security, stability, and upward mobility is pervasive. From those currently enrolled in educational or training programs to those working in low-wage jobs to those not actively pursuing human capital investment at all, nearly all the people I interviewed note the importance of education and work experience to escape poverty. When I ask what they think struggling people should do, they generally reference education and work. Their descriptions of their own educational and work histories and aspirations reveal the esteem in which they hold educational ventures.

"I Don't Have Enough Paper Behind Me"

Bebe, the young woman who cares for a woman's children in exchange for a free place to stay, directly ties her desire for education to her career goals: "I want to finish high school, I want to get me a job, I want to work in a day care center, I like being around kids, and I want to work around kids, and in order for me to do that I have to have a high school diploma."[37] She's right, and many child care centers require education beyond a high school diploma as well; even so, such jobs provide notoriously low pay.

Mandy is also ambitious. A mother of three and a high school graduate, she's currently unemployed but occasionally serving as a substitute teacher's assistant, and she wants to further her education to get a good job. She tells me, "I don't have enough paper behind me to get in to what's good for me." She believes her lack of education is what's holding her back. She continues longingly, "Like if I'm making enough money, I don't have to, you know, struggle, I can buy a house. I can take my kids somewhere. You know like I can do things with them. I like a job that offers you a salary. I don't want an hourly pay job anymore." The childhood she imagines for her children is nothing like her own; she and her mother, a drug user, were homeless at times.

Kim, who we met at the beginning of this chapter, tells me, "Let me get this little piece of paper, then I'll find a job." She points to her lack of a GED or high school diploma as keeping her from getting a job, though she does have extensive work experience. She's currently preparing for the GED exam and tells me:

> You don't have that piece of paper, they don't want you. . . . Just because I don't have that piece of paper, that's my struggle now with that one, you know, other than that . . . I mean, I guess I could find a job, but it would be something that I really don't want. But if push comes to shove, I would take it.

I ask what kind of job that might be and she says, "Burger King, McDonald's, something like that . . . minimum wage." Kim's convinced she could get a job without a GED, as she has in the past, but she clings to the notion that a GED will open better doors for her, rewarding her for her human capital investment. While having been employed in the past without a GED might signal to her she doesn't need it, instead she views her past employment as insufficient and believes a GED will make a difference. She has a great deal of confidence in the power of the GED to yield what she sees as better employment.

Bianca also thinks that lacking her GED is what is keeping her from a job. A mother of three, she dropped out of school in the tenth grade to work in a gas station full-time to support her mother, who suffered from rheumatoid arthritis and was caring for her own mother, Bianca's grandmother, who was significantly debilitated by diabetes and related complications that are far more common among the poor than they are for middle-class people with diabetes. Like Kim, I meet her through a program aimed at preparing her for the GED exam. She has already completed a training program in medical assistance that did not lead to a job. She may have been drawn to the medical field in part due to her family's medical problems, as well as her own history of cervical cancer. She sees the GED as the ingredient to make the medical assistance course pay off: "So that's why I'm here then for my GED. . . . Because I want to pursue my medical field. . . . When I have my GED . . . then I accomplished everything." A GED is unlikely to provide the job opportunities she thinks it will, but instead of ceasing to believe in the achievement ideology, Bianca may just keep revising its terms, setting her sights on another credential that she thinks will let her capitalize on the two she'll already have.

Inez, a single mother of one small child, has a gruff voice but a welcoming and friendly manner. She has a history of low-wage work in a meat-packing plant and a sports stadium, in addition to a few years dealing drugs and some time in prison. She is intent on education as the route to changing her life. She believes she can achieve stable employment and an escape from poverty if she completes her GED, and she is certain all this would have happened sooner had she simply stayed in school; when I ask her if there was one thing she could change about her life she says without hesitation, "I wish I never dropped out of high school." She tells me, "Well, the job that I want, and that's why I'm taking the GED classes, is to work with kids. I would like to work in a day care center. . . . That's the job I want and that's the job I'm gonna get." In fact, her criminal record might keep her from working in child care.[38] Inez wants to have her own center, a dream even further out of her reach. She believes the GED is the key to open the door to these opportunities but this is rarely the case.[39]

Neoliberalism calls for this kind of focus on what people can do as individuals to assure their financial well-being to the exclusion of recognizing the structural barriers that make that increasingly difficult. But as more people achieve college degrees, the educational bar to assure occupational and financial security also rises. Individuals such as Inez accept the burdens neoliberal society places on them, but inequality is built into the structure of the system. Neoliberalism has no answer for how those at the inevitable bottom could climb the ladder, even if they do everything right: if they do ascend, others fall to take their place. Someone must be at the bottom, and they aren't always people who shirk their responsibility in a neoliberal world. And neoliberalism ensures that those at the bottom will blame themselves for their position.

Participants implicitly acknowledge a barrier when they reference the importance of education in achieving stability, although they tend to suggest that not getting an education is an individual decision. Those who are in GED programs are naturally likely to believe that such programs would change their lives. Dominique describes the circumstances that led her to pursue a GED: A prospective employer at a cleaning service told her outright that she had been turned down for a job because she didn't have a high school degree. Dominique, who's in her mid-forties, is shy and soft-spoken for most of our interview, but she speaks with obvious frustration when she notes that she couldn't imagine how a high school degree would help her clean homes or offices, though she seems to understand that an employer overwhelmed with applications might narrow the field in what amounts to an arbitrary way. She explains, "They said the reason they do that is because they don't have enough jobs to go around. So you got a hundred applications, you could get rid of seventy-five without that. Now you narrow it down to twenty-five, you know." And she's not wrong. A high school diploma or GED is an easy marker to use as a proxy for things like persistence, dedication, and punctuality. Katherine Newman described a tight labor market in fast food in New York City, where there were fourteen applicants for each open position and hiring managers did indeed use educational credentials to reduce time sifting through the large numbers of applicants.[40] So Dominique's experience is not unusual.

KWRU member Jessie has a forthright manner and tells me, "It just seems like . . . you have to have a high school diploma to even work at Payless. Like how stupid can you be to work at Payless? You don't even have to do anything but ring people up. It just don't make any sense nowadays." Jessie's acquainted with the skills required to work a cash register, as she worked at a large drugstore chain in the past.[41] She's planning to get her GED and dreams of being a computer technician or a nurse. For either of these career aspirations to become reality for Jessie, she will need more than a GED.[42] Jessie says that she has faith that her life will improve "as long as I keep my eye on the prize," and she blames herself for her poverty: "I'm my own person. I make my own decisions. If I made a decision that was wrong that made the situation worse, I did it."

"You Need to Keep Working to Be What You Want"

Participants in this study subscribe to the notion that one needs education in order to get a good job; beyond their personal experiences they describe a view that education is the answer for people in general. While many of them have set their sights on a GED, others are skeptical. Gail, herself a high school dropout with a GED and a job as an administrative assistant making under $17,000 a year (her salary approaches the federal poverty threshold for a family of three),[43] looks at me with certainty from behind her slightly tinted prescription glasses when she says, "a high school diploma just isn't enough. You need to go to school. You need to keep working to do what you want and be what you want." She herself has no plans to go to school, and with her husband's salary her family is scraping by; she also likes the job that she got as part of a welfare-to-work program, and if she got a better job she might lose medical benefits.

Bebe has little hope of even a high school diploma, but she too notes that higher education is important: "If you don't have a college degree or something, you can't get a job." KWRU member Marisol's neatly painted eyebrows make her look permanently hopeful and happy. She tells me her own goal is to get her GED, but she also says wearily, "There's hardly no jobs for like people that only have a GED, a lonely diploma." She's been volunteering at the KWRU office, doing general office work and answering phones and would like a job doing these types of tasks in the future. Savannah tells me, "If you want to get a really good job, you have to have a degree, a bachelor's or something in college. . . . You have to have a degree in college in order to get a really good job to live comfortable." Yet the chances Savannah, Marisol, and Bebe will obtain college degrees are slim, given their financial barriers, time constraints, and prior academic experiences.[44]

Carole, another enrollee in a GED exam preparation course, tells me, "You have to have education behind you. You have to." Carole also extols the virtues of a college degree; while she is working to study for her GED, she aspires to one day go to college. She wears her curly dark blonde hair pulled into a tight ponytail, revealing a broad smile and a cautious confidence. Carole believes that a training program would make it very likely that a client would get a job: "They can place you into a pretty good job" that "would probably pay pretty good." Karen, the sister of a KWRU member, was at one time homeless and addicted to crack, and has been on welfare. She was raised in foster care and she relinquished or lost custody of three of her four older children. Now she has been in recovery for seven years, is married to the father of her three-year-old daughter, and is home full-time with their daughter; her husband financially supports the family, and they live in the home left to her by her foster mother, substantially reducing their cost of living due to near-zero housing costs. While they live in poverty, she does not face as much material hardship as she once did. Karen speaks passionately about the importance of education and says she thinks the welfare training and job readiness programs are a waste of resources:

> What about the people that are on welfare, that doesn't have a high school diploma? What kind of job are you preparing them to go to? They should take them back to school. . . . You're sending [people] to these job readiness programs, that don't have a high school education! They're not going to get a job in a law firm! They're not going to get a job on a computer, or, getting paid like anywhere between, 13 to 15 dollars an hour. No, they're

going to get minimum wage. So that they're going to go to Burger King, McDonald's. . . . Welfare just wants them out of their system. So they're pushing them anywhere they can go. And that's it with the welfare. What that's gonna do is start the cycle all over again. They're going to end up being burnt out, on these, these McDonald jobs, end up going back to welfare, starting that program all over again. It's a vicious cycle. You know? And, and I think that, um, if the politicians had any kind of heart for family, where they want families to succeed and not set them up for fail[ure], send them back to school. Send them to school. Let them get their . . . if they don't have a high school diploma, let them get their GED, send them to a trade school so they can be off the welfare permanently, not just for a moment. That's all they're doing, it's just, momentarily solving the problem.

Karen thinks a meaningful education would lead to permanent escape from welfare and poverty; she holds up human capital investment as the answer. Her belief in education reflects her confidence in the achievement ideology; she believes someone should provide aid for people to go to school, but assumes that educational support alone will fix poverty and end the need for welfare.

Kia, a high school graduate who took community college courses, then became certified as a home health aide and as a medical assistant, is back in school again to be a paralegal while also working the night shift at a bank, all while being the single mother to three children, aged seven, four, and two. She believes strongly in the power of human capital investment. Friendly though businesslike with me in most of our interactions, she is passionate when she discusses the importance of education in terms of what she wants to say to a friend who is not in school:

You're home, you don't have any children, you on the street, you're not working. Go to school! Go to school! That's why they make so many certificate schools, you can go to culinary or art school, you can go get a medical assistant certificate. They're doing all this for like people that don't want to put all them years in college. At least you have something under your belt to get you a better job. Because, like, pretty soon they'll say, "Do you have a degree to flip a burger, or did you go to school, or culinary art school to do this?" They want you to have it, that's why when you fill out an application: What have you done with yourself since high school? Fill in the gap. And you don't have anything to write down, and they're going to pass you by, because they want somebody who's determined, and who has done something with themself to want something for themself, somebody who's going to bring something to their company. And they don't understand, and I'm just sitting there, I'm like, "Okay well, you're not for me."

Kia's belief that her friend should invest in education and framing it as the path to a better future demonstrates her strong belief in the power of individual agency. Her commitment to the achievement ideology blinds her to barriers her friend may have to face in furthering her education and leads her to denigrating her for not following the human capital path.

Study participants also tell me that they want their own children to stay in school and finish school, as a means to attain a measure of security as adults. KWRU member Jessie, who dropped out of high school, tells me that she wants her four children's lives to be:

> Hopefully better than mine. I'm not gonna say push, I'm gonna just back them 100 . . . like 300 percent and let them know even if they fail this much that they can make it, yes, you can. . . . Because I'm the mom that went through that and I don't want to see any of my kids go through that. So I'm gonna see them all the way through high school, college, whatever you gonna do, trade school. You ain't gonna do what I did.

KWRU member Rosa, who dropped out of high school during the ninth grade, tells me, "I want to show my kids that staying in school is the best thing you can do because if you don't, you ain't going to get nowhere in life." Rosa has seven children, but she doesn't have custody of the three oldest, teenagers who live with their father. She wants those children she does have with her, ages seven to twelve, to make different choices in school than she did.

Barriers to Building Human Capital

The commitment of the people I interviewed to teaching their children to invest in human capital strategies demonstrates their faith in individualism and the achievement ideology. They hope that people like Paul Ryan are right that culture and choice drive poverty, that if poor people had better attitudes, they (presumably unemployed) could get jobs (and presumably then not be poor).[45] This perspective unfortunately fails to recognize the extent of the barriers to upward mobility poor people face.

Even the fragile stability of the middle class[46] requires a bachelor's degree. The data on job training programs such as those some of the participants in this study are planning to complete are mixed. Job training programs are not typically linked to employers and recipients of their certificates often find they remain jobless.[47] GEDs also buy little. Research shows that people with GEDs are no better off than high school dropouts in terms of their likelihood of getting good jobs, and that employers also view GEDs as less valuable than high school diplomas. In addition, neither those with GEDS nor those with standard high school diplomas have had good job prospects in the postindustrial economy without additional training; jobs available to workers without advanced education or specialized skills do not pay well.[48] Russell Rumberger, author of *Dropping Out: Why Students Drop Out of High School and What Can Be Done about It*, said in an interview, "The things that employers generally most look for or think are important, especially at lower-end jobs, are the things like perseverance and tenacity, and those kinds of qualities that are not measured by the GED."[49]

At the same time, the route to a bachelor's degree can be perilous, even for those who can find a way onto the path. From financial institutions that offer loans to schools themselves, there are a number of entities eager to exploit dreams of upward mobility for profit, and there is a problem of institutions offering substandard credentials (to those students who finish) and imposing crushing debt.[50] Even those not seeking to exploit dreams for profit but to expand educational access to a larger group of students are misguided, perhaps willfully ignorant, about the high cost and low return of such access. The Obama administration sought to restrict the access of poorly performing for-profit colleges to federal financial aid dollars to protect people from exploitation at the hands of for-profit colleges and debt they would never be able to repay. The efforts have met with mixed success.[51] However, the problem of crippling student loan debt is hardly confined to for-profit colleges.

In 2012, 71 percent of four-year college graduating seniors had student loans. Among such students, the average student graduated with a debt of $29,400, a 25 percent increase in debt levels since 2008.[52] Noncompletion—in which case they will have debt but have no credential that might help them pay it off—is a serious risk.

Another significant barrier to mobility exists in the interconnection between poverty and mental health problems. A recent Gallup poll found that those living in poverty were twice as likely to have been diagnosed with depression compared to other Americans.[53] According to a *JAMA Psychiatry* article in 2014, millions of low-income Americans suffer from parasitic infections that are associated with cognitive impairment or mental health disorders.[54] Both greater exposure to violent conditions—something many participants reference—and disparate health care and behaviors contribute to these adverse outcomes. Economic insecurity affects people cognitively as well, so much so that poverty reduces the ability to make the best long-term choices.[55] As psychologist Johannes Haushofer commented to the *New York Times*, "It's circumstances that can land you in a situation where it's really hard to make a good decision because you're so stressed out. And the ones you get wrong matter much more, because there's less slack to play with."[56] So poor people suffer greater consequences from poor choices than do better-off people.

Research into the impact of violence on poor people can and should spur efforts to improve the conditions under which poor people live and their access to quality health care. Neoliberalism hamstrings such efforts. It also makes inequality inevitable. It is difficult to ameliorate trauma, mental health problems, and adverse health conditions without addressing the structural forces that create these problems. Addressing violence and trauma and mistrust directly will not change the fact of deep poverty without systemic change.

Evidence also suggests that the traits associated with beating the odds impose a high price on the poor. It's unclear how much control poor youth or their parents—or the participants in the research for this book—have over whether they'll possess these traits which vital to achieving upward mobility. It is clear that these traits are rare, and that even if they could be chosen the choice would be difficult. The same traits associated with academic and professional achievement for disadvantaged youth—self-control and resilience—carry health risks ranging from visible aging of their cells, higher blood pressure, more body fat, and higher levels of the stress hormone cortisol.[57] Poor health outcomes represent a serious downside of being a poor person who's an effective striver, and this health research further demonstrates the patent unfairness, as it also shows that the traits associated with success are associated with *good* health for better-off people.

Agency and Ambition

"It Doesn't Just Happen; You Have to Make It Happen"

The achievement ideology revolves around what people think and do as individuals, guided by the notion that we control our own futures. The emphasis on education in many participant interviews reflects this ideology. Similarly, they emphasize individual ambition. Gail demonstrates this perspective when she says, "I think that if you have the ambition to be more than just average then you do it, you'll exceed to try to do the most you can to get the income you want and need." Describing her general outlook, she says, "I feel like there's nothing I couldn't do." The achievement ideology leads her to believe she can achieve whatever she desires.

Participants who believe in the power of their agency to effect changes in their lives see opportunities to make decisions that will improve their circumstances. KWRU member Maureen, who has not had a job in two years, feels crippled by depression and anxiety. She left her job at a fast-food restaurant where she worked from age fourteen to thirty-one as she could see that her two children were struggling emotionally and academically because of her unpredictable hours. Her children showed measurable improvement when she quit, but she acknowledges that it was a difficult trade-off as her financial struggles have deepened, leading her to engage in shoplifting and then selling the stolen items to make ends meet. Now she is preparing for a sentencing hearing following a conviction for shoplifting. But she says her situation will improve because "I'm gonna make it improve." When I ask another participant, Polly, if she thinks her situation will improve over time, she says that it will "if I put myself and my mind to it."

A recovering addict who long ago lost custody of her older children, Carole speaks with determination about her future with her two younger children. She leans in toward me as she says:

> It takes work and if you don't think to plan little footsteps, it's never gonna happen. Your dreams can come true, but you have to map out a plan for yourself to get there. You know what I mean? And you have to put action into it. . . . If you want anything, [if] you're gonna get anything, you've got to work hard for it. Whatever you put into life is what you gonna get out of life. You gotta work for whatever you want, okay?

Like others I interviewed, Carole has a strong conviction that individual effort and persistence will lead her to the successful life she craves. Undoubtedly, her efforts to conquer her addiction required great effort and persistence, and may have reinforced her belief in the power of her own agency to achieve her goals. She needs to continue to believe in herself to maintain her commitment to sobriety. Her success in this realm may be an indication that she does have the fortitude to persist even in the face of substantial barriers to economic mobility. But hard work and dedication are not sufficient to yield success, and indeed only in a minority of cases will they do so, in combination with a number of other factors, including luck.

When I ask Tina, a peripherally involved member of KWRU, what people who are struggling to survive should do, she says:

> I think they should work hard and try to get themselves together the best way that they know how and try to, you know, just pull themselves out of the situation that they're in, as hard as it is. As hard as it is, I found that it can be done. It's hard. I'm not going to say that it's not hard, but I think it can be done.

KWRU membership has not disrupted her belief in the American Dream and that hard work leads people to "deserve" to get ahead, which also correspond to her beliefs about what people who are struggling should do. Recognizing that it is an uphill battle doesn't stop Tina from believing that anything is possible with hard work. She doesn't want to admit that upward mobility might simply be impossible for some people, particularly by "just pulling themselves out of the situation that they're in." Tina continues: "It doesn't just happen; you have to make it happen, you have to push yourself, you know. Life is all about hard work." Tina's conviction in the power of individual agency and hard work is apparent. Similarly, Karen, currently unemployed and not actively looking for work, believes all will work out for her and she'll find a good job

> because, if you don't [think positively] you're gonna be a victim of your own circumstances. If you think beneath your level, that's where you're gonna stay. You've got to think . . . you've got to have great expectations in life. And you have to go for them, you know, you have to reach for them. And it's like, whatever it takes, prepare yourself to get there, you know, don't go outside the law, don't go outside the realm, to do it. 'Cause I learned that lesson too. Things are not just gonna, just, land in your lap. You have to, you know, you have to work and plan.

"Where There's a Will, There's a Way"

As chapter 3 will describe in more detail, there are a small number of participants who recognize that structural barriers constrain individuals' agency and that individual blame is misguided. KWRU member Colleen survived a childhood shuffling between foster care and her father's care. Both her parents struggled with drug addiction. Now twenty-nine and a mother of three, she wears her long curly hair in a low ponytail as I interview her for hours in my office; she meets me there after she's done with work for the day. Her master's degree makes her the study participant with the highest level of formal education. Colleen says she learned in a college sociology course that poverty and lack of jobs are a widespread problem: "It was the first time I ever heard anybody say to me or suggest that all of these things and you read these stories and I'm like, 'Hey, these are everything that I went through. These are all the people that I know. This is everything around me and it must not just be something that happened to me.' This is something that's going on in society." A longtime KWRU activist, she tells me, "Like when you see so many people in the situations that they're in, you can't ever say it's that individual's fault. These are large segments of society. This isn't just one individual that's on welfare." This view, more typical of sociology professors than of mainstream U.S. adults, is predictably rare among participants in this study. Most, unlike Colleen and some other KWRU members, focus on personal power to accomplish goals. Blaming people for anything less than success is pervasive among those I interviewed.

This individualistic ideology often includes contradictory ideas. Although participants' own lives clearly evidence the impact of structural factors in shaping their poverty, the achievement ideology's pull is strong and powerful. KWRU member Helen tells me, "You can't blame the homeless people for being poor. That's not their fault." But then she adds, "There is a lot of young people out there that just want to be on their ass and do nothin' and go to these shelters to live for free . . . half of them could be out working." Helen is in her late forties and slightly overweight; at first glance, the lack of gray in her straight red hair makes me think she looks young for her age, but her wrinkled, weathered face counters my initial impression. She has an extensive history of poverty and unemployment punctuated by periods of temporary and part-time employment. Evidence suggests that in this she resembles welfare recipients, many of whom have extensive work histories.[58] Helen has a part-time job at the time of our interview. A nominal member of KWRU and a former activist, she has spent time with members who discuss the macroeconomic forces that shape employment prospects, which may have influenced her comments. She draws on her own experiences as well as a general sense of the job market. She contradicts herself throughout the interview, at one point saying, "There ain't shit out there. I'm serious. There is no jobs at all." Then, moments later, criticizing people she knew who weren't working, she said, "There's jobs out there." When I ask her about this reversal, she says, "No, there is none, but maybe if they look." Much research shows that the labor market, not a lack of desire for work, drives the unemployment of welfare recipients.[59] Later Helen returns to the other point of view: "They're closing down all these factories, all these jobs, there is none, so what are you supposed to do with the people that want to work? There's a lot of people out there that want to work and can't." Helen is correct: Deindustrialization was particularly disastrous for the working poor in Philadelphia, and abandoned shells of former factories litter the landscape of North Philadelphia neighborhoods. Later Helen says, suggesting perhaps the weariness of anyone seeking a solution to poverty, "I know there's no jobs out there, but they should really try to find something. . . . I know it's hard, but at least try to get a job. . . . They need to get off [welfare] and get a job."

One potential answer to the problem Helen references is that poor people might relocate to a place where jobs are more plentiful. Yet this potential bridge over structural barriers has so many obstacles that it does not constitute a meaningful alternative. Moving itself costs money, and for poor people who lived with family before it may involve taking on new housing costs. Moving to an area without public transportation may require a car and all the costs that accompany it. People may face housing discrimination, and places with more jobs typically have higher housing costs than places with few. Class-based and race- and/or ethnicity-based job discrimination make it far from certain a move will pay off. Moving also disrupts the local social ties the urban poor do have that help them survive—in addition to housing, this may include child care, emotional support and connection, and other kinds of support.[60] The catch-22 poor people face as they consider their options, under pressure to subscribe to individualism, makes it almost natural that they would speak in contradictions. While few study participants contradict themselves as blatantly as Helen does, many do simultaneously bemoan the lack of jobs and decry people for not working. Even in recognizing barriers that poor people may confront, participants assert that nothing is insurmountable. Jen, twenty-four, says, "There's ways to work around everything," listing a few individualistic strategies people can employ to better their circumstances or weather a financial storm. Karen, contemplating going on the job market at some point in the future, similarly tells me, confidently, "Where there's a will, there's a way." Most participants strongly assert that individuals have the power to change their own lives.

"It's My Own Fault"

The logic that hard work always leads to success leads to the corollary that poor people cause their own poverty. Inez, a poor single mother whose aspiration to work in a child care center I referenced above—a dream decidedly out of reach due to her lack of a high school diploma and her criminal record for nonviolent drug offenses, despite her current efforts toward getting a GED—tells me it's people's own fault if they're poor. Maria, who's twenty years old, lives with her mother and is pregnant with her first child at the time of our interview. She tells me, "It ain't nobody else's fault but theirs," even though her plans for a future out of poverty depend on her mother's willingness to provide child care, a resource not everyone has. Savannah, who lives with her father and has no housing costs, says, "If you work hard then you can have, you know, whatever you want. Whatever you do in life, it's upon you. . . . If you want to get ahead in life, if you want to do more, you want to have more, I think you should get off your lazy butt and do it." Stacie, who has a college degree but is unemployed and facing eviction in the coming weeks, says, "I think everybody is responsible for their own actions."

The focus on what we have the power to do through our own actions inevitably leads to blaming poor people for their poverty.[61] For desperately poor study participants, this means self-blame as well. Mandy, broad-shouldered and tall, with a commanding presence, tells me:

> I made myself poor. . . . I played a big part in my poverty. . . . Nobody told me to go out here and have three kids knowing that I'm going to struggle to take care of them. You know nobody told me to take the steps that I took to get where I'm at, you know. Nobody told me to do any of those things. I made those decisions so I in turn inflicted some of my suffering on myself. . . . That's my fault that I don't have enough money to be comfortable . . . because there are jobs out here that you can get. There are little side help you can get. You can baby-sit. You can, you know go out and mow somebody's lawn. You can take out somebody's trash every week. There's a way. The same way I'm teaching my kids you got to learn how to work for your money, I can be out there doing it.

Mandy has a high school diploma but as a single mother of three children, including one infant, she cannot realistically work outside the home now. The cost of child care would be prohibitive, not offset by any wages she would receive based on the kind of job she could get. She does have an extensive work history, but the jobs she's had have never paid a living wage. The research showing that the stressors the poor face constitute an economic disadvantage likely have more to do with her poverty than the part she played in it; her mother was a drug addict and they were homeless at times, and her stepfather molested her. She was homeless again when she ran away at age fifteen.

Personal responsibility and a sense of striving as an individual permeate participants' notions about survival and mobility strategies. A participant who chose "Shy" as her pseudonym is homeless, and living in a KWRU Human Rights House at the time of our interview. Shy is warm and friendly and always greets me with a hug. She says, "Basically, it's me havin' to change my situation. Nobody can change my situation but me." Most participants tell me any difficulties they face are their own fault. Nina, whose constant smiling and seeming self-confidence contrast with her comment, says, "Sometimes I feel like it's my own fault." Nina receives cash assistance and food stamps.

KWRU member Rebecca, who finds our interview upsetting, tells me, "I blame myself . . . and how hard I tried, it's still my fault. It still comes down to me." Rebecca cries as she tells me this. Blaming themselves for their poor economic circumstances caused great pain to the people I interviewed. Rebecca described the bind in which it places people like her:

> It is kind of hard, you know, because you don't want to think about yourself like, "Oh, I'm struggling." You don't want to think about yourself like that. You want to think about, "I can do this." . . . You want to think positive and all, and you just got to step back, take a look at your life. . . . And then just better yourself from then on forth.

Participants like Rebecca feel as though they've repeatedly fallen short, disappointing themselves and failing to be the sort of role models they would like to be for their children. Rebecca's teenaged daughter, born when she was a teenager herself, is pregnant when I interview Rebecca, meaning she will be a grandmother at thirty-three. She's striving to achieve stable housing for her daughter and grandson, along with her eleven-year-old son. At the same time this agentic attitude can be empowering. For those who believe their own efforts will yield the futures they want, they see themselves as the only barriers to success. So they cautiously but confidently assert that once they make the right moves, they'll achieve their goals. Refraining from making those moves is a way to protect their self-esteem as it staves off potential failures that perhaps on some level they do anticipate. Even if they're wrong to blame themselves and wrong to believe anything is possible with hard work alone, these perceptions are nearly ubiquitous in the United States. It would be surprising if most of those I interviewed didn't share these views.

"I Am Very Independent"

Gail, who portrays an understated confidence, says, "I am very independent and I don't like to turn to people." She credits her father with this perspective:

> My dad always raised me that, to be strong, do what you have to do, basically to be a survivor. So I went, I mean my first job I was fourteen, fifteen, fourteen or fifteen years old. So I worked my whole life to where I really didn't, I automatically [be]came independent. I got pregnant when I was young. I was stubborn. I felt as though I didn't need any help. This is my baby, I'm going to work and I'm going to do what I got to do to take care of him. So I really basically through my life didn't turn to too many people.

Gail's mother died when she was two. She feels close to her father, and talks to him every day and sees him every week.

Jen says, "Whatever I get in life is all from me, and only me by myself and where, however far I go is only gonna be, 'cause that's as far as I took myself, and there's nobody else to help me." In fact, based on her account, she would not have her job if her mother had not filled out the necessary paperwork as she is functionally illiterate. Yet she still claims to be independent.

Mandy says, "I believe, like I said independence is a big thing for me. I don't know how independent that I am but I believe in it. Like my mother she did it all by herself. So watching her do it just made me stronger knowing that I don't need anybody. . . . I need help sometimes but you don't depend on other people. You find a way to make it work for you." In fact, Mandy's mother could have benefited from housing support that would have kept them off the streets.

Silva argues that betrayal causes working class people to cling to neoliberal ideals: "Over and over again, working-class youth experience bewilderment and betrayal in institutions, learning that they can depend on others only at great cost."[62] The participants in my research did not report feeling betrayed by institutions—though it seems evident the American Dream itself has betrayed them—but they did report instances of feeling betrayed by other individuals, including family members, and certainly some of them avoided reliance on others because of such betrayal.

Denise, a high school graduate with some community college experience, has recently returned to Philadelphia after six years with an abusive husband out of state. She's living with her mother, yet focuses on her own sense of independence as a crucial factor in her positive sense of self-worth:

> I feel very independent, very strong-minded about my decision and choices now than I did in the past. I feel like I could do anything I want to do as long as I put my mind to it and just research it. . . . I feel that good about myself that I can provide for a future, and that's what I'm trying to do now, you know, something that I don't have to lean on somebody else to do for me. I'm actually making a decision and choice this time. I don't have to lean.

Denise again tells me later that she is "an independent person," and doesn't like to accept assistance from others. This drive to be independent, not accept help from others, to do it "on my own" is an understandable response to a widespread individualistic ideology, and along with other factors, it fosters an avoidance of social ties, the subject of the next chapter.

The Limits of Individualistic Ideology

Study participants may have espoused individualistic ideology, but for the most part their lives and circumstances disproved the theory that personal effort and persistence are sufficient to lead to success.[63] One of KWRU's leading activists speaks with a forceful but quiet determination:

> You go down to the John Deere Plant, in southern Illinois, they had something like, you know, nearly two thousand what, three thousand

workers. . . . They laid off all the workers and hired back three of them. . . . What happened to the 2,997 workers? Some of them became homeless. That's how you become homeless. It's structural, it's not, you know, "Oh, I made the wrong choice."

This leader has done work with homeless people in a variety of locales and is generally better informed than most participants about the specifics of poverty outside Philadelphia. Few of the people I interviewed see these wider structural forces at play, though at times cracks appear in their general acceptance of the achievement ideology.

"There's No Jobs"

A few participants lack confidence that education is a panacea. These participants directly tie their recognition of a lack of jobs to acknowledgment of the limits of education's reach. Becky tells me, "I don't think there's anything out there for people that have education anymore." She herself is not in the job market because of debilitating illness, and she dropped out of school in the seventh grade so her mother would not have to put her younger siblings in foster care when serious illnesses struck both the adults in the family. However, these participants generally cling to education as the best option, in recognition that although it provides no guarantee, it does proffer the best bet; their individualistic ideology is more limited but still powerful.

A number of participants disrupted individualism by acknowledging the limits of hard work. Even as they focus on what individuals should do to get out of poverty, they acknowledge constraints on their personal capabilities to succeed. Alyssa, for example, a married mother of four young children, is working as an administrative assistant at a social service agency where she was previously a client. She describes a pattern of small raises over the four years she's been working there, "Which, at first I thought it was good, but, now, how about I need a raise again." The limitations she faces as an administrative assistant have become a problem, as three of her four children have been born since she took the job, stretching her salary ever thinner. Her salary is less than the poverty line for a family of three and she supports six people—including her husband, a stay-at-home father. Other participants, like Dominique, note the crippling force of student debt. Referring to a young college graduate, a former coworker at a restaurant: "And then she's stuck with a big college loan. . . . It's not fair really. They get everybody to make them big loans, give them the hope, and then when they're done it's not there." Dominique's experience has led her to be particularly skeptical of education. She says,

> When I was waitressing we had a busboy and the other waitress that were out of college, they finished college, they got good marks, okay, and the waitress kept going on her days off to job interviews and all, and she's so sweet. Sometimes she'd come in and she'd just bust out crying. Why was she crying? Because nobody was hiring. They said not enough experience, and she was like, "How do I get experience if I'm just out of college, if nobody's gonna hire me?"

Dominique is nonetheless studying to get a GED, which suggests that recognizing the limitations of building human capital may not prevent people from seeking it. Among study participants Dominique is unusual in knowing college graduates; most have no direct knowledge of whether a college degree would guarantee financial security.

Many lament the catch-22 of job experience—you need to have a job to gain job experience, but you need experience to get a job. Bianca tells me, "Like you see like in the paper they have a lot of things about like medical, for medical billing, for LPN, for medical assistant, but they also say that you have to have so many years experience, so much time experience. . . . You got to at least have the chance to get the experience."

Kia acknowledges it's very hard to get a job without experience, even with educational credentials, of which she has many, including a high school diploma, two years of community college, and certificates in home health aide work and medical assistance. Nonetheless, she tells me of a friend, "So she actually wasted that money that she paid back going to school for. Because they want you to have experience, and she's like, 'Well how am I supposed to get experience if you don't hire me? I'm coming straight out of school.' And they want you to have that experience, you know?" If pursuing education is the only possible route to a job, even acknowledging that it may get you nowhere may be unthinkable, which may be why Kia is seeking a paralegal certificate when we speak and why she characterizes education as the key to getting a job in another part of the interview. The apparent contradiction in Kia's assessments lays bare the fact that it is nearly impossible for people such as those I interviewed to acknowledge that education might not be useful, when it is the only thing they perceive they have the agency to control. If no one else is responsible for your poverty, you alone have the power to change your circumstances, and the only thing you think you can do is seek education, then admitting deficiencies in that pursuit would be paralyzing.

Conclusion

Participants in this study reflect the societal shifts outlined in the Introduction; they subscribe to the notion that through individual effort and persistence they can achieve a better life, even in the face of a structure that provides little opportunity to do so. In their view, investing in human capital through education is a reliable path to upward mobility. Structural constraints are absent from most of their narratives; they wholeheartedly embrace the achievement ideology, clinging to the belief that their effort and persistence will enable them to thrive in the future.

This ideology guides their approaches to escaping poverty, whether they are actively pursuing those approaches, planning them, or simply aspiring to them. Ultimately, they may need human capital to escape poverty, but it won't be sufficient. Rather, many poor individuals like participants in this study obtain credentials only to find their opportunities for stable and well-paid employment no wider than before. One limiting factor is the low ceiling on the education that is most accessible; another is the dearth of jobs that pay a living wage. Believing in the achievement ideology is, in this respect, misplaced confidence in a future far from guaranteed. And yet it provides a great deal of hope to many of the people in this study.

In keeping with others' findings, the lives of participants who are pursuing human capital illustrate its costs and uncertain rewards. Participants refer to effort and merit as causes of inequality and place the responsibility for the existence of poverty squarely on the shoulders of the poor themselves. Rather than recognize structural barriers or systemic causes of poverty, they frame their difficulties as the result of poor choices and prescribe—for themselves and others in their situation—familiar individualistic remedies of attaining additional education, training, and work experience. This individualism serves to make it difficult to build social ties, including sustainable ties.

Their individualistic perspective on the world is common in U.S. society. Participants in this study, while economically worse off than most Americans, are otherwise quite similar to their fellow citizens. They desire a better life and believe personal effort is the way to attain their goals. They want to achieve their goals on their own as a marker of their successful independence, which is also part of what leads them to avoid developing social ties, the topic of chapter 2.

2

I Stay to Myself

Avoidance of Social Ties

I'm a house person, I like staying home. . . . I stay to myself; I
don't ask nobody for nothing.
—Nicole, 21, North Philadelphia resident

Kelly, lonely and grieving the deaths of two close family members, tells
me the only person she would ask for help if she needed it is her grandmother, whose health is failing; the prospect of losing her grandmother
to illness in the near future compounds her sense of isolation. Her dra-
matic eye makeup makes her sad eyes look bigger.

While isolation clearly worsens the pain of her grief, when I ask Kelly
to tell me about her neighbors, she says, "I don't usually talk to them. I
stay to myself. . . . I don't have no friends. I stay by myself. . . . I can't trust
anybody."[1] When I ask her what it's like to help others she says, "Right
now I need to help myself." With few people to turn to and few resources
of her own, she does not feel as though she has extra resources to give to
others. Kelly lives with her mother and her young son; his father was de-
ported to his native Dominican Republic. She has a negative relationship
with her mother and she says that her sister, who passed away, was more
of a mother to her than her actual mother. She says that her mother
thinks "I don't know nothin' . . . treating me like something's wrong with
me. . . . She's not there like a mother's supposed to be there." This is why
she says she would not ask her mother for help. While clearly Kelly is
receiving help in that she lives with her mother, she would benefit from
more social connection. When her grandmother passes away, she will
be terribly isolated. Unlike most of the other participants in this study
who were not KWRU members, she is not attending programs at any
social service agencies, which compounds her isolation. She has little
companionship apart from her son.

Kelly is one of the most isolated of the study participants. But "I stay to myself," "I'm not an outside person," and other variants of choosing to isolate oneself and avoid ties with others are common refrains in participant interviews. KWRU member Marie, forty-two, tells me the best thing about the neighborhood where she and her family live in a house rented with a Section 8 voucher, is, "I don't know nobody. They don't know nothing about me." Marie has begun to build ties through KWRU, as the next chapter describes, but like many KWRU participants, she avoids ties in general. The life she describes apart from her involvement in KWRU sounds horrific:

> Those streets are brutal. . . . I don't want to go outside. I'm scared. . . . I'd rather just keep life like it is right now. I'm in the house. The doors are shut. . . . So when it's dark outside I'm always in the house before it gets dark. But if I get caught out there I'm on my way in here. . . . I'll only do what works for me. So I don't go, even during the day I don't go nowhere. I don't want to know nobody. I don't want any new people in my life. I don't want to try anything else new. I don't want no more new friends. I don't want anything.

Many scholars decry what they see as an increase in social isolation. Robert Putnam argued in *Bowling Alone: The Collapse and Revival of American Community*[2] that the latter part of the twentieth century witnessed a decline in formal group membership of various types; the title of his book refers to his observation that people continue to bowl as a leisure activity, but they bowl alone instead of in leagues as in a bygone era. Stacie, an intensely religious participant who mentioned going to God for emotional support, not to friends, for example, is facing eviction. She tells me,

> These days like people are more so to themselves and in the house, you know what I mean? It's not like people would come out and have block parties and stuff like that, where I live anyway. . . . It seems like people are just like really to themselves.

Stacie is reserved and poised, soft-spoken without being timid. When I ask her if she has friends in her neighborhood she is close to, she tells me, "I have a lot of associates. . . . I don't really hang out with anybody. . . . A friend is someone that, you know, we can talk about anything, go out, hang out, talk about the good, the bad. . . . An associate . . . I just say hi and bye to them." The desire to avoid interactions with others extends beyond neighbors. Denise, who also connects her avoidance of others to her commitment to human capital investment, elevating her aspiration for education above any desire for social connection, confides, "I don't have many friends, I don't choose to. Basically right now I'm just on a track where I'm trying to get my education back on track. Yeah, I got enough stress. . . . I don't trust nobody.[3]

The networks poor people can access tend to have meager resources, so immense need may quickly drain those resources.[4] Yet, as Harknett notes, "social networks play an important role in providing financial and in-kind support to poor families."[5] Indeed, for those living in financially precarious circumstances, having others on whom to rely can make the difference between homelessness and a safe place to stay.[6] Yet distrust can be high and pervasive.[7] At times poor people work together; at times they self-isolate,[8] illustrating the complexity of these mechanisms and the fact that the poor are not a monolithic group.

This chapter describes the varied reasons participants from both groups report "staying to themselves," avoiding potentially valuable ties. It shows how the individualistic ideology described in chapter 1 breeds social isolation. It also discusses varying reasons for avoiding social ties: general distrust of others, the sense that their neighborhoods are dangerous and therefore it's best to avoid contact with neighbors, pervasive stigma about the poor, and fear of obligations to others or others' inability to return their favors. My findings resemble others': poor people isolate themselves from their peers while trying to become upwardly mobile.[9] This chapter relies on interviews with KWRU members (again noted in the text as members of KWRU) as well as nonmembers. The desire to avoid social ties is a common one, even for KWRU members, who must push past this to become involved in the organization.

Individualism Breeds Social Isolation

As noted in the previous chapter, the focus on individualism leads people to both focus on agency's power as the strategy for survival and success and to avoid social ties; development of and reliance on ties contradicts their perspective on the importance of going it alone. So this is one of the four main mechanisms I identified that hinder the formation of social ties among the poor.

For participants in this study, developing a social tie with another, a tie that provides resources, threatens a strongly held sense of individualism. Building relationships implies a need for those ties; this challenges the common self-concept described in chapter 1 of individuals who believe they can and should succeed independently. People want to be self-reliant and avoid seeing themselves as dependent; therefore they try to refrain from asking others for help. As Silva argues, people make "a virtue out of not asking for help; if they could do it, then everyone else should too."[10]

Structural forces as well as individual feelings both shape social isolation.[11] Kia, a twenty-six-year-old African American mother of three children, exemplifies this. She balances working the night shift at a bank part-time with studying to be a paralegal. In spite of the difficulties her financial situation and schedule present, she expresses her commitment to keeping to herself. Her siblings and parents live in Philadelphia and they've had no rifts in their relationships, yet Kia has resorted to living in her car with her children and to renting a single room in the past, even though she told me she could have stayed with her brother or sister. She explains, "You can't always stay with people." She believes those who are struggling should further their education and avoid relying on others for help. The myth of individualistic success is one of the strongest barriers to the formation of social ties among the poor. As such, it does real damage to the lives of poor people, rendering them alone and with fewer tools to survive.

"I Like to Be Independent"

For many participants, forging ties with others and getting assistance with daily needs poses a threat to their sense of independence.[12] They mention this issue most frequently in relation to the difficulty with getting help. Dominique, a participant in her forties, says she has more difficulty asking for help now than when she was younger, because "I feel like I should be at a certain point. You know, I really should. . . . I feel at my age, I should accomplish something." And yet, without a degree, she is unlikely to achieve her goal of a well-paying job. Stacie, who has a fifteen-year-old son, is facing a potential eviction, but she tells me, "I wanted to know that I could do it on my own. . . . I didn't want those people [who helped me] to become crutches to me."

New KWRU member Stefanie tells me, "I don't feel comfortable asking people for help." She and her daughters live with her parents but she pays them rent and purchases her own food. For Leslie, receiving help "shows that you can't do it yourself . . . it shows that you're incapable of doing what you want to do so that you have to ask for help, and then you become dependent."[13] She also lives with her parents, buying food at times and contributing to utility bills when she can, but doesn't see her reliance on them as dependency.

Stefanie and Leslie do not want to get help from others in part because it flies in the face of the argument that one can accomplish all one's goals alone. It contradicts their emphasis on personal agency, something they already have difficulty holding on to, as both of these women rely on their parents for housing and frequent child care. Stefanie contributes a great deal of what she has to her family's expenses. Leslie acknowledges the broad and deep support her parents provide without viewing it as dependence on others. Like Stefanie and Leslie, Kelly lives with a parent, but her mother's assistance is fraught with emotional complications due to their strained relationship.

Reliance on Others and Isolation

Even as many espouse the importance of individual effort and personal educational attainment to achieve their goals, the study participants who are best off rely a great deal on the support of others. Most rely on strong kin ties. Jasmine, twenty, is currently in a program to improve her math skills. Others in the program are preparing for the GED exam, but as a high school graduate Jasmine doesn't need that. She has a medical assistant's certificate and wants to become a registered nurse. Jasmine exhorts others to finish school. She tells me, "It don't matter if you have kids, it's up to you to go back and finish," crediting her own agency for her educational achievements. Yet she also makes it clear that help from her kin made it possible: "My mom and my grandmom wasn't going to let me stay home. If my grandmother had to retire early [to provide child care] for me to go back to school, that's what she was going to do." Jasmine found an alternative arrangement and her grandmother continues to work. Jasmine has two family members on whom to rely—not an impressive kin network, but still more than others might boast—and this allows her to avoid social ties outside her family. Other participants do not have this advantage. With a social tie, even a temporary one, Stacie might be able to borrow money to make rent when she's short, and she might even be able to move in with a social tie if she is evicted. If such a tie were sustainable, it would be even more productive.

Participants like Jasmine reflect how "individual effort" works in practice; many of those who think of themselves as independent actually get substantial help, particularly in the form of housing and child care, from kin, but also in the form of moral and emotional support. They value self-reliance, privacy, individualism, and self-sufficiency without necessarily practicing it.[14] Maria, who's pregnant with her first child, tells me that she'd like to get a job working in an office, and if she needs additional education beyond the high school diploma she has, she'll be able to go to school because her mother will watch her baby. Jasmine tells me, "I got a lot of motivation at home. I got people like, 'Go ahead and do it if you want to do it, go ahead.'" I ask her, "Do you think that encouragement and support from them have helped you a little bit?" She says yes; "You need somebody there like, 'Go ahead, you can do it, it ain't hard, trust me, you can do it.' Or even if it's hard, it is hard. You got people like, 'I'll help you.' You know, so, don't think you gotta do it by yourself." When I ask her about the best thing in her life Jasmine immediately tells me about all she's done, emphasizing that she's only twenty and has accomplished a good deal on her own. She values the support of her family, and as her comments reflect, recognizes the value of her kin ties in helping her along. Yet she doesn't recognize that others' struggles might suggest not a lack of trying, but a lack of support such as that she receives.

Many of the people I interviewed who are not involved with KWRU have extensive help from kin; in part this help has been the resource that has prevented them from falling far enough to reach out to strangers for aid. Nicole, Maria, Kelly, Leslie, Diva, Polly, Savannah, Denise, Jasmine, and Kim all live with their parents. When I ask Diva how people who are struggling to survive manage, she extrapolates from her own experience and tells me that they might "move back with their parents, and, live, you know, have their kids live with them at their parents' house," not realizing how fortunate she is to have that option when she has no job and two children. Her parents live in the Philadelphia suburbs in a large home and her father is a physician. She says if her parents didn't have the money to provide this support, "I would still find a way," but it's not clear that one exists.

Jen's experience illustrates how solid social connections dwarf the importance of human capital. Of all the people I interviewed, her literacy level is the lowest, but she has the highest paid, most stable employment. Jen wants to do things on her own and claims that everything she's achieved she's managed on her own. She says, "Whatever I get in life is all from me, and only me by myself and where, however far I go is only gonna be, 'cause that's as far as I took myself, and there's nobody else to help me." Yet she is functionally illiterate and has used her social connections to get work and in her words, to "fool people" into believing she is more skilled than she is. Granovetter[15] pointed out the influential role of social connections in attaining employment; the lack of them depresses outcomes as well.[16] Jen's mother met her at the job interview for the position she currently holds and filled out paperwork for her, and found her an apartment through a friend and obtained a reduced rent for her. Jen has a good job at a hospital and is in an educational program now to improve her basic literacy skills. She aspires to complete her GED someday and eventually go to college, though given her literacy level that may be unlikely. Her supervisor now knows of her illiteracy but has chosen to support her rather than fire her, partially, Jen thinks, because it might look bad that Jen fooled her.

These participants' words and the characteristics of their lives illustrate a glaring contradiction: Most rely on help from kin while describing themselves as going it alone; they treat the advantages of kin ties as if they are irrelevant to the question of whether reliance on others is wise. In this way, having help from kin allows them to maintain the individualistic ideology that leads them to avoid nonkin social ties; they can avoid extrafamilial social ties *because* they have kin ties on whom to rely, to which they grant themselves access as exceptions to avoiding ties. While a few, like Kia, rely less on kin ties than they could, others espouse the virtue of self-reliance while relying on others—just not others outside their immediate families.

Very occasionally those without kin available do manage to acquire substantial support through social service agencies, though such programs are limited. Housing assistance proves particularly valuable. Carole has recently obtained housing through the Pennsylvania Department of Human Services (DHS) due to her status as a former drug addict in recovery, with two small children. She will be able to live there for a substantial period of time, rent-free. She tells me, "Thank God I have DHS in my life because they placed me into my own apartment. . . . I have eight years to be there. . . . I plan on taking advantage of all my, you know, the help that I've gotten out there, you know?" She plans to use the time without worrying about housing costs to pursue education, hoping to go to college after completing her GED. I ask what she would do if her rent was $500 a month and she says, "I wouldn't be able to do it." The housing stability and cost savings allow her to invest in human capital. She continues, "I'm really trying to succeed in life. . . . I just want to keep on going forward and keep on achieving. . . . So, now I'm going to school and I'm taking computer classes . . . and I'm just trying to keep on moving up."

Mandy' relationship to government-sponsored help is similar to Carole's. Mandy has a Section 8 voucher and she got help with the paperwork from people at a housing shelter, and then from the office of a city council person. As mentioned in chapter 1, she says, "I need help sometimes but you don't depend on other people." She depends on institutions instead of individuals, which leaves her ideology intact, keeping her from building social ties.

"Pride Is a Big Thing"

Gail blames her pride for making her refrain from asking others for help. She explains, "I don't want people to think I really need them." Nina also reports, "I don't like to ask nobody for nothing. . . . Pride is a big thing." Carole says her difficulty in getting help is "pride, I guess. My ego gets in the way." She further explains, "I don't want nobody to take care of me. I want to be able to care of myself." Carole's main source of pride is staying sober, which she has done for a year. Participants in the study take pride in doing things independently and seek to avoid associations that might threaten their views of themselves as capable people accomplishing life's tasks on their own. They also aim to protect the image others have of them.

Tina explains why she keeps her distance from others and doesn't ask for help or build friendships with others: "It's like I don't want anybody to feel sorry for me. I don't want people to think that I'm lazy," evoking the notion that anyone who needs help must not be working hard enough. The achievement ideology, as described in the prior chapter, holds that hard work leads to success. Need for assistance therefore signals laziness. Rosa says, "Having other people help you out, is a little bit embarrassing." Once, when KWRU member Rosa was homeless, she asked to shower at a cousin's house; the cousin wanted to charge her and her daughter money to bathe; she may have been recalling that incident. Bebe, Rosa's niece, describes a young woman she knows, in the depths of poverty, who regularly receives help from her mother and sisters with all her expenses—food, rent, utilities. She comments, "But that's not a way to live, everybody helping you out." Bebe's discomfort with reliance on others is common. Yet living in isolation, struggling alone without help from those around you is not a way to live either. The notion that they should be independent from others serves to isolate people from others who might aid them; it also induces guilt and shame when they do forge ties, deepening their troubles.

The priority on independence to the point of avoiding social ties extends to participants' hopes for their children as well. Alyssa tells me, "I don't want them to depend on people. 'Cause it's just, okay, you, you should be able to do it for yourself. You know what I mean, like, if you depend on somebody, you're always going to want them to be there. No, depend on yourself." She has lived with her family in adulthood and no longer does so, though she still uses the furniture she got as hand-me-downs from family members. Rosa has similar aspirations for her children: independence that necessitates social isolation. She reports that she hopes when her children are adults, "that they have their own business, their own house and they don't have to be depending on nobody but their own." The dream of entrepreneurship is a common one for Americans, including the poor,[17] yet it usually remains an unfulfilled dream or a failed attempt, and is connected to individualism.[18] Small businesses have a very high failure rate,[19] and without a foundation of adequate capital they are more likely to fail.[20]

Isolation Pervades Poor Neighborhoods

"I'm Not an Outside Person"

Many participants avoid social ties due to a desire to avoid contact with their neighbors, considering their residential neighborhoods a source of fear, stress, crime, and violence; as Kia says, "I'm not an outside person." Other researchers have reported this as well. Those who live in neighborhoods of concentrated poverty face intense social isolation. The spatial concentration of poverty creates disadvantaged environments that become progressively isolated socially and economically.[21] Deindustrialization and the increase of concentrated poverty have left those in such neighborhoods with few social ties, which exacerbates high levels of unemployment and poverty.[22]

Carol Stack found "a cooperative lifestyle built upon exchange and reciprocity"[23] in which social networks of kin, fictive kin, and neighbors were crucial to the survival of very poor people.[24] The non-KWRU participants do not have this sort of cooperative lifestyle, and KWRU participants only begin to develop it within KWRU, as I describe in the chapters that follow. It simply is not something most participants find within their neighborhoods; many do not have it within their families either.

Mistrust: "I Can't Trust Anybody"

Participants' residential neighborhoods are sites of fear and distrust,[25] and participants avoid neighbors and thereby cut themselves off from the most proximal, available ties, ties that could provide welcome assistance.[26] The importance of neighborhood ties is perhaps greater for poor people than for wealthier people because they have less access to transportation and therefore the places where they meet others are more restricted.[27] They are also less likely to have stable jobs that might serve as sources of ties.[28]

Lack of trust pervades many poor neighborhoods,[29] in what Silva describes as "a world without solidarities and without safety nets, leaving them wary and distrustful in their interactions with others."[30] Exchange networks require trust, which in Judith Levine's words, "is inherently entwined with social capital, an invaluable resource for producing safe communities, connections to the labor market, political clout, and survival strategies under economic stress."[31] While residents' skepticism about unknown others is an understandable defensive, adaptive, and protective move, it can have severe consequences in limiting the reach and power of social networks.[32] Trust alone can't fix the underlying problems of poverty, but it can make lives better. Kia, focused on education and work and fiercely independent, says, "I don't know my neighbors. I make it so you don't know nothing about me, I don't know nothing about you [laughs]. . . . You know, it's just so hard to trust people these days. I don't know, they might be out to hurt you or harm you."

Sometimes the lack of ties extends to friendship with others who aren't neighbors or even to family. KWRU member Rosa tells me, "I just don't like nobody getting into my problems." She says she even likes to "keep away from my family. . . . If I have a problem, I deal with it on my own."

Kia tells me that even if she's having a bad day, she wouldn't go to anyone to talk about it "because everybody's got their own opinions, and sometimes I don't want to hear other people's opinions." Given Kia's own references in our interview to those she thinks are making poor decisions, it's understandable that she would be wary of others' opinions: she fears they would judge her similarly. KWRU member Helen, who has a habit of laughing nervously, tells me if she needs emotional support on a bad day: "I talk to myself. I don't talk to nobody about my problems. I just talk to myself [laughs]. Because it's none of their business [laughs]. I guess, I don't know. . . . Because then if you tell them your problems and they go around and tell everybody else, 'Oh, she did this, she did that.' So I just keep it to myself." Even as Helen reports feeling close to several family members, including her mother-in-law, she is quick to say she doesn't trust them.

Participants frequently report avoiding neighbors to escape such gossip, prying questions, and anticipated judgment. Kia and Helen are reluctant to make friends with neighbors or even to consider acquaintances who aren't neighbors as friends; this stems in part from fear of people knowing details about their lives. While it might be easy to trivialize the preoccupation with avoiding gossip, the notion is closely linked to distrust and to the other factors in the avoidance of social ties I discuss in this chapter. Participants prize an air of independence that revealing their problems would disrupt. As people who make stigmatizing judgments of the poor, it makes sense for participants to avoid airing their own problems.[33]

Residential neighborhoods are a main source of potential social ties, but if those neighborhoods give residents pause about associating with each other or prompt them to stay inside and avoid contact with one another, they can never develop social ties of any kind with each other.

Danger: "I Think I'm Safer Inside than Outside"

Participants cited physical safety and security more than any other reason for avoiding interacting with others in their neighborhoods. KWRU member Alice, a white woman in her forties, twice-widowed, with two children at home, tells me, "My block itself has drug dealers on it" and "once I go home . . . we're in the house. We don't go back out unless it's an extreme emergency . . . [I] lock the door after I come in. . . . I don't bother with nobody." KWRU member Lina, a single mother of a toddler and an infant, describes the immediate neighborhood of the KWRU Human Rights House where she is staying as chaotic and frightening: "It's just loud and there be fights and stuff on the block. And you can't really bring your kids outside. . . . I keep my kids in the house 'cause they be, they like fighting and shooting and stuff on the block. And they be jumping people." KWRU Human Rights Houses are quite cramped; whole families share a bedroom and several share facilities. The organization's meager resources mean that the housing they offer is usually in the poorest and most dangerous areas of the city.

Most of the participants in this study describe their neighborhoods as areas fraught with danger, rooted in violence and the drug trade. They frequently note that selling drugs is one way to survive for people who are struggling, and at times express sympathy for people who turn to selling drugs, but they try to avoid drug dealers to guard their safety. Savannah says, "There are people that stand on the corners and sell drugs. . . . It's not a good thing. But, I mean, that's the only . . . for them that's the only way they get to make ends meet." Savannah herself sold drugs briefly in the past, telling me, "I'm not proud of myself. . . . It's something I'm not proud of. . . . I was trying to support myself . . . enough that I could get my own money to get out" of a bad relationship. Paloma tells me her children cannot play outside "because it's way too dangerous. You know, there are drugs . . . there are people who do have guns and, you know, it's a rough neighborhood." Yet she also tells me she has neighbors "who are still very nice but deal drugs to survive. . . . It bothers me that I have a neighborhood that has to deal drugs to survive, but where else am I gonna go? Do you see anybody on my block with a fancy car? . . . You ain't gonna see them in no fancy coats. They sell enough just to pay their bills. I don't see nobody getting rich quick around here." Paloma's empathy is striking, particularly given that the father of her children has long suffered from drug addiction, which broke up their partnership.

Some recount horrifying events they've witnessed that give them ample reason to avoid others around them and to protect their safety by "staying to themselves." KWRU member Tina says, "This neighborhood, you don't go out after dark. There's a lot of drugs in this neighborhood. . . . The delivery pizza man from Oxford Avenue, they just shot and robbed and killed him two weeks ago. He just went to the door to deliver pizza and they shot him in his head and took his money." April also reports shootings in her neighborhood: "I see people getting shot every day. You hear the guns . . . people shootin' when you sleep at night." April lives with her two children, ages four and five. Until recently she lived with her boyfriend of nine months, but he was abusive and she now has a restraining order against him. Her experiences with him compound her fear of violence.

Even with crime rates low by recent historical standards,[34] the possibility of crime generates caution. And these fears are well founded; rates of violence go up as concentrated poverty goes up.[35] And while the nationwide rate of violent crime has been on the decline since the early 1990s,[36] Philadelphia has not experienced the same pattern. In fact, during my research period, violent crime was on the uptick.[37] A number of participants reported experiencing violence or seeing their children experience violence; personal experience with violence in their neighborhoods understandably leads people to retreat from their neighbors.

When I ask KWRU member Carmen to tell me what the worst thing
is about living in her neighborhood with her two children and her new-
born granddaughter, where she's lived for the past three years, she says
directly, "The shooting. These kids, these young kids, that are selling
drugs, buy these guns and . . . they're trigger happy. It's like, you know,
my gun's bigger than your gun type thing. . . . People die, innocent people die. It's usually the innocent ones that die." She shares a story about
violence hitting close to home:

> This summer just past, a friend of mine got shot right in front of my steps.
> You know, right before the kids get out of school, you got this yellow tape,
> you got blood on your step, you know what I mean? Yeah. I was really
> hoping my son didn't see it. He didn't see it. He didn't see the body. He
> seen the after effect, but he had to like jump through the bushes to come
> in because they had my whole house taped up so nobody could come in
> or leave out. . . . When it's noisy out it's okay, people are out, you know
> what I mean? When it's quiet, something's gonna happen. . . . [My daugh-
> ter] was telling me, "It was real quiet mom and something told me to . . ."
> Because she was down there at the corner, she was like, "Something told
> me to come up." And she said no sooner than that they started shooting.
> Fourteen shots were fired.

Carmen's eighteen-year-old daughter and ten-year-old son have grown
up exposed to violence and have learned to constantly be alert.

Carmen may be an exception to the rule that people in poor neighborhoods are isolated from one another. She tells me, "Right now the
best thing that I like about living here is my neighbors. . . . We all look
out for each other." She describes a community in which she allows her
daughter to stay alone in part because her daughter can call a neighbor if she needs help. Her neighbors call her if they see something that
concerns them with one of her children, and she and her neighbors
borrow money from one another when they run short. She certainly
assumes that the shooters she mentioned do not live in her neighborhood. It's possible that Carmen's neighborhood is more connected than
most poor neighborhoods. It's also possible that the other members of
her neighborhood are not as connected as she is, and that her KWRU
membership supports this connection because it has heightened Car-

men's willingness to trust others. Her next-door neighbor, Mandy, is a study participant but not a member of KWRU (Carmen referred me to her). Mandy doesn't describe avoiding her neighbors specifically, but she also doesn't describe their neighborhood with the same warmth Carmen does. Carmen expresses significantly less poverty stigma than most participants in either group. This study does not include interviews with the other neighbors on whom Carmen relies to see if their impression of the neighborhood agrees with hers, but my research and others' suggest that Carmen is an outlier; I ask all the participants in the study about their feelings about their neighbors, and she is the only one to speak so warmly.

Pauline, another KWRU member, has a more common response to violence in her neighborhood. Her fourteen-year-old niece who lives with her was recently hospitalized with severe injuries from a neighborhood attack with a knife and a razor blade. Motioning with her hand from her cheekbone next to her ear down her jawline to her chin, she tells me, "They sliced her face from here to all the way down here. . . . All of it was hanging open. They tried to cut her throat. . . . She got a mark over here. They stomped her. They did everything. . . ." Pauline paused a moment, and took a deep breath, "They pulled out her hair. . . . She had bald spots. . . ." Pauline could not even recognize her niece when she saw her; her injuries required fifty-eight stitches on the outside of her mouth and thirty-seven on the inside, and seven more on her throat where the group of attackers, teenage girls themselves, had tried to cut her throat. She says:

> Because they know the girls that took and cut [her], they know them and they'll tease [her], "that's why your face is cut. And if you keeping running off your mouth and getting smart and stuff and having a lot of mouth, we're going to take and put another slice on your face." . . . [She's] been in the house for two weeks. She don't socialize with nobody. She goes to school. She [goes] in the house.

Ongoing threats keep Pauline's fear of her neighborhood fresh and current.

While Pauline isn't the only participant to have had someone she cares about experience violence, a number are cautious without having experienced it themselves. KWRU member Stefanie tells me there are a lot of drugs around her neighborhood, and they lead to violence: "There was a commotion going on right here and me and my mom was outside. And they had a shoot-out right in front of my house. . . . My mom told me and my godsister and my brother to go to the back room and just lay down on the floor because the way they were shooting . . . they shot and the bullet went in the house next door."

As Jane Jacobs argues in *The Death and Life of Great American Cities*,[38] when we retreat to the comfort of our private spaces in an effort to protect ourselves, we may be making our streets and neighborhoods less safe. When families with children use public spaces, people who commit violent crime are the ones who retreat. When we remain cloistered in our own spaces away from others, we deprive the streets of our eyes and ears and company as potential witnesses that can deter crime. And of course, when we grow to know and trust our neighbors, they grow to trust us as well and we all look out for each other, adding a degree of safety we don't have when alone and unprotected in a frightening crime-ridden neighborhood. To break the isolation, we have to spend time outside, taking risks both real and imagined. But being outside sometimes provides kids with space in which to be active in healthy ways, to get vitamin D, to burn energy, and to stave off the boredom four walls and a television can represent.

Poverty Stigma

As described in chapter 1, study participants tend to blame themselves when they fall short of their aspirations of success and to blame people for the economic instability those others face as well.[39] They often see themselves as their greatest barriers to success. They share the stigmatizing views of poor people and recipients of public benefits so common among politicians and the public. According to Sharon Hays:

> The mere mention of welfare, for many people, brings to mind not just poverty, but a whole series of daunting social problems: teenage pregnancy, unwed parenting, divorce, abortion, drug abuse, unsafe streets, volatile race relations. . . . The image of [welfare recipients] as deviant and dangerous people, suffering from forms of immorality that seem almost

contagious, is so ubiquitous that it tends to seep into one's consciousness almost unnoticed.[40]

Participants in this study reflect the effects of contempt for the poor, which goes beyond fear and distrust to divide them from their neighbors. KWRU member Marie reports, "It seems like they don't have no life, and so they have no ambition, they have no goals, they have nothing." Marie's own goals to get a job someday are vague. She is suffering from clinical anxiety, which makes it particularly difficult to imagine her future, a difficulty common among the poor as it is. April tells me, "You got a lot of bums around here. Because I see them every day. . . . You know, you see the people walking around that's on drugs. You see people sleeping on the street. You see it all around. You see prostitutes selling their bodies. You see everything around here." When I ask Nina, who has taken great care with her appearance, to tell me what her neighbors are like, she responds, "They're dirty. They're trash. They're on drugs. I don't speak to none of them people." This may be part of the reason there's only one person in the world she considers a friend, someone she's known since high school.

Nina's words reflect a common stereotype. The popularity of the notion of drug testing welfare recipients suggests the power of the association between illicit drugs and poverty. Politicians have frequently put forth proposals to test recipients, with the rationale that public funds should not be used for illegal substances, that recipients are fortunate to have taxpayer funds, and that they should not have full control over those funds. On the one hand, the notion of welfare recipients as criminals using illicit substances is a well-worn stereotype and fits with notions of undeservingness. On the other hand, there is also a common thread underlying proposals for drug testing and food stamp restrictions: a stigmatizing paternalism. While drug testing seeks to prevent spending on drugs, SNAP (Supplemental Nutritional Assistance Program) restriction proposals seek to prohibit the purchase of steak, seafood, or other "luxury" items.[41]

As of the middle of 2015, elected officials have proposed drug testing applicants for TANF (Temporary Assistance for Needy Families) or food stamps in at least twelve states, in defiance of the results of such programs in Florida and Michigan. Such programs have proven to cost more than the benefits withheld from those few who test positive, and the U.S. Court of Appeals for the 11th Circuit and the Michigan Court of Appeals, respectively, declared the laws as written in Florida and Michigan unconstitutional.[42] Similarly, during his term as Pennsylvania governor, Tom Corbett accused the unemployed of being drug users in complete defiance of the evidence, saying, "There are many employers that say, 'we're looking for people but we can't find anybody that has passed a drug test.'"[43] Such statements translate into policy and have been doing so steadily since the 1996 welfare reform. Despite abundant evidence that the stereotype describes the exception rather than the norm, U.S. policies crafted by both Democrats and Republicans focus almost exclusively on how to force the poor out of dependence and into work—to save them from their lack of morality by coercing them, through an incomprehensible system of carrots and sticks, to enter the labor market that will somehow be their salvation.

Such beliefs lead study participants to stigmatize those around them, the people who live in their own neighborhoods. Leslie is a young unmarried mother of one child, living with her parents in a poor neighborhood. Short and slender, with her strawberry-blonde hair in a ponytail, she shares with me her aspirations of marrying the father of her child, getting a good job, and moving away—typical hopes for many poor young mothers. She says of her neighborhood:

> I loved it growing up. . . . It was a great thing to be from. Nowadays it's not. . . . They all have kids that they don't take care of. Nobody has any respect for others. . . . A major problem . . . I'm definitely seeing a lot more renters than owners. . . . But the homeowners that we have on the street, never a problem from any of them. Anybody that buys a home on the street, never have a problem with any of them. But it seems like the problems that we have like just on the street, like I'm not too sure about the whole neighborhood in general about as far as like their rental percentage to the owner percentage with houses, but I know on this street like the rentals have always been a problem.

Her parents own their home, and Leslie attributes perceived neighborhood problems to renters—people somewhat worse off than her and certainly more likely to be poor than homeowners are.

Many participants in this study live in poor neighborhoods; those who do not reside in the poorest neighborhoods live on blocks where all their immediate neighbors are as poor as they are, due to high levels of class segregation in Philadelphia, even within neighborhoods. Many tell me they live in "the ghetto." Many of those who live in West Kensington call it "the badlands," and the name says it all for them. The stigma about poverty and about welfare receipt keeps them apart from their neighbors. When I ask them what they think about poor people or people on welfare, they frequently report their impressions of neighbors, blaming poverty on individuals and seeking to distance themselves from other poor people. When I ask how people struggling to survive manage, Kelly tells me, "Some people go out there and sell drugs." Nicole says, "People steal, people rob and stuff like that. . . . Prostitution . . . there's a lot of stuff that they do . . . to make money." KWRU member Pauline also says, "They would steal. Lie to get what they want." Similarly Nina and Rosa say poor people get money by working as prostitutes, strippers, and escorts, and by selling drugs. Inez ties her assessment of what others might do to her avoidance of those others. When I ask her to tell me how people who are struggling manage, she says, "Well, since I don't want to be with nobody, I don't know," but then offers that sometimes people sell drugs, and "probably go around and rob a bank." In each case the disapproving tone revealed the stigmatized view participants held of people engaging in these activities, even for Rosa and Inez, who themselves admitted selling drugs in the past.

"They Don't Need Welfare"

Welfare recipients do not like being on welfare, and are painfully aware of the stigma it imposes.[44] Welfare recipients tend to portray themselves as different from others on welfare and see themselves differently from the stereotypical welfare mother. KWRU member Helen draws on her perceptions of her neighbors and her experiences as a former welfare recipient to set herself apart from them:

A lot of people in my neighborhood ain't working. . . . That's stupid because they're young people, they could get a job, they don't need welfare. . . . Because you're lazy and just want to stay there and do nothin' with your life. I want to do something with my life. . . . All they use the money for is beer and alcohol and drugs. . . . But most of them should be working. . . . Most of them people who was in the [welfare] program [when I was] are lazy. That's why they couldn't find no jobs.

Helen has tried to find steady work, but has only been able to find part-time, inconsistent work.

KWRU member Lina, currently receiving welfare to support herself and her infant and two-year-old, acknowledges commonality with welfare recipients, saying, "We all on the same boat, like we all getting like food stamps and cash and stuff so I don't feel any different," and "I can't really like go out real fast and get a job or something like that," but nonetheless notes, "I think everybody on welfare should get off and get a job." Kim, a current welfare recipient, unemployed but with an extensive work history, tells me:

I feel like if you can work, get up and work. . . . And if they don't make them go to GED or get a schooling or get a training, they're not gonna do it. They're gonna sit back and wait for their money. It's free money. "Why should I go work if I could sit here and wait for a welfare check?" That's what a lot of them say.

Kim is studying for her GED and wants to use it to get a good job and get off welfare permanently. Maria is pregnant with her first child during our interview, and about to become a first-time welfare recipient. She tells me, of welfare recipients, "To me, if they're not sick, they should be out getting a job. Some people have all the kids and put them right on welfare. It shouldn't work like that. . . . Some just being greedy and abusing the money. And they getting it. . . . I think it's most of them." In each of these cases, participants describe themselves as exceptions to the rule rather than questioning the stereotype. Rather than doubt the common perceptions of welfare recipients, they take the truth of such stigmatized notions for granted, voicing their support for policies like drug testing for welfare recipients and restricting food stamp usage. In so doing, they echo the public statements of officials.

Study participants express the same sentiments researchers like Edin and Kefalas document in *Promises I Can Keep: Why Poor Women Put*

Motherhood Before Marriage.[45] Many of the poor mothers they interviewed set themselves apart from others in, or close to, their situations—they distinguish themselves from mothers who are worse off. Similarly, Gail, a former welfare recipient, tells me, "I just think that [in] certain cases people abuse it and they shouldn't. . . . Personally I think the system just makes it a little too easy and they don't push them as much as they should to help them better themselves." Yet she acknowledges that welfare has been crucial to her own survival. She says she has "to strive to be better and keep being better, not just to stay in one place."

Many participants in this study include current and former welfare recipients, and they harshly criticize people who shared this circumstance. Participants' comments suggest they believe urban legends of welfare cheats as easily as people who have never been on welfare do. Meanwhile, they dissociate themselves—and others they judge to truly need it—from those who abuse the system.[46] For example, Mandy, a current recipient, says, "I believe that anybody that wants to sit home and wait on a check has problems. They really are lazy. . . . I believe it's a lot of people that don't want to work. . . . Probably the reason they started the welfare reform was because people, they kept having babies and didn't want to work." Mandy believes the difference between her and other welfare recipients is that they want to be on welfare and she does not. Yet she also blames herself for her poverty.

Leslie, a former welfare recipient, says:

> I think there needs to be some kind of another welfare reform. Like I know that they did reform it I think recently, maybe in the past couple years they reformed it again. But obviously it's not working. You know. If people are still walking in the [welfare] office head to toe in Polo and whatever other kind of clothes that are like ridiculously expensive with their nails done. Well, stop paying $100 for a pair of pants and go buy yourself some food.

April, currently receiving Supplemental Security Income (SSI)[47] and a former welfare recipient, says:

> I see some of these girls out here that they don't care, they love to stand in the line. They love to stand in the line at the welfare office and get their

little check, you know, and some of these girls I see the big gold earrings on, the nice clothes and sneakers on. They love that kind of stuff. Because it's free money. They don't care 'cause it's free money to them. . . . Lazy. . . . I mean, these people that I see standing in line, they can get a job. It don't look like nothin with 'em. It's lazy.

Such statements echo the message of an image that circulated on social media in 2014, which denigrates and dehumanizes those who receive food stamps. In various iterations, it contained a photograph of a bear with versions of this text: "The food stamp program is administered by the U.S. Department of Agriculture. They proudly report that they distribute free meals and food stamps to over 46 million people on an annual basis. Meanwhile, the National Park Service, run by the U.S. Department of the Interior, asks us, 'Please do not feed the animals.' Their stated reason for this being that . . . 'The animals will grow dependent on the handouts, and then they will never learn to take care of themselves.'"[48] A number of sitting Republican legislators and candidates for the Senate or House have shared the image. The comparison of food stamp recipients to animals suggests the scorn prevalent on social media and in the comments of politicians such as Pennsylvania attorney general Tom Corbett when he was a candidate for Pennsylvania governor: "The jobs are there, but if we keep extending unemployment, people are just going to sit there."[49]

In *A Place on the Corner*,[50] Elijah Anderson illustrates how people define themselves partly by whom they oppose by using sets of discursive oppositions; thus, the regulars set themselves apart from the hoodlums, and the wineheads struggle to set themselves apart from other wineheads. Snow and Anderson[51] also found this distancing, a kind of identity talk, among the homeless people they studied. The authors encountered homeless people who described themselves as different from other homeless people and refusing to associate with them, claiming that they were responsible workers while others were lazy. In similar fashion, welfare recipients think poorly of welfare recipients—they think of them as generally lazy, people who cheat, or people who don't need the money, while simultaneously justifying their own welfare receipt.[52]

Such views reflect the power of the story of the welfare queen, a woman defrauding the government of taxpayer dollars in welfare benefits. This story, first circulated during the Reagan administration, had its roots in one incredible instance of a woman who was probably a murderous, kidnapping psychopath, as well as being extremely unusual in her ability to game the welfare system, yet it had a real effect on the policy debates surrounding welfare and welfare reform.[53] In reality, welfare recipients on average have two children and a very low standard of living.[54] As Josh Levin writes, "Linda Taylor showed that it was possible for a dedicated criminal to steal a healthy chunk of welfare money"—as he implies, most people lack her depravity, which was manifest in a shocking number of heinous crimes. The image of what Levin calls "fur-laden thieves bleeding the American economy dry" that President Ronald Reagan extrapolated from this case had no actual support.[55] Reagan told the story of this "welfare queen" as though it were representative of the system.[56] Those seeking to cut funding for programs for the poor couch their efforts as "eliminating waste, fraud, and abuse" but, as Eric Schnurer writes, "none of the savings actually come from fraud, but rather from cutting funding and tightening benefits" because fraud by recipients is so rare.[57] Reagan accomplished welfare savings through these means and the practice has persisted.[58]

"I Call Them Dirty. . . . They're Trashy People"

Investigating rhetoric and practices at welfare-to-work agencies, Chad Broughton[59] found this attribution paradox among the clients: they subscribed to the ideology about welfare recipients' faults and failings, but did not apply those understandings to themselves. Broughton refers to this process as "othering," "by which, in this case, welfare recipients shift the stigma that welfare receipt carries from themselves to other welfare recipients."[60]

This "othering" also happens in regard to how poor people see other poor people in general, beyond welfare-related stigma. Indeed, people use varied criteria to characterize those with whom they do not want to associate in a variety of situations. This is part of what Michèle Lamont called boundary work: "We constantly draw inferences concerning our similarities to, and differences from, others . . . a significant portion of our daily activities are oriented toward avoiding shame and maintaining a positive self-identity by patrolling the borders of our groups."[61]

The poor differentiate themselves from other poor people by asserting their values of hard work, responsibility, and morality. They define themselves in opposition to and better than others in similar economic positions.[62] They separate themselves as good and deserving from others whom they define (or whose definition by the media and politicians they accept) as essentially bad and undeserving. People who live in poverty find ways "to connect themselves to the morality of the American middle class while simultaneously creating a sense of moral superiority over other groups of poor Americans."[63]

Stigma is a barrier to developing social ties because people avoid inclusion in a stigmatized social network. Study participants often invoke popular images of lazy and greedy welfare mothers, and refer to poor people as dirty and homeless. KWRU member Rosa, for example, describes poor people this way, "You don't have sneakers to put on your feet. Your hair's a mess; it's not washed. Your body is dirty. Your clothes is all holey and dirty. That's what I call poor." Rosa points to things that would set someone apart from and below her in the hierarchy; she didn't fit her own description of poor in any sense, although she was de facto homeless, living in another KWRU member's home temporarily, with nowhere else to go. Kelly explains, "Poor is to me when you don't have nobody, you in the streets. Like the homeless people out here." Even as lonely as Kelly feels as I described above, she lives with her mother, indicating she has more than "nobody." And she is quite right that homelessness is a sign of having no one.

Participants in this study define poverty in different ways, typically in ways that exclude themselves. Usually people define poverty as KWRU member Alice does: poor people are those who "don't have nothing." Betty tells me someone who is poor is "in the street, in a big box, and they don't have a shelter. A homeless person." Nina says, "when you can't afford nothin'. You can't afford to put clothes on your back, you can't afford to put a roof over your head. That's poor." Alyssa says, "living in the street. And not having nothing. That's poor." Rosa explains, "when you got to live in the street and you're homeless and have nothing. That's what I consider poor." April offers a more elaborate image:

> Poor is when you ain't got no working stove, no heat, no hot water. You barely got a place to lay your head. You don't have a bed to sleep on. You

got to sleep on the floor. You don't have a phone, you don't have TV, no radio, you don't have nothin'. . . . That's what you call poor.

April, who lives in an apartment with her two small children where she barely affords the rent on disability payments, has heat, hot water, a bed, a phone, a television, and a fully functioning kitchen. This reflects a careful definition of the stigmatized status as different from how she sees herself. Most definitions of poverty vary depending on the participant's own circumstances. It's notable that April, who has never been homeless, does not define poverty as homelessness the way Rosa does, but only as lacking some of the things she has. April's description essentially fits Rosa's situation, since Rosa has no legal claim to the resources April names, but Rosa turns to people poorer than herself to describe poverty.

Given such detestable definitions of poverty, when I ask people if they think of themselves as poor, many understandably say no. Indeed, given the existence of poverty stigma, it makes sense that most people define poverty as a state worse than their own and offer descriptions of poverty that make them seem well-off by comparison. They frequently consider themselves better off than their neighbors and other people struggling in poverty with whom they come in contact.

Poverty stigma reinforces isolation; many poor people avoid inclusion in a stigmatized group and have minimal opportunity to connect with better-off people. Non-KWRU participants harbor pervasive stigma about poverty that causes them to avoid associating with others who are in many ways like them. While KWRU participants still harbor such beliefs in ways that discouraged their formation of such ties, the group's mission specifically sought to dismantle that stigma, as I describe in chapter 3; some members began to recognize that personal failings alone could not cause all poverty. But fundamentally, most participants in this study, including the KWRU members I interviewed, viewed many potential social ties with disdain, blaming others for their poverty and seeking to distance themselves from these others rather than aiming to foster relationships with them.

The Occupy Movement may suggest the possibility that the tide will turn. It seems likely that participants' views reflect the rhetoric they hear; just as in the era of welfare reform welfare recipients spoke of the need to encourage work and reduce dependence,[64] so too, poor people may—a little more often—react to other poor people with a sense of commonality rather than contempt. Occupy Wall Street captured the collective consciousness for a time and raised awareness of inequality, pointing to a poverty not of individuals' doing. The slogan, "We are the 99 percent," is a direct reversal of the message of the image of the bear that park visitors shouldn't feed—we are one.

Reciprocity

Poverty leads to lower levels of trust, interactions, and reciprocal exchanges. Research suggests that the poor get, as well as give, less social support than do those of higher economic status, even though they may need more support.[65] Avoiding relationships with others enables participants to avoid requests for help from those others. This has the positive effect of preserving precious resources and avoiding expectations of reciprocity that they could not fulfill. There are powerful norms of reciprocity in society,[66] but it's difficult for the poor to reciprocate due to their own acute needs and limited resources.[67] Reciprocity can resolve the tension between getting help from others and maintaining a sense of independence—they are able to feel like they "pay" for what they get, in a sense, so are not dependent.[68] Reciprocity is both a burden to participants who fear their inability to give back and a reminder of how others have sometimes taken their aid for granted without acknowledging the need to offer anything in exchange. Social ties, if they serve any useful purpose for participants in this study, come at a price, and many participants report their unwillingness to pay it as a reason for staying to themselves.[69]

Reciprocal obligations can serve to hold the poor back; excessive claims on group members constitute a potential negative to social capital.[70] This is a real risk, and most study participants report experiencing such difficulties: they helped others in the past and found themselves without much in reserve, but hold out hope their network members will reciprocate when they need it. Sometimes that reciprocation materializes, but sometimes it doesn't. However, the negative experiences some have confronted lead them to be cautious and distrustful.

Receiving help from others elicits feelings of gratitude while simultaneously leading to feelings of feared dependency. Reciprocity is nice, but the obligation involved is weighty and instrumentality can feel ugly and impersonal. Participants describe the prospect of owing others favors or money as part of reciprocal obligations as something to be avoided; for some this is a terrible situation, especially if they fear not having the resources to pay back what they owe.[71] Dominique tells me, "I don't know if I'd ever be able to pay it back." At forty-four, Dominique is unemployed and studying for her GED, aware that her job options consist of minimum wage jobs. KWRU member Dora says that if you can't pay someone back for a loan, you'll have to do something else for that person or they will hold it over you later in some way.[72]

Just as awareness of norms of reciprocity can stop many from asking for help out of fear of their own inability to reciprocate, such norms can also hinder some people from giving help because they fear others' inability or unwillingness to reciprocate. Giving help involves complex and sometimes contradictory emotions and responses. On the one hand, giving others help is positive: not only do participants in this study enjoy a sense of pride in doing a good deed or a favor for someone in need, but often they also recognize that giving help could be an important survival strategy as it can be an investment in future help. When those I spoke with, who are struggling themselves, give help to others in their lives, they hope they are increasing their chances of being able to draw on help in the future and often specifically told me so. However, more often they report that those are poor investments. Given the level of poverty study participants experienced, it's unsurprising that many feel the last thing they can do is help others. Providing help to others is only an investment in help for oneself in the future if others actually help in the future—otherwise, helping others can seem like an unwise expenditure of scarce resources.

Often, participants describe giving help to others as an activity they have experienced negatively. They feel others took advantage of their generosity or failed to obey norms of reciprocity. In these cases, participants' perceived investments in future help as a survival strategy did not provide the return they expected or desired. The reciprocity relationship depends on others holding up their end of the bargain. Sometimes it doesn't work in this manner, although participants usually feel it should.

KWRU member Jessie tells me that giving help to people can be "stress-ful sometimes. . . . You feel as though you give, give, give, give, give and you don't get anything in return. Basically you're being taken advantage of sometimes."

"They Were Robbing Me Blind"

It's often relatives who take advantage—expecting child care but not offering it in return, wanting too much in return for housing, wanting money but not lending any, getting housing but not offering anything for it, and pressing the boundaries of help offered, such as when Jen's sister has her babysit but doesn't return until hours later than they agreed.[73] Alyssa tells me about the time not long ago when she and her husband and their kids lived with her mother-in-law and had to pay to share housing. Although it seemed on its face a reciprocal relation-ship, she felt her mother-in-law was taking advantage of her and it was not an even exchange, and a few months ago they were able to move out on their own: "I had to pay her $150 every time I got paid, plus I had to buy food for the house, plus they got all my WIC. They were robbing me blind in that house." This happened to Bebe as well; her mother expected her to contribute monetarily, even though she was still a minor.[74] Bebe's mother was also violent and would not allow her to enroll in school.

Participants tell me heartbreaking stories of family members who refuse to share food with them. Betty explains that her welfare check and food stamps were for the house, and her husband kept his earned income for himself. If they ran short on food in the house, she would often skip meals so their daughter could eat, while he would spend his money on food and entertainment for himself.

Many participants speak of a general failure of others to observe reci-procity norms. Inez has a couple of relatives she considers part of her social network and to whom she reports providing support, yet does not consider them reliable, productive ties. Experiences of reciprocity with kin reinforce participants' impulse to stay away from others. Nina describes her father's girlfriend's expectation that she pick up the res-taurant check when they go out together, even though the woman has more money than Nina, and her mother's requirement that she pay for gas and share her food stamps in exchange for a ride to the store. When I ask her if she's pooled resources with anyone, she says, "I wouldn't dare." She does not want to risk being taken advantage of even more. Nina feels many people in her life take advantage of her and do not reciprocate to the extent she thinks would be fair and appropriate. While many participants have relied on kin ties at some point for support, in general their negative experience of reciprocity within family led them to avoid building such ties outside of kinship. Leslie, who lives in her parents' house with her son, experienced reciprocity in a positive way— she and her fiancé, who sometimes stays there too, contribute money to her parents' household but her parents refuse it when Leslie's money is particularly tight. She says of the arrangement, "It's kind of like we all kind of try to wash each other's back, like if they need something, if we can do for them then [we will]." However, this positive experience does not outweigh Leslie's other reasons for avoiding nonkin social ties.

"It Doesn't Pay to Ask for Help"

Some participants avoid potential social ties due to a sense those ties would refuse their calls for help. Inez explains that she doesn't like to ask her family for help because when she does they usually decline. She is willing to participate in reciprocal exchanges but says those around her are not. She reports helping them but tells me they are unwilling to reciprocate, so she doesn't even want to bother to ask any longer. She explains to me she feels that they take advantage of her and it makes her angry, upset, and sad. She says:

> It hurts when they want to take advantage of me. I feel like crying. Because when I want to go out it's like . . . it's like they turn around and say, "Can you do this? Or can you do that?" But when I turn around and ask them for help, they're like, "Oh, I can't do it." Or, "You got to do it on your own." Or, "I'm busy. I can't take care of him." I'm like, "My God. I do favors for you all, but you can't turn around and return a favor for me?"

KWRU member Rebecca feels similarly. She says, "Asking people for help to get by and all, it doesn't help. . . . And it puts your self-esteem down because if you do ask for help . . . I asked [my sister] one time . . .

and she wouldn't lend me $5. So it doesn't pay to ask for help from friends or family or anything." Even with family nearby, Rebecca has been homeless, and her sister and mother initiated proceedings to take custody of her minor son from her on the basis that she doesn't have stable living arrangements. I accompany her to family court and we learn that they have failed to appear, so she is able to retain custody of her son, but the fact remains that they punished her for her poverty instead of taking her in. The fear that others won't help, or recollection of unfulfilled past requests, leads to reluctance on the part of many participants.

Some people do not want help because they are afraid they will not be able to return the favor; avoiding social ties is one way to escape this possibility. It also reminds them to refrain from expecting reciprocity from others who may not deliver. April, unemployed, living on a low fixed SSI income and recently rid of an abusive boyfriend, is in a precarious financial situation and concerned about her inability to fulfill norms of reciprocity: "I don't want to get no help from nobody when I know I can't give it back." Asking for help (or getting help) implies a debt, and the people I interviewed are aware of this. KWRU member Dora, who does rely on her sister and on a boyfriend, doesn't want to rely on others. She tells me, "I didn't want to ask . . . because I didn't want to owe anybody."

Help is a complicated issue for those who struggle to get by on a daily basis. Many study participants depend on help from kin or, if they are members of KWRU, from other members, and they are grateful for it. As chapter 4 will describe, KWRU has a strong set of reciprocity norms to which most members conform. Most retain their general feelings against reciprocity, but find that the group's reciprocity norms and pooling of resources make the investment worthwhile, creating a difference between other social ties and KWRU ties. Yet in every context, it's difficult to ask for help and getting help implies indebtedness, as part of a norm of reciprocity. That means giving help to others should lead to receiving help as well, yet sometimes others fall short of reciprocal expectations and people are left feeling used and taken advantage of. Due to the fraught nature of reciprocity and the desire to avoid burdensome ties, particularly because the help they may provide feels so uncertain, participants stay to themselves in part as an effort to purposefully limit their social networks. Focusing on what ties cost them instead of the benefits they offer presents one more reason for participants to isolate themselves from potential ties.

Conclusion

Most study participants do their best to avoid social ties outside the most limited of kin connections. Building relationships implies a need for those ties; this challenges their common self-concept that they can and should succeed independently. Participants like Kia, who has lived in her car with her three children instead of asking her parents or siblings to take her family in, exemplify a deep commitment to individualism. The myth of individualistic success respondents like Kia believe, bolstered by neoliberalism, is one of the strongest barriers to the formation of social ties among the poor. As such, it does real damage to the lives of poor people, rendering them alone and with fewer tools to survive, as do other factors such as distrust and danger in poor neighborhoods, poverty stigma, and reciprocity's pressures and failings. These varied factors in social tie avoidance keep participants from building social ties with nonkin that could provide significant support and, over time, sustainable ties.

In fact, many participants have few ties among their direct neighbors, few if any friends they count on for support, and weak or absent relationships with their kin. This leads to profound isolation, and for many the negative effects are apparent: they have experienced homelessness, they are depressed, and they spend much of their time inside. Their isolation hinders their ability to develop ties with others and therefore limits the social capital they have.

To be clear, social tie avoidance does not necessarily cause people's lack of supportive social ties. Virtually all study participants in both groups except for a few long-term KWRU members espouse individualistic ideologies in their interviews, but some people would embrace social ties if they had access to a supportive social network. Some participants only avoid social ties after bitter experience, as they suggest in their stories of failed attempts to invest in social ties and draw on their investment. To some extent their disappointment was inevitable: for the poor, kin and other potential social network members have meager resources and therefore limited ability to help each other. And sometimes social ties are reluctant to help even when they could.[75] KWRU members develop mutually supportive and sustainable ties and rely on those ties while maintaining individualistic ideologies. For those who are not members, frustration and disappointment as much as ideology lead them to avoid social ties in the future—not just with those who have let them down, but with anyone.

In some ways retreatism is a luxury regardless of its cause. Many non-KWRU member participants can afford to retreat from nonkin social ties because they have the means to avert homelessness without them, usually by relying on familial ties. These participants see themselves as accomplishing a great deal independently, though they receive quite a bit of help. Their perceived independence comes at a high price, even more so for those who lack kin ties on whom to draw. Nearly all KWRU study participants, without reliable family support, have experienced homelessness—isolation created acute need, which eventually led them to form social ties with unfamiliar others to facilitate survival, through the organization. Need outweighed fear, judgment, and pride, leading them to enter a situation of reliance on nonkin others, a situation I turn to in chapter 3, which discusses how people come to KWRU and therefore begin to build social ties with others.

3

The Only Way We're Going to Survive

Social Ties as a Survival Strategy

It was worth it. It was something different. It was something
I was never hearing in my life. It was something that I was
feeling like being left out, being homeless . . . they make
me think more of me [at KWRU]. . . . I want to help them.
'Cause that's the only way we going to survive—if we help
each other.

—Marie, 42, who received temporary housing from KWRU

Cate was waiting to meet with her caseworker at the welfare office when
KWRU came in to hand out fliers:

> They came with fliers; a whole bunch of people came with fliers. . . . They
> denied me my rights in the welfare, they said, "No, come back in three
> more months," because according to my income it was too much. So I
> told one of the girls that gave me a flier, I said, "Listen, I'm having prob-
> lems, they don't want to open my welfare and this is my problem." And
> she told me, "Okay, Cate, come to one of my meetings." . . . So I went to
> one of their meetings, you know, and when I went to one of their meet-
> ings, they told me, "Okay, Cate, meet me tomorrow at the welfare office."
> [We met there and they] said . . . "Cate, stand right there in the middle."
> I was standing in the middle, they went around, round circling me, and
> then she pulled my hand. . . . They were just saying, you know, we want
> to talk to the head man there. . . . You know, that's all they were saying.
> And then they'd say, "Up and out of poverty now." And I didn't know
> none of the song[s] . . . but I'm sentimental and I was crying. . . . [A
> KWRU activist] said, "This is the problem. This woman has not had . . .
> it's been a month. She's been out of a job and everything. They came in
> here and they say she [has to] wait for three more months. How the hell

is this woman going to wait for three months for a check when she got three kids, plus she's losing her place? She was evicted out of the place."

Cate came to KWRU because she was desperate, not because she had become free of the multiple reasons described in chapter 2 that lead poor people to avoid social ties. It's possible that before she came to KWRU she did not fear that other poor people were dangerous or violent, or have pervasive poverty stigma, tightly held individualism, or fear of reciprocity. But none of those things would have prevented her from taking the hand that reached out to her. The barriers to building social ties that poor people experience do not typically change when participants seek help through KWRU. Yet intense need, coupled with a lack of kin ties able to provide support, leads people like Cate to KWRU for help. When needs are great enough and kin ties are weak, destructive, or absent, poor people in Philadelphia may end up at KWRU where they receive assistance that helps them survive, ranging from aid navigating available services, to food, to a place to live. The help they receive from KWRU can extend beyond these practical supports to include knowledge and tools to see their way through future difficulties and a new perspective on their place in the world. At times it also begins to chip away at the individualistic ideology and break down the avoidance of social ties.

This chapter describes KWRU's public face. It also describes how KWRU study participants learn about KWRU, and the overall distinctions between KWRU participants and non-KWRU participants that make KWRU members willing to ask for help from the organization. It describes the aid they receive, including refuge from homelessness and assistance finding a way not to fall through the holes in the public safety net neoliberalism has left in tatters. KWRU leaders say it is not a social service organization. In fact, it does offer services to those with economically unstable lives, helping people who live with homelessness or housing insecurity to secure permanent housing, and it assists those who are having difficulty getting welfare benefits for which they are eligible.[1] The group's aid to members is a critical way of building organizational strength, and it has transformed participants' lives. This chapter relies on KWRU members' experiences learning about the organization and getting help from it, even in the face of the obstacles to doing so described in chapters 1 and 2. Some non-KWRU members' experiences are mentioned, with their non-KWRU membership noted.

KWRU's Public Face

"HUD House Occupied" reads the headline next to a short caption and a picture appearing in the October 1999 issue of the *Progressive*. The caption reads "On June 22, a group of more than fifty people led by the Kensington Welfare Rights Union took over, repaired, cleaned up, and occupied a vacant Housing and Urban Development building. Nine people involved in the takeover were arrested and charged with conspiracy, criminal trespass, and criminal mischief."[2] KWRU reported that a month later, many of the demonstrating homeless families were awarded housing vouchers as a result of the protest.

A 2004 article describes a tent city KWRU erected:

Last July they staged one of their signature protests less than a mile from their storefront office: a tent city to dramatize homelessness. . . . The routine is similar for every tent city. . . . [A] small army of Kensington volunteers descended on the vacant lot, cleared out the trash, and tipped the crew of a city garbage truck to make an extra pick-up and haul it away. In a neighborhood where burned-out apartment buildings are as common as livable homes, they tramped down the weeds, built a kitchen lean-to, raised tarps and pitched a few nylon tents. A painted bed sheet read: "Welcome America's Poor." . . . On July 4, KWRU broke camp at dawn. Everyone got ready to march. . . . As they paraded to the Constitution Center later that afternoon, the group held aloft some 25 plastic mattresses they had slept on all week, each one now painted with an American flag on one side and a slogan such as "Homeless in America" or "7 Million Unemployed Poor" on the other. Almost immediately, the police arrested [two of the leaders]. The two went quietly. Chanting "Hey, ho, poverty has got to go!" [members] locked arms with the college students [volunteering with KWRU]. There was pushing and shoving, and the KWRU protestors landed on the ground several times but got up again. In the end, the group circled the building, marching past television cameras and tourists. They left a demand for economic human rights at the center's gate.[3]

In August 2004, KWRU activists traveled to New York City to participate in the protests surrounding the Republican National Convention. They marched from Philadelphia through New Jersey to New York over the course of several weeks, calling their journey "March for Our Lives."

> Initially, they were going to erect tent cities—they call them "Bushvilles," a reference to the Hoovervilles of the Depression—on the outskirts of New York, where they could both house and mobilize the area's poorest people in preparation for the Republican Convention. This year, though, police foiled [the] plan by destroying the Bushvilles as soon as the group could set them up. So . . . [they] decided to take the campaign on the road, creating a mobile Bushville that would camp out in a different town every night. Most days [the] group, wearing matching white T-shirts, walks 20 miles through the grimmer precincts of New Jersey. Each night they show up on the doorsteps of churches, asking for a place to sleep. Sometimes they camp outside. Once in a while they'll rent two rooms at a seedy motel, one for men and one for women. They pool their food stamps to buy sliced bread and cold cuts and subsist on a diet of sandwiches and soda.[4]

In addition to KWRU's actions to secure housing vouchers and those to publicize homelessness, they engage in political activism on issues they see as connected—including military action in Iraq, which, members note, costs money that could have gone to social welfare.

KWRU's political activities bring a combined strength of voice to issues affecting members, and as noted, some bring about real change in protestors' access to benefits. They also serve occasionally to make KWRU visible to potential members. Shy, a thirty-nine-year-old member, became aware of KWRU through news coverage of a protest on television; she recognized her cousin among the protestors.

Learning about KWRU

Shy is unusual; most members learn about KWRU directly from other members. Sometimes people have found out about KWRU through neighbors, family, coworkers, or friends who are members of the group.

After Colleen first heard about the organization she tried to find out how to contact them, but she wasn't able to find them in the telephone book. She explains:

> My dad found [the] Kensington Welfare Rights Union phone number through a food shelter . . . a food bank, St. John's, on Kensington Avenue. He would go to eat most of the time at the mission and he got it from one of the nuns that worked there, he got their number.

KWRU's recruitment efforts can be effective. A fifty-nine-year-old member who chose the pseudonym "Why" tells me that the former director of the organization came to speak at the community college where she was a student. KWRU activists go to welfare or housing offices, hand out fliers, and talk to people who have come to those offices for assistance.

KWRU also conducts what it calls "food distributions," where members spend time in poor neighborhoods giving out food to people and telling them about KWRU. Becky, a fifty-eight-year-old KWRU activist who lives with her daughter and grandchildren, tells me she learned about the group when activists were distributing food and other items:

> So what happened from that was my grandchildren went outside playing, they went down the corner and on the very corner was this great big tent, and at the tent . . . they had come back from it at the corner and they brought a bunch of bananas. . . . And I said to them, "Where did you get the bananas at?" And they said some lady on the corner gave them to them. Some nice lady on the corner gave them to them. . . . And with all the stuff I had been through it was like, "there is no nice people out there. . . . Who's giving you something for nothing?" You know, "I got to go see who this is." . . . And I went down the corner to check out the person to find out why somebody's giving my grand kids something. . . . [And the former director] was on the corner giving bananas and sneakers and everything you could think of. . . . She tried for over a year to get me involved in the organization.

Becky was suspicious at the beginning and wondered why these strangers would help her. It took her a long time to overcome that suspicion and get more involved. But she comments:

If, you know, if there's anything [KWRU] can do that they're able to do to help you they will. If there's anything I can do to help them, I will. It's like, it's not about me, it's not about any one individual, it's about all of us as a whole. It's about leadership and there is a lot of leaders, a lot of good, strong leaders. It's about leaders that stick together. . . . It's like if I turn around and I call [a fellow member] tomorrow, and I say . . . "I'm hurting. I don't have any food," she's gonna find a way to get me food. . . . It's closeness that goes even deeper than that. We have all been through the same thing. Each and every single one of us has been through hell and back again. And every one of us have our own stories. You know, but at the same time we all, we respect each other.

When we speak, Becky is completely positive about KWRU membership. Helen, forty-five, has basically dropped her membership when we speak. Like Becky, she tells me that KWRU members were giving out fruit and vegetables a half-block from where she lived at the time. She says, "They was giving out food. They said, 'If you don't come to the meetings you can't get no food.' So I said, 'Well, I don't really need the food, but I would like to find out what the meetings is about.'"[5]

The difference between knowing about KWRU and joining did not necessarily relate to having a personal connection to a group member. Eight non-KWRU participants tell me they had heard of the group when I ask. Two are employed at an agency located not far from the KWRU office and knew of the organization, perhaps because they had seen the sign. However, I recruited three other non-KWRU study participants from KWRU members, which meant that they had an acquaintance involved with the group. While not all members joined out of a sense of desperation, it seems likely that the study participants who knew others in KWRU but had never joined might have done so if and when they faced a crisis.

A Lack of Assistance

"If My Own Family Won't Help Me"

Low-income people often turn to social ties for support,[6] but among study participants there are serious obstacles to doing so, as described in chapter 2.[7] Both groups include people who have relied on immediate kin but despised every minute of it, but a few non-KWRU participants have richly supportive relationships with their parents. Most in both groups face obstacles that hinder them from widening their networks to include nonkin ties, and those in either group who have kin on whom to rely typically rely on only one kin tie rather than an expansive and interconnected network. Low-income people with readily and steadily available support are rare.[8] Some of the non-KWRU participants have family members who provide housing, either free or low-cost, or they have housing subsidies. Some non-KWRU participants receive cash assistance from welfare, having not hit time limits yet; some are in welfare-mandated training or job search programs to maintain their benefits; some cobble together enough to live on with spouses or grandmothers by working low-paid jobs. Some very successfully navigate available social services to obtain food stamps, medical assistance or low-cost clinic care, occasional grants to pay utility bills, and go to food banks to supplement their diets. KWRU participants generally differ in terms of kin support; they conform to what Shira Offer said of her participants: "The most vulnerable and disadvantaged mothers, those in greatest need for support, are the least likely to have it available from their networks."[9] Twenty-one out of the twenty-five non-KWRU participants in this study had received housing assistance from family members. KWRU members typically lacked kin ties who would provide social support this extensive. Not everyone in desperate circumstances can rely on kin for that support.[10] Like Matthew Desmond's[11] participants, in the absence of kin ties many KWRU participants seek other kinds of ties.

Those who are homeless, unable to get food stamps, or trying to escape domestic violence who do not have family members on whom to rely confront situations with no obvious remedies. KWRU members in this study seem to get less support and to get that support from fewer sources than do non-KWRU participants. Family and friends are not there for KWRU members to the same extent as they are for non-KWRU members, and twenty-three out of the twenty-five KWRU member participants have experienced homelessness. In addition, non-KWRU participants have more intact personal networks. These networks provide real, material help, most evident in their housing situations: only nine of the twenty-five have experienced homelessness; KWRU participants have experienced homelessness because they lack kin ties with whom they could stay. While some non-KWRU members, such as Kia, eschew reliance on kin, most have relied on kin to prevent homelessness at some point.

Karen's mother signed her house over to her, so now Karen owns a house. But she is far from secure because her family relies solely on income from her husband's seasonal employment as a bricklayer. Jen pays reduced rent for her apartment, a deal her mother secured. Leslie's reciprocal relationship with her parents, who refuse her monetary contributions to the household when her funds are tight, is very unusual. None of these women are KWRU members.

In harder times, non-KWRU member Alyssa, who has a job but didn't graduate high school—she has a GED—had accepted support from her family under terms that others might consider unacceptable; as she describes it, staying with family members was a nightmare. Her mother demanded money from her when she lived there, although at the time she was receiving welfare, was in school, and had few surplus funds. When she lived with her mother-in-law, she had to pay her even more and provide food as well. When we speak, Alyssa and her husband are providing a home of their own for their children. Alyssa wears glasses and has dark curly hair she keeps pulled back in a neat, high ponytail. She acknowledges the continued support of her family around her:

> My area rugs, they came from my grandparents, my end tables and my coffee table came from my grandparents. My dining room table came from my grandparents, a lot of stuff in my house was stuff from other people. . . . My mother-in-law gave us the fridge . . . my bedroom stuff all came from other people . . . my bunk-bed sets for my daughters came from my mother-in-law. The crib my son has . . . came from a friend of mine . . . some of the clothes my kids have were hand-me-downs from like my mom, my little sister, you know? Things like that.

Even when they no longer provided housing support, Alyssa's family provided items important for the family's well-being.

Poor people without family to rely on seek help from agencies[12] such as soup kitchens, food banks, and homeless shelters, as well as programs that help pay bills or provide vouchers to purchase necessities.[13] Beyond material support, social service agencies can act as resource brokers, connecting poor people to each other and to other organizations.[14]

Participants who are not members of KWRU seem to have more positive experiences in using social services than do KWRU members. For example, Inez has a strong relationship with a woman at a social service agency; she tells me that when there was a fire at her mother's house, "Miss Patty" had "helped me out with furniture for my brother's room, my nephew's room and downstairs." But the sort of emotional connection Inez reports feeling to Miss Patty is unusual, and Inez's own description suggests that Miss Patty provided her more service than she could realistically give to many people, giving Inez her personal phone number and maximizing the services she received. Miss Patty also soothed feelings Inez might have had about taking help, as Inez quotes her to me, "You know you are a smart woman, you can do everything on your own but don't do everything on your own." Typically, social service agencies provide a good deal of material support but rarely provide emotional support. As I'll discuss in this chapter and the two that follow, this is one of KWRU's unique strengths. However, agencies can and do serve as sites that provide opportunities for clients to build connections with one another, as Mario Luis Small documents; his book *Unanticipated Gains: Origins of Network Inequality in Everyday Life* demonstrates the role child care centers can play in the lives of parents.[15]

While many low-income parents remain fearful of DHS, focusing on its power to remove children from their homes, some non-KWRU members have found this resource invaluable. Carole explains that she received furniture, appliances, and toys for her children from DHS. Gail tells me, "DHS also provides help for kids, not just coming to attack their parents for what they're not doing right. 'Cause that's what people mistake DHS [for]. 'Oh, my God, DHS is after me,' but they don't realize that DHS also can give you a lot of help on things you need." Carole tells me, "DHS helped me with . . . some furniture, [a] refrigerator . . . it was all brand new stuff."[16] Non-KWRU participants also have greater success in getting support from agencies; KWRU members report frustrating experiences. Rebecca, a KWRU member, tells me she had tried in the past to get help from agencies, but without success. A number of KWRU members I interview report that KWRU is the first organization that has actually provided them with help.

Of the twenty-five KWRU members I interview, only seven have received housing assistance from family members and all but two have been homeless. Cate tells me, about receiving help from KWRU: "My mom was in Puerto Rico . . . my brothers can't help me, you know." Lack of kin ties, or kin able to assist them, brings people to KWRU for help in meeting basic needs. Becky explains to me that she received help from a family member on only one occasion—a temporary place to stay; she expresses her surprise that KWRU provided help when she says, "If my own family wouldn't help me, why would somebody else?"

Getting Help from KWRU

"They Said No; That's When I Went to Welfare Rights"

The most common reason to seek out KWRU's help is a threat to housing. Others come because they lose their welfare benefits. CC, forty-four, became homeless when she left her abusive husband. She heard that KWRU provided housing, so she went to the organization for help. KWRU has put her in one of its Human Rights Houses, but until she gets her own stable housing she cannot regain custody of her five- and seven-year-old children.

> I don't have no lawyer, I can't go in there and fight. I don't want nothing he got now, all I want is my children, so. . . . And because I don't have decent housing, that's why I don't have my kids with me. That's why I'm here at Kensington Welfare Rights. 'Cause I get $158 every 2 weeks. Where can I live for $158?

James, thirty-four, tells me he and his wife became homeless when living in another state, so they then moved to Philadelphia to stay with family members. He says, "[My relative] told me about the Kensington Welfare Rights Union, how they fight for affordable housing and I was like, 'whoa that's what I need.' . . . So out of selfish reasons, you know what I mean, me and my wife, we started coming to the meetings." Now James, his wife, and their children live together in a house they rent with a Section 8 housing voucher that KWRU helped them get.

Paloma, twenty-eight, wears a confidence born of her intelligence and quick, biting wit. Like CC and James, she also came to the organization for help when she became homeless.

> Well, I become homeless at nineteen, saw this lady giving out food, she said that . . . if you needed housing, come to the meeting the next day. And I needed housing. I was living in a rented room because my boy-friend and I had an apartment . . . that we lost because we had gotten sick [missed work and were fired] and couldn't pay the rent. So we moved out of that apartment and moved into a small room, renting [in] . . . a house full of rooms that were for rent. The house was falling apart but it was cheap. That's all we could afford. . . . So I went to the meeting. I was very embarrassed about my situation because when we had gotten home that previous night, the place was locked up because Licenses and Inspection had closed it down. . . . So we spent the night out in the park. It was one of the scariest nights of my entire life.

Jessie, twenty-six, came to KWRU for help with welfare, but soon learned they might be able to help her with housing as well. She tells me, "I was having problems with my welfare. They kept cutting it off." Her grandmother, who lived near the KWRU office, had seen it and told Jessie about it. She continues,

> So me and my ex-husband, we were driving past it and we went in and we told them . . . my welfare was being cut off. . . . And then I found out that they help with housing, so then I told them that we didn't have nowhere to live or whatever. And so like a couple days later they had put me in a Takeover House.[17] . . . So my whole motive to go in there was just to get help with my welfare. . . . But once I went in . . . then I heard people talking about housing, and I was like, "Wait a minute. I need that too. I don't have nowhere to stay." So that's where I got involved with them.

Jessie lived in a Takeover House for a while, which led to temporary housing through the Office of Emergency Shelter, but when it didn't lead to permanent housing she ended up living in a KWRU Human Rights House, where she is at the time of our interview.

Colleen, twenty-nine, describes her life before KWRU. She left one job for a better-paying one, $7.00 an hour as a receptionist at a hair salon, but found she couldn't afford child care for her son while she was working.

> So I call up the caseworker. All I was receiving at the time was medical assistance and food stamps. I called them up, this is February or March, and said to them, "I don't have any way to pay daycare on Monday. I don't know what I'm gonna do." "Well, that's not our problem. You need to call the subsidized child care line. Here is the number." So I called the subsidized child care line and then they told me, "Well, due to welfare reform and TANF, anybody who's on TANF gets top priority, and if you're not on TANF you're on a six to nine month waiting list." . . . I can't go to work Monday, like I have no money to pay the daycare on Monday. "That's all we can do. We'll put your name on our waiting list.". . . I said, "Okay, well, I can't work Monday. I guess I quit my job." So I called up the caseworker and said, "I had to quit." "Well, now you can't get anything." "Well, what do you mean?" "Because you quit your job, you're not eligible for anything." I said, "I quit my job because I couldn't pay for my child care." They told me no.

Had Colleen shown up for work and left her child with no one to care for him, she might have faced prison time, as we witnessed in two high-profile cases in 2014.[18] KWRU helped her navigate the process to get TANF and subsidized child care, and when we speak she has a job as a social worker and remains active in KWRU.

Marisol, twenty-five, tells me,

> I got here because I have a welfare problem, they didn't want to help me or my kids with medical or with any other benefits they give. . . . I got involved because I had a welfare problem, I was pregnant, they had me running around, and a friend told me, "Look, there's this place called the Kensington Welfare Rights, they probably help you with your welfare."

Marisol didn't believe they would be able to help her but she decided to try anyway. She continues, "So I got here and a couple people from here helped me out, and like I said, we was in a struggle for like two months, but they did help me out." Marisol was fleeing an abusive relationship when she came to KWRU, and when we speak she is hopeful about getting a housing voucher with KWRU's help.

Like Marisol, Stefanie, twenty-one years old, was having a problem obtaining assistance from welfare. She says, "I was on welfare when I . . . was pregnant with my daughter. And they told me when I turn twenty-one, that I could get food stamps. When I turned twenty-one, I went over there to . . . get food stamps. They said, 'No.' I gotta wait til I'm twenty-two. That's when I went to Welfare Rights."

Alice, a forty-seven-year-old member, tells me,

> I came here with a welfare problem. . . . The welfare problem was, since I had two children at home yet, it was just giving me enough cash for the one. And they kept it up for about two and a half months. And I kept calling my counselor. The normal routine. And, they said "well we can't do nothing about it." I said "fine." I came here, explained the situation to [KWRU and they] called them up, within a day or so everything was straightened out.

Alice has been a fixture at the office since soon after she joined, helping out however she can, including spending many hours answering the phone.

"I Knew I Needed an Organization to Know How to Survive in This World"

KWRU members mentioned receiving help from the organization navigating welfare, health care, and utilities, with money, transportation, child care, and information about schools, legal services, obtaining Section 8 and other housing help, clothes, food, furniture, and other material items. At the time of my research, a typical day in their office in West Kensington includes phone calls from people with specific concerns or problems; people call whose houses are in various states of disrepair, hoping that KWRU can find somewhere else for them to stay or help them do some repairs. Sometimes people call whose children have been taken by the state. Many such people have lost custody of their children because of their failure to provide appropriate housing. KWRU focuses on housing issues, helping individuals find homes and repair their homes, and demonstrating for affordable housing in the city, state, and country.[19] One KWRU participant tells me about how she became a member: the roof literally caved in at her apartment and she called a KWRU member she had met recently, to ask for help. The member asked about the landlord and, learning he hadn't been around, she said that KWRU members would come by. "Pack your stuff up, we're gonna put it in storage, and you're getting out of there. We'll call License and Inspection. More than likely you're gonna fail inspection and this will qualify you to get emergency housing." The study participant told me, "I knew nothing about that. . . . I was so into my own little world trying to survive that I didn't know that I had other resources, you know what I mean?"

My very first meeting with a KWRU member is not an interview, but an opportunity to witness these services in action. I accompany Paloma to the house of an elderly woman who can't speak English. I sit on the couch in the immaculate living room while Paloma calls a utility company. She identifies herself on the telephone as a representative from the Kensington Welfare Rights Union, explaining that she is calling on behalf of the woman who lives there, and requests that the woman be put on a budget plan. This action allowed the woman to pay off her utility bills without losing service.

The group also responds to problems raised at meetings. As noted above, Cate met KWRU activists at the welfare office one day and they invited her to come to a meeting. Then they met her the next day at the welfare office and staged a highly successful protest. She tells me that when she got her benefits because of KWRU, "That's when I knew that I had to become from an organization to know how to survive in this world, because I was all by myself." Marie typifies members' understanding of their relationship to one another when she tells me, "That's the only way we going to survive, if we help each other," and she pools resources with other KWRU members.

KWRU provides a place to stay for new homeless members and assistance that helps them to overcome barriers to securing food stamps, welfare, and medical care. For long-term members, a brief stay in a KWRU Takeover House or Human Rights House can lead to a Section 8 voucher, providing the opportunity to secure housing with more longevity and stability. A KWRU house serves as a de facto homeless shelter, and KWRU members have the impression that staying in one enables Section 8 waiting list members to claim an immediate need to be pushed up the waiting list. Staying in a KWRU house also signals to organization leaders a commitment to the organization, which they reward with Section 8 vouchers when they receive some directly (as happened shortly after the City Hall protest, when city officials released five vouchers to KWRU to distribute to members). Eight of the twenty-five KWRU study participants are living in KWRU Human Rights houses during my research; another two are staying rent-free with KWRU members. Seven have Section 8 vouchers they secured with KWRU's help. An additional three received housing help from KWRU members prior to our interview.

Through KWRU, Walter has received vital medications to manage a chronic condition. He explains to me:

> I have no health care. . . . The network made arrangements for me to hook up with a free clinic . . . and I was able to get some pills for my [medical condition], otherwise I'd be in bad, bad shape. . . . But one of our supporters is a nurse . . . [and] has connections with nurses and doctors and they hooked us up, you know.

Through fund-raising efforts, grants from nonprofit foundations, and speaking engagements for KWRU leaders—the speaker splits his or her fee with the organization—KWRU is also able to provide financial help to members on occasion in order to pay a bill. For example, Helen describes getting financial help from KWRU directly to get her heat turned back on.

"They Educate You Here"

In addition to the kinds of practical aid KWRU offers—aid that can be substantial—KWRU provides members with tools to survive, which, as they describe it, they can continue to use even without direct KWRU assistance. The significance of this to members is intensely meaningful; they feel they have received not just help to facilitate survival, but the ability to navigate their difficulties in ways they couldn't before they found KWRU. Cate says:

That's how I learned how to survive, through KWRU. . . . If I was to become homeless, I know what to do. . . . I learned like if want to get something notarized, I know where to go that it's free. . . . And I know lawyers, legal aid service, I know a lot of people from the legal aid service. I know a lot of doctors that are free [that] KWRU knows that they will see me free, they don't charge. And I know, if I was to be homeless, I know where to go, to a hospital that I can go take a bath and they give me socks, panties and bra. . . . And I know where to go . . . [to a soup kitchen] to eat every day. I would have my meal. . . . I know that. Before I wouldn't know that.

Involvement with KWRU provides these participants with concrete survival skills, a way to get the necessities of daily life when their personal and financial struggles seem insurmountable. KWRU members also gain knowledge they can use to help others, such as how to procure financial assistance to pay for rent. CC, who lives in a Human Rights House and expects to receive a voucher through the organization, tells me:

Different things, like if they found they self a house, where they can go to get money for they last month's rent and security deposits and all that. . . . They can go right to . . . OSHA. . . . They can go to TAG, Tenants Action Group. They give out money. Then you can get vouchers from different people to go to the Salvation Army. They give you furniture for how many bedrooms you got. . . . I didn't know [that before]. . . . They educate you. They educate you here. All you gotta do is listen.

Carmen explains that she too learned a lot of practical information about what people can do to navigate the system and get the help they need. She is proud she knew a way to help her neighbor get her utilities turned back on, even though the neighbor had lost her job and didn't have sufficient income to pay her bills. She tells me:

I had a neighbor across the street. . . . They cut her phone, her gas, her electric, she lost her job . . . and she had to pay $150, that was her agreement with the . . . with the Section 8 voucher, but she lost her job. She wasn't in there long enough to collect unemployment, and she was kind of like juggling, paying one person to pay another person to try and keep them all on, and then finally just didn't work anymore and everybody just cut her off, so . . . I had to help her out . . . getting a doctor's note . . . having the doctor write a note for her to get her utilities on. . . . I was like, "How cool are you with your doctor?" She was like, "No, she's pretty cool. . . ." I was like, "Well, call your cool doctor up so we can go down here and get this note." She was like, "You think they're gonna turn it . . . ?" I was like, "Yes. You get a doctor's note all your utilities will be on. You're gonna have thirty days to make an arrangement. This is only good for thirty days. In thirty days if you don't have your things all set up you got to go back and get another doctor's note."

Carmen was willing to do whatever might be necessary for her neighbor to regain her utility service, and she used the skills she has acquired through her KWRU participation to help her neighbor successfully navigate the system. Jessie also tells me that she learned about the existence of different programs through her KWRU involvement and has shared that information with others. She says:

Now I'm not ignorant to the fact that there's so many places that can help. Like I've heard situations . . . and I can actually turn around and be like, "Yes, well, there's this person by this name and this phone number that you can call and go and they'll help you, and there's this program and that program." I've learned so much in so many places and so many people that I'm no longer illiterate to the things or to the places and programs that I can go to to help me to better myself. . . . There was a time I heard someone, they couldn't pay their rent. "Oh, wait a minute. There's TAG on 12th and Market. Go down there. They can help you. And if not there, there's another place here, you know." And, "I need a lawyer . . ." And I go, "Wait a minute. Go to CLS [Community Legal Services]." . . . You know, there's like a lot of places. Like I've learned a lot of programs and places and phone numbers and people that I can help someone else with. . . . So now I'm no longer illiterate to the places and programs that there's out there to help people that we don't know about because they don't . . . they don't put it on TV. . . . You know, they don't put it on radio. They don't put it on nothing to let us know that it's out there.

Jessie feels that KWRU has pulled the wool from her eyes; while she remains frustrated at what she perceives as lack of publicity about social programs, she feels good that she has acquired information she can now share with others, doing a sort of public service. Colleen tells me she's gotten information too:

> All the time . . . from people at KWRU. I think [Paloma] has helped me out a lot in the past on where to go for a particular issue or contact a lawyer who's in KWRU, to get information about Head Start, you know, I'm trying to get my son in. . . . I've talked with [someone else I know through KWRU], because she's a therapist, about therapy for my son through the mental health system and things like that.

"You're Not the Only One Who Has Problems"

While in general KWRU does not completely change the mindsets I've described in chapters 1 and 2 that tend to be a barrier to the establishment of social ties, KWRU members do learn that other people have problems similar to theirs, begin to see the extent of poverty on a broader scale, and learn about the structural and political reasons for poverty. This mitigates their belief that agency determines people's circumstances and leads them to begin to question the achievement ideology. In this respect the power of the individualism I described in chapter 1 lessens, as does poverty stigma, although their isolation from their immediate neighbors generally does not.[20]

While members do not let go completely of individualism or stigmatization of the poor, they develop trusting, cooperative relationships in KWRU. KWRU provides a community independent of a neighborhood and a safe environment for members *not* to stay to themselves. In this environment, KWRU members begin to feel a sense of community and commonality with one another, seeing emotional as well as practical benefits of building social ties instead of avoiding them. Alice says she's learned, "You're not the only one that has problems." Marisol says she too has learned a lot, and now "I feel like . . . that in the situation I'm in now, that I'm not by myself." Colleen explains it this way: "I know I'm not the only one. . . . I thought I had a really unique story. I thought I did . . . [but there are] thousands and millions that are out there," suggesting that poverty's breadth signals systemic explanations rather than individual ones. Walter also speaks to me at length about another KWRU member:

> She went to school, she struggled, she worked, she has a family, she got married, she's not a single mother, she's married. Her husband has a technical degree in mechanics, he can't find a job. And she's not alone, this is not some exception to the rule. People are not poor because they're stupid, people are not poor because they're not married, people are not poor because they are in the inner city. People are not poor because they're black or nonwhite, people are not poor because they're not you. They're poor, and they're you. Something is happening, in this society, and the problem is not stupidity, the problem is structural.

For some like Jessie, who tells me deep poverty is a relatively recent obstacle, KWRU is providing a context in which to explore information about poverty. She explains:

> KWRU has taught me a lot more about poverty . . . because to be honest with you, as I was growing up I never needed for anything. . . . So I didn't consider myself low class. At all. . . . My eyes just opened to a whole new world once KWRU came into my life. Like I was ignorant and naïve to the things that were going on. Like KWRU says they try to raise awareness of what's going on in the world with poor people. . . . And poverty, and that's something I didn't know about. . . . Because I didn't consider myself to be low, poor. I thought I was doing good because my parents . . . took very well care of me. . . . You couldn't tell me there was anything wrong with us because . . . there was never a time we didn't have. It wasn't until I had my own children [that I struggled]. . . . Then when I got into KWRU that's when I, you know, learned that there was a lot of things that I did not know about.

Jessie actually grew up in a poor neighborhood and was far from wealthy; her feeling that she wasn't poor is merely relative. Prior to her KWRU involvement, Jessie had completely accepted the idea that poor people caused their own poverty, evidencing her acceptance of the achievement ideology. It is incredibly difficult to overcome such entrenched ideas.[21]

Even in the face of the Great Recession and high unemployment, people continue to blame the poor for their poverty and the poor continue to blame themselves.[22] Jessie continues:

> Like I knew there was people on the street, but whenever I seen people like that, being naïve what I was taught was they're probably on drugs . . . and whatever, whatever. That was my big thing. I just thought you made yourself that way. You know. Because you shouldn't be on the street, you shouldn't be hungry, you shouldn't be asking nobody for a quarter. You did it to yourself. But now I know that that's not true. I know there's no way in hell that you could do yourself that way, like you could actually be like, "Well, I'm gonna be poor today. I want to starve. I'm not gonna take a shower today." There's no way that if you had a choice . . . that you're gonna pick that. So that's like one of the things I learned from being with KWRU was like you don't make them decisions. . . . Something has happened in that person's life to make them be where they are today. It wasn't a decision that you made because there's no one in this world that would decide they're gonna be poor and they're gonna live on the street and they're gonna sleep on a vent. There's no way.

Jessie is living in a Human Rights House, and she's lived on the street. Her experiences and her time with KWRU have changed her perspective on the causes of and blame for poverty; she's seeing limits on the reach of individual agency, as described in chapter 2. What KWRU has achieved in Jessie's case is unusual but not wholly unique. Other KWRU members report explicitly changing their minds as a result of KWRU's teachings and activities. Several participants say that through KWRU they learned poverty was not their own fault and that they shouldn't be embarrassed or blame themselves, nor should they blame others for their poverty. Maureen, thirty-three, says that KWRU has "changed my perception of what poor's like. . . . [Before I thought] that it was just people being lazy and not doing the right things, but it's . . . then, you know, once I saw them and I'm in the situation I'm in, you know, it made you realize it's not. . . . It's not just here, it's everywhere, you know." Maureen is currently living with her sister because she cannot afford to live independently.

Shy has one child, a young adult. Outgoing with a ready, broad smile, she tells me that the travels she has gone on with KWRU have opened a world she never knew existed by showing her that poverty is widespread, even in areas she always thought were safe from poverty. She had never been that far from home before. She says:

> I went on that bus tour. . . . I went to Utah, Tennessee, Mississippi, Virginia, New Orleans, I went to all these different places. . . . I seen the same thing I seen here. Poor people, people sleepin' outside, people sellin' they belongings tryin' to be able to eat and I was like, "I ain't know this was goin' on in the world." How I know in my wildest dreams, there's people in California starvin'? When I think of California, I think of the stars, the TV shows, the game shows, and y'all over here hungry, y'all goin' through what I'm goin' through. So it was amazing. It was, it was scary but it was amazing, like, there's somebody else out here worse than I am. . . . I thought it was in Philly, one little section, my section. I didn't know it was like that. So, that was a trip that I'll just never forget. I went to Miami, Florida, and it was goin 'on in there. . . . And I thought they was more rich, uppity people in Miami, Florida. They on the beach, chillin'. No. They was homeless, sleepin' on the beach.

Similarly, Carmen says being on the tour opened her eyes. "Homelessness is just not in Philadelphia or Pennsylvania, it's everywhere . . . and the stories are all the same, just different faces. You hear the same things over and over and over and over again." The traveling KWRU members do with the organization provides them with experiences most poor people never have: seeing other parts of the country, and the world. Gaining a perspective on the lives people live elsewhere enables members to entertain alternative explanations for poverty. Shy was truly shocked by what she witnessed, as it called into question her long-held ideas about poverty being rooted in individual actions and personal failures. She explains:

> I got all my knowledge from KWRU. Because before I really got into the union, and really dealt with them and been all over the world, I thought it was our fault. Yeah, I really thought it was my fault that I, I just can't

get there. Like, it's just my fault, like, "I'm just not tryin' hard enough. I'm not stickin' with this, I'm not doin' that." And, to a certain extent, it is my fault but then again, since I've made my mistakes, okay, I'm thinking I could fix it, like, you know. But you can't fix it if there ain't nothin' out there. . . . So, yeah, for a while I thought it was, like, poor people's fault that they were poor. But as I got with the union and I learnin' national stuff and been all over, it's impossible for it to just be poor people's fault, all the poor people I see.

Now that she has changed her mindset in part, Shy can articulate the ways in which she had blamed herself for her poverty. Yet, at another point in the interview she espouses the achievement ideology: "You just like, you gotta work and strive for what you want and then you make it." The achievement ideology has great power in the United States, and it's unsurprising that Shy could have begun to rethink her views and yet still believe in the achievement ideology. What Shy has learned through KWRU has challenged her stereotypes about poor people; she has even begun to stop blaming herself and others for being poor. A big part of the change for Shy is seeing the extent of poverty. She has begun to recognize that poverty is a more systemic problem than she once believed and she now contends that there is a governmental role in the perpetuation of poverty, calling the achievement ideology into question. She is anxious to learn more, and she believes the more knowledge she gains the better prepared she will be for an uncertain future. Whereas some might consider her "empowered" if she embraced individuality and invested in human capital, KWRU offers her and others a chance to be empowered through a shared mission and response to a rigged system.

However, KWRU's ideas about the sources of poverty do not sway every KWRU participant. Those who recently joined the organization or who are more peripherally involved are particularly immune to the organization's tenets; most of those who exhibit a strong denial of poverty stigma were in leadership roles. Others, like Shy, Carmen, and Jessie were able to note the point at which their KWRU involvement began to change their ideas and teach them new things. These participants offer sometimes contradictory or conflicting opinions about the causes of poverty, as they struggle to process new information and come to terms with how it challenges what they thought they always knew. More peripherally involved members, such as Naomi and Helen, claimed to have learned nothing from their time with KWRU. Like Shy, Carmen, and Jessie, these participants still blame the poor for their plight at times and focus on personal responsibility as the answer to their problems. Helen says that her KWRU involvement "made me think about doing everything on my own because that's the only way it's gonna get done. That's the way I feel. I even told them that. If it wasn't for me doing things for myself, I would have never got to where I'm trying to get." Most members, however, on balance find that KWRU involvement opens their eyes.

"The Problem Is Not an Individual Problem"

Walter acknowledges that at times he has felt ashamed of his poverty, as he imagines all poor people must at some point, but he tells me his shame dissipated as he became involved in activism to combat poverty. This allowed him to take part in mutual relationships with others. Some KWRU leaders acknowledge to me that politicians, members of the media, and social service administrators have accused them of taking a vow of poverty, the implication being that as individuals, these leaders have what others perceive to be the intelligence, eloquence, education, or experience to get a stable job but they choose not to. I ask one leader about this vow of poverty claim, that they want to stay poor to make a point. He explains:

> I realize that the problem is not an individual problem. And so, if I got that job, I would have to weigh it against my responsibilities, because I don't want to let people down. If I take the job, and it allows me to sustain myself. . . . But the problem is not an individual problem. . . . I have this commitment. . . . I realize that I might get a job today, but [I might] get laid off the next day. I mean, you know, it's like [you] cannot be one of many trying to get a better chair on the Titanic. . . . You get a good chair, would you take the good chair? No, I want to get those chairs and turn them into a goddamn raft, to get the hell off the Titanic!

KWRU's stated mission is the eradication of poverty. Many members, even some activists, recognize that this is an unlikely outcome of their efforts. Yet they value the sense of being part of a group, both for the support it provides and for the sense of belonging and community it offers. This is curtailed when people avoid social ties, as described in chapter 2.

Although the participant who chose "Why" as her pseudonym is doubtful that KWRU will end poverty, when I ask her what people who are struggling should do, she nevertheless says, "I think they need to join together . . . they have to unify, they have to . . . become one. You know, because you can't do it by yourself. You need the organization, you know. And that's what makes them sit up and take notice. You know, otherwise they think they don't have to do anything." Many KWRU members express this sentiment in interviews: the answer for those who are struggling is to find an organization, so they can work together with others to successfully improve their lives. While they do not turn against the idea of human capital investment, this perspective stands in stark contrast to the strategies described in previous chapters to avoid social ties in order to focus on individual actions.

Where most participants discuss individual decisions they can make and actions they can take to survive or to manage, KWRU activists mention working together with others. I ask Paloma, "What do you think is the best strategy?" She says:

> Organization . . . because two heads is better than one; three heads is better than two. Fifteen is better than five. You know. A unified strategy is much better than someone by themselves trying to get by. I think that if people unite and create organization among themselves and really study why what's happening is happening and then formalize their strategy to counteract why these things are happening, then that helps them truly survive.

Paloma has been a KWRU member for nine years when she tells me this. She is receiving cash assistance from the state and has housing support KWRU helped her get, but she will soon reach her five-year lifetime limit. The decision to join KWRU may come from desperation and acute need, but for many members it changes their thinking about the ways to alleviate their poverty. The organization's emphasis on collective strategies to combat poverty centers on people joining together to help one another and to fight poverty through collective action. It's a message leaders and activists espouse and help to craft; even when rank and file members don't use the rhetoric of fighting poverty as a collective to describe their own goals and activities, they do internalize and express to me a newfound importance of working together in order to survive.[23]

"The Best Thing"

Many KWRU activists and leaders told me that working together is the solution to poverty. When I ask participants what they think people struggling to get by should do, many non-KWRU members offer individual-focused strategies, as described in chapter 1; others pause and hesitate before simply answering, "I don't know" or "hope and pray." To be sure, some KWRU members feel similarly uncertain of what to do or propose individual strategies when I ask this question, but they are more likely than non-KWRU members to suggest that a collective can bring about change.

One KWRU activist, involved for eight years, tells me poor people should "figure out what they can contribute to this process to bring about a change. Organize with a group of people who's willing to do, by any means necessary, to have those basic necessities, and when you get with that group, go all out." The sense of affection and loyalty to KWRU and its ideals pervaded responses to my question about what strategies people who are struggling should embrace, as the excerpts from KWRU member interviews below demonstrate.

Becky, a longtime member of KWRU whose health generally keeps her from attending rallies:

> People in every single solitary corner all around, they have to organize. They have to organize big enough and strong enough so that the people can make the change . . . you pick to organize and you pick to fight. . . . When you get involved in the organization they'll take you step by step . . . they'll teach you how to survive. . . . Join the organization. Get involved with them . . . as an organization, you can do it.

Carmen, for whom having a group of KWRU members at the welfare office made all the difference:

Try to work. . . . Stay focused. . . . Get involved in a group. Join a group, don't do it by yourself. . . . When you're involved in an organization . . . if I was to go down to the welfare office by myself, I'd get no results. Because I tried. I didn't get no results. I go in with a group of people . . . I got seen right away, they didn't want no problems, they didn't want no uproar, whatever it was, but I got seen right away.

It makes sense that many of the more committed members related this to me, since it's part of what the organization leaders teach them.

The founder of KWRU, Cheri Honkala, tells me that when people are struggling, they should

> get support of other lower income people that understand the plight they're in . . . because it's very hard then to feed into our own internalized oppression.[24] When everybody is constantly in direct or indirect ways telling you that you're a loser, it's really hard not to buy into that. . . . They have to get involved in a larger fight to build a movement in this country calling for changes. . . . Only when massive amounts of people begin to participate in building a massive social movement for economic human rights are we ever gonna see any kind of changes, and as long as they remain, you know, ashamed and invisible, we're never gonna change anything.

Cate says, "They need to be in an organization to fight it. . . . You got to be in an organization, so when something happens, we could pick up each other fast. Because normally when you're by yourself, you're just dropped and that's it." Colleen, a member for six years, tells me that she would advise others to

> get connected with other people who are struggling and help find the solutions and to help, you know, work together to address these issues, because you're gonna be torn down if it's just yourself. You're gonna get burned out, you're gonna be . . . you're gonna have a lot of heartache, a lot of heartache through the process, and if you have other people, a collective to share your thoughts and ideas and to share your frustrations with and know that you're not alone, I think that that was . . . I think that was the best thing.

Shy, an active member of KWRU and a frequent participant at protests, agrees with Colleen, also connecting what she thinks other poor people should do to what she feels worked for her. She says:

> Me, personally, I found the union. Like, KWRU to help me and to guide me and to teach me more and to know what's goin' on in the world. Because if you poor or you just can't find your way, you need to learn, things is about learnin'. You need to learn more and learn your rights and know what you facin', what you gotta deal with in order to even make it. So, if you poor and you not doin' nothin' or talkin' to no type of organization like KWRU, you gonna be lost because you don't know what's goin' on.

The strong feelings that KWRU evokes suggest the power of its model and the potential for good that organizations based on the KWRU model could do if they had adequate resources and a supportive political environment.

Social Capital

KWRU offers a great deal of assistance to its members such as practical help with welfare, legal services, food, clothes, housing, and information. Unmistakably, KWRU provides social capital to its members. This support is social capital because like other forms of capital, it can be drawn on and invested in. Different types of ties tend to provide different types of capital. "Strong" ties, such those to family and friends, generate bonding social capital as well as emergency assistance including cash, company in times of loneliness, and the chance to confide in others.[25] "Weak" ties[26] tend to offer social leverage, generating bridging social capital that may allow for upward mobility.[27] Often poor people have only bonding social capital, if they're fortunate enough to have that.[28] But even bonding capital to cope is not universal; those most in need are most at risk of being isolated.[29] KWRU offers bonding social capital that helps members cope on a daily basis, but not bridging social capital that would allow for leverage for upward mobility.[30] Certainly some staunch activists and leaders move on to other things, gain employment and housing over time, and still consider themselves part of the wider antipoverty network of organizations. Yet KWRU's goal is not to help individuals get out of poverty but to develop a social movement to end poverty for all.

Individual circumstances and decisions alone cannot generate social capital. Structural forces play a large and underlying role. Structural factors impose constraints on individual behaviors. Robert Putnam notes the phenomenon I identified in chapter 2 when he says that "social capital is often lacking in disadvantaged areas, and it is difficult to build."[31] Indeed, William Julius Wilson discusses how deindustrialization and middle-class flight left inner cities without social capital, leading to high unemployment and welfare use. The spatial concentration of poverty creates disadvantaged environments that become progressively isolated socially and economically.[32]

Conclusion

KWRU provides housing and welfare assistance and often a great deal of emotional support as a community of like-minded individuals with shared experiences. KWRU members are a unique group of poor people, organized to end their own and, they hope, others' poverty. In the process they engage in daily activities like many others: taking care of their children, running errands, trying to find ways to make ends meet, and socializing with others. Activists also organize other poor people through food distributions, knocking on doors, and protest demonstrations. The Kensington Welfare Rights Union is a distinctive organization offering services to those on the financial brink in exchange for their membership in a movement to end poverty. As people grow more involved, KWRU provides them with a political education about the structural roots of poverty and encourages them to let go of self-blame and their individualistic focus on the achievement ideology. The organization helps people deal with daily survival while simultaneously organizing them through demonstrations and other events. In working together with others in the organization people begin to build social ties, overcoming the factors that tend to cause tie avoidance.

People learn about KWRU in a variety of ways, but they seldom join the group unless they need help with something very urgent such as medical issues, hunger, domestic violence, family conflict, utility services, lack of housing, or issues with welfare. The need for housing is acute among the desperate population that comes to KWRU for help; the lack of strong family ties deepens the need and pushes people to KWRU's doors, while the help the organization offers pulls them in.

Cate went to a KWRU meeting after encountering a KWRU activist at the welfare office. Alice was having trouble getting welfare benefits for one of her children when she came to KWRU for help. CC had fled an abusive relationship, leaving behind her youngest children, when she turned to KWRU; the organization provided her a temporary place to live and was helping her secure a Section 8 voucher to establish stable housing in order to regain custody of her children. As I have described in this chapter, most people first come to KWRU when their situations are dire. Many have recently escaped from domestic violence. They do not decide to invest in social capital at the expense of human capital; they are just desperate for help.

The decision to *continue* as an active KWRU member, however, does represent a more or less conscious decision to focus on social ties to facilitate survival. KWRU offers some members housing, which typically is more stable than a homeless shelter, if not as stable as housing to which individuals would have their own legal claim. KWRU also offers support in preventing the loss of electrical and similar services, and access to welfare payments. These varied benefits come at a cost, as described in chapter 4, but also offer the opportunity to build sustainable ties, as discussed in chapter 5.

Involvement with KWRU provides members assistance in overcoming immediate difficulties and skills to survive daily life, but what members learn from KWRU is not limited to practical information; some of them also begin to comprehend the broader reaches of poverty and question whether they are really at fault for their circumstances. To sustain assistance from KWRU, members must give in return. The next chapter describes this reciprocal dynamic.

4

What Goes around Comes Around

Reciprocity in a Poor People's Social Network

I said [to a KWRU leader], "You gave me this—it wasn't a palace—but you gave me and my daughter a roof over my head and we worked for that. We worked for that." . . . I said, "Look, you find me a place, I be right there. If I get my housing I'm not going anywhere. I'm gonna come back here and fight for those ones that are still homeless." . . . I go to every function, international meetings. . . . I do everything. Everything.

—CC, 44, KWRU member who was once homeless

I meet Stefanie, a young Latina mother of two girls, when she has just walked into KWRU for the first time to get some help securing food stamps. Her long dark hair is pulled back into a smooth ponytail, revealing small gold-colored earrings. I interview her the following week. She and her girls live not far from the office, in West Kensington, with her mother, father, and brother. She pays rent to her parents, purchases her own food, and pays Rent-a-Center every month for her bedroom set, but the state views her as part of their household and therefore she cannot qualify for food stamps. She counts two women as close friends, but both are out of state and neither is a source of support. She plans to volunteer in the office, answering phones and assisting others who walk in for help. She explains working in the KWRU office in terms of reciprocal obligations:

> There's some people out there that be like, "Oh, I'm not gonna go do that, they're not gonna pay me for that." But you're helping other people, they help you, you know what I mean? . . . That's how they pay you back. They're helping you.

Stefanie explicitly points out the way social capital mimics financial capital under KWRU's reciprocity norms—KWRU doesn't pay money for her labors, but it "pays" in support.

Membership in KWRU provides social capital, and norms of reciprocity organize this social capital within KWRU's membership. Social networks are built on reciprocity.[1] Although not all KWRU members understand this as quickly as Stefanie does, reciprocity is a crucial component of KWRU membership. Virtually all my interviews with KWRU members include some reference to this principle. This lays bare the double-edged sword of social capital—to invest in it, one must give away time and other resources. As chapter 2 emphasized, most participants in this study had a strong inclination to safeguard those resources for themselves, and this ensured that they had minimal social capital.

The service KWRU requires of its members is substantial because members have so few resources. New members learn that they need to give their time by volunteering at the office and participating in protest rallies. Due to the limits of Philadelphia's transportation system, especially in poor areas, most members had to travel hours to fulfill these obligations.[2] The only transportation available for free in Philadelphia is walking, and in bad weather showing up to the office to volunteer or at a rally to add to the strength of the protest might require hours in rain, cold, or heat. Members I spoke with typically walked to the office, even from far away; some took city buses when they had tokens or money for the fare.[3]

There are both positive and negative aspects of reciprocity, as I touched on in chapter 2. Many participants recount good feelings about giving and receiving help. In a context where most people believe in individualism, both giving and receiving help from others elicits complicated emotions. Stack argues that "poverty creates a necessity for this exchange of goods and services" and that the "powerful obligation to exchange is a profoundly creative adaptation to poverty."[4] While she studied poor people over four decades ago, my findings suggest that when poor people create a network similar to the one she found, these insights still apply. Participants in KWRU as well as nonmembers report feelings of gratitude and security from reciprocity, yet many see it as negative when one party in an exchange relationship is unable to fulfill reciprocal norms. When participants feel used, such as when they've provided help only to be left in the lurch when they confront needs of their own, they perceive the relative weakness of reciprocity norms to keep others in line. When they anticipate that others may not reciprocate, they hesitate to provide assistance; they also hesitate to accept aid when they worry about their own inability to reciprocate.

People I interviewed shrink from both giving and receiving help because they fear their own inability to reciprocate and others' inability or unwillingness to do so. The positive side of giving others help is that people often enjoy a sense of pride in doing a good deed or a favor for someone in need, and in the context of reciprocity they also recognize that giving help is an important survival strategy, as it can be an investment in future help. When those I speak with, who are struggling themselves, give help to others in their lives, they know they are increasing their chances of being able to draw on help in the future, either from the particular people they assisted or from others as part of the logic of generalized reciprocity. On the other hand, participants also experience giving help to others negatively, when others take advantage of their generosity or fail to obey the norms of reciprocity. In these cases, participants' perceived investments in future help as a survival strategy do not provide the return they expect or desire. Certainly, norms of reciprocity apply to the study participants as well, so sometimes they help others because they received help in the past and either want to give back and are happy to do so, or because they feel they must return the favor out of a sense of obligation. And they can be resentful about having to fulfill the norms of reciprocity themselves.

As this chapter will describe, KWRU mitigates the problems reciprocity entails. For KWRU members, reciprocity operates as a responsibility to the collective; the organization makes demands of its members. They need not worry so much about paying back individual members for help others have given them, but they must fulfill obligations to the organization or risk losing the help it provides.[5] Reciprocity can thus be a pathway or a barrier to social support and social capital, and while social capital within KWRU does not provide any upward mobility, it does guard against the worst consequences of dire poverty, including homelessness and starvation. KWRU members who obey the organization's norms of reciprocity will always have a place to stay and something to eat, because the members do what they can to take care of each other.

This includes providing food to the membership at events and through food distributions to the larger community, and providing housing to homeless members. Reciprocity is what makes these things possible in KWRU, because financial capital is scarce.

This chapter begins by describing reciprocity within KWRU and its centrality to the organization's functioning. KWRU facilitates specific reciprocity and *requires* generalized reciprocity within the organization. For the most part, this reciprocity functions very effectively. Members who would not trust each other outside the organization find themselves sharing extensive resources; reciprocity builds the foundation for sustainable ties. The private safety net KWRU offers is even more valuable in a neoliberal era when the public safety net has grown so weak. This chapter also describes the problems with reciprocity and what happens when it breaks down. It relies on interviews and observations with KWRU members.

The Centrality of Reciprocity in KWRU

KWRU members have a strong sense of generalized reciprocity, and while KWRU facilitates specific reciprocity, it requires generalized reciprocity. In my use of the term, specific reciprocity refers to an individual repaying the specific person who did him or her a favor.[6] Generalized reciprocity refers to helping others because one has been helped, almost as if paying into a communal fund.[7] Paloma tells me her perspective:

> Life's a circle. What you do, you receive good or bad. And I think that I've always lived my life with that ideology. That if I help someone, someday I'll need some help and get it because of it. . . . I give freely. I don't give to receive something from you. I give because it's the right thing to do and I think that God rewards that. And the way he rewards it is not by millions of dollars, but by having that guardian angel look out for you in your life. And I think that guardian angel works overtime with me probably.

Tina, who nonetheless espouses an individualistic ideology at other times, tells me more simply, "What goes around comes around. If you help somebody, you'll get it back."[8] The sense that members get from

KWRU, that others in their social networks often face similar barriers, fosters trust and facilitates generalized reciprocity.[9] In her interview with me, KWRU founder and former director Cheri Honkala tells me that people who struggle

> pretty much operate an underground barter system. . . . "You pick up my kids, I'll watch your kids," "You help me get through this financial crisis this month, I'll go through my own financial crisis next month," "This month I've got food stamps and I've figured out how to stretch them all month, so you give me some cash and I'll use my card to buy some of the food that you need this month." Life is all about an exchange.

As the founder of the organization, Cheri Honkala's perspective points to the importance of reciprocity and how it operates to shape the group's mission, activities, and norms, as well as the perspective of other members, as quoted above. I found in my other interviews and observations of the organization that the importance of exchange was real as well as envisioned. Within KWRU, reciprocity functions as currency. Members could never pay dues; while the organization has some other sources of capital, it operates largely on the time and resources that members provide to satisfy the norms of reciprocity established by the group. James embraces KWRU's norms of reciprocity. James tells me he gets a lot of help, "from any and everybody," including KWRU. I ask how he feels about that:

> Depends on what kind of help and who the person is, you know what I mean. . . . I hate asking people that look for favors, when they do a favor . . . but at the same time . . . the reason why I got these relationships with different people is because it's always been like a favor for a favor . . . the bridges is both ways, you know what I mean.

When he first got involved with KWRU, James lived in a Human Rights House. He feels that within KWRU reciprocity is generally very effective. It is, he said, built on a mutual understanding of helping one another. Reciprocity relates to KWRU's relationship to the service it provides; because it is not a social service provider, members must pay for service and because members cannot pay in money, they must pay in other ways. Whether members receive minor help, such as information about available government benefits, or more major help, such as group activism to restore their benefits, KWRU asks them to do something for the group in return. When they oblige, they solidify their membership in the group and begin to develop ties by engaging in reciprocal exchanges with the organization. Noncompliance with this initial request for reciprocity generally causes their involvement with the group to terminate. But reciprocity between participants and KWRU transforms assistance into social capital; it allows participants to invest in future support and repay help they receive. Reciprocity therefore allows participants to alternately draw on and invest in support from this tie to the organization; this quality renders the support social capital, distinct from support available from social service agencies.

Members' reciprocity takes many forms, including volunteering in the office, going to rallies and demonstrations to help KWRU have enough people for a successful protest, distributing food in neighborhoods, and talking to recipients to expand membership. KWRU seems to foster the attitude that allows for indirect, or generalized, reciprocity among members of the organization, as evidenced by several members' remarks that "what goes around comes around." But in effect this dynamic operates as direct reciprocity between the organization and its members, because KWRU's enforcement of norms focuses on forms of direct reciprocity in which the member is one actor and KWRU is the other actor in the exchange. In contrast to participants who are not members of KWRU, members can participate in reciprocity within KWRU without feeling cheated when they do not receive a direct recompense from the person they help. KWRU presents the opportunity for generalized reciprocity in a bounded community.[10]

When members fail to participate in the group's activities, or do not participate as much as or in the way that KWRU dictates, KWRU may refuse or withdraw help. At times this seems to arise from a lack of mutually understood expectations, or a member's doubt that KWRU will repay her involvement with help. In some cases this doubt arises from issues of timing—thus when both a member and KWRU feel that it's the other's turn to invest time or help, neither will act until the other does, and reciprocity breaks down completely. KWRU membership has requirements other than reciprocity, but reciprocity is one of the most crucial. As I explain later in this chapter, when members lose their membership it is typically a failure to meet reciprocity norms that causes it.

How People Learn about Reciprocity Norms

Members learn about reciprocity norms in a variety of ways. Long-term members rarely tell them explicitly and no formal information describes these expectations. But Jessie learned about them in very explicit terms; a friend of hers who is also a member told her what to do:

> So once I got involved she told me like, "Keep yourself known, keep yourself seen, you know what I'm saying? Don't just come in here and say, 'I need help' and then fall back and expect us to remember that you're here because there's a lot of people that come in on an everyday basis for the same thing." So she said, "Keep yourself seen. Keep yourself known. Let them know that you're here and you're really interested in them helping you. Not only them helping you, you helping them to help you." So that's what I did.

Jessie explains that at first she was very involved and in the office "all the time," but over time her involvement declined. While she still went to rallies and demonstrations, she couldn't work in the office full-time anymore, as she tried to balance school and additional children. She says:

> They [got] mad at me. . . . They just thought that since I got my place [temporary housing] that I didn't think I had to do it anymore. But it wasn't so much that, it was I couldn't give that much time anymore.

Jessie chose to make more of an investment in human capital than she had previously, but she continued to invest in social capital through KWRU. She continued to go to demonstrations, rallies, and on trips, to show the organization

> that I still cared about it. I still needed help from KWRU even though I was in my transitional [housing]. . . . So I still made myself seen, you

know, but it was that they wanted me there the way I was before and I couldn't do it, you know, I had the children. . . .

I don't think they ever understood. To this day they still don't understand. . . . They just think that once you're involved you should always stay involved on a regular basis.

Jessie is maintaining her membership in KWRU even while reducing her involvement. She aims to maintain a level of involvement as a way to fulfill reciprocity norms and invest in social capital with KWRU. Indeed, she is living in a Human Rights House at the time of our first interview, drawing on the KWRU social capital in which she is still investing.

When Reciprocity Works in KWRU

Marisol is a striking example of how effective reciprocity can be in KWRU. She frequently puts in time volunteering at the KWRU office; she's doing this on the day we meet and on the days of our interview, and they are helping her to secure housing. She tells me, "Like when I used to live alone with my daughters, so like I had a neighbor who would like ask for help all the time, that was an everyday thing, and I would help her for the first couple of times, but then I started saying no, because the more you help the more they take advantage of you, they don't want to do nothing on their own." By contrast, within KWRU, she describes:

I feel that they helped me like when I got here, it was three years and a half, I told them, "Look you help me, I promise . . ." They told me, "Look, I need you to help us with the organization, and the same way we're helping you, you can help somebody else." So I thought about it and I said, "You know, that's really true." And . . . I feel comfortable right here and I get some chance to help others.

Strikingly, she retains some resistance to reciprocity; she says at another point in the interview, "I don't like to rely on no one," in part because she feels like even if she asks for help, "You know what? I don't get it anyway." It seems likely, though she didn't clarify, that she meant outside KWRU. She feels that KWRU members are her only friends and they "have been very great to me" and even as she continues to struggle she feels the organization needs her. "That's why I'm here," she says, talking about volunteering at the office.

Other participants agree about the efficacy of reciprocity in KWRU, and point to its ability to transform their effort into future support, and therefore social capital. Those who comply with norms of reciprocity in the organization view the exchange as beneficial. They express their gratitude for help they get through KWRU during a difficult time. Carmen says getting help such as KWRU offers, "makes me feel special . . . like people actually care." Through her involvement with the group, Cate reports learning how to navigate complex welfare rules and gaining increased self-esteem. Cate says getting help from KWRU "feels like you're secured. People are securing you. . . . Like before it's like I felt doors was locked. When I feel that people's helping me, doors are opening." To do her part for the organization, Cate has let new members stay with her, travels with the group, goes on food distributions, and brings in other members. Cate takes reciprocity very seriously. She has received invaluable help—and she has given invaluable help. For her, reciprocity's promise that initial support can develop into an opportunity to build social capital makes her life appreciably better.

KWRU provides temporary housing for CC in a KWRU Human Rights House. CC has an adult daughter and a thirteen-year-old daughter, as well as two younger children who live with their father, a man she left due to their abusive relationship. She desperately wants custody of them but a lack of stable housing has stood in the way. When a protest yields five housing vouchers from the mayor's office, she's assured she'll receive one of them, as she tells me and as other participants agree. CC works in the office helping those who come in for assistance, goes to rallies and demonstrations, travels to international meetings, and gives out food and clothes with the organization. She tells me her perspective on the help she's received from KWRU: "It feels good. . . . If somebody gonna help you. 'Cause you can't be by yourself. . . . You can't make it in this world by yourself unless you rich. You know what I mean? You need somebody that [you] can lean on at some time. . . . So it feels good when you can get help."

Working with KWRU is an important survival strategy; CC invests in future assistance by doing so. KWRU's system of requiring reciprocity provides the assurance that members who give their time increase their chances of receiving help from the organization in the future. For participants like CC, reciprocity functions to make social capital into an investment that matures over time. Pauline says that when she helps KWRU, "I know I'm a get it back. I might get it back a different way but I'll get it back." She helps out in the office regularly, making phone calls to caseworkers and helping people who come in. Like CC, she experiences KWRU as a place where she can invest her resources and expect to draw on them later—reciprocity transforms support into social capital. Walter explains to me his view of help with KWRU: "Well it's mutual . . . and so when it's mutual it feels good. You're working together to improve your immediate situation, as well as your long-term situation. . . . It's a good feeling and it's reciprocal." Social service agencies typically provide a one-way relationship when they supply support, with no obligation for the recipient to provide anything in return. But reciprocity in KWRU allows the recipient both to pay back the source of help and to invest in future help. Reciprocity transforms a one-way support relationship to a two-way exchange relationship. Capital implies a resource one may both invest in and draw on. The reciprocity mechanism in KWRU therefore transforms what might otherwise be social support into social capital.

The Difference between Reciprocity in KWRU and Outside It

James describes a contrast between reciprocity within KWRU and reciprocity outside it. He knows that people give help to those who have helped them, but he disdains the sometimes instrumental perspective people have about social ties *outside* KWRU. He says, "I don't like it when . . . the only reason [is] because they want something in return." He describes this as a functioning mechanism: "Everybody can always remember me helping, you know what I mean, like any and everybody all the time. . . . The reason why I have all those bridges to stay at all those relatives is because I done helped them on numerous occasions, you know what I mean. [They're thinking,] 'I'm giving him help just like he would give me help.'" Yet he prefers social capital that arises from relationships built on a mutual understanding of helping one another in KWRU, which he refers to as "the network."

Sociologists describe the distinction to which James refers as *negotiated exchange* versus *reciprocal exchange*. As sociologist Linda Molm[11] theorized the distinction, *negotiated exchange* implies parties acting with an instrumental, obligatory view, while *reciprocal exchange* implies greater trust. When others only provide help when promised specific returns on that help, it smacks of obligation to James in a way he does not believe applies to KWRU.

For James, reciprocity among family members tends to be negotiated exchange, while KWRU represents reciprocal exchange. He says, "When you get help from family members it's always, like 'you owe me one.'" James sees extended family as built on obligation and instrumentality; he says extended kin have helped him because they felt they had to, whereas KWRU is there for him based on "mutual understanding." As the near-universal experience of homelessness among KWRU participants reflects, KWRU members often do not feel they have family members on whom they can rely, and their stories suggest that James correctly identifies a reason KWRU members could not rely on family. While some live at a distance from their families and some have never gotten any help at all from them, a number of participants got help from kin that came with material or emotional bills they couldn't pay.

Negotiated exchange characterizes reciprocity between people much of the time, and can yield gravely needed assistance. Yet its explicit obligations can give people pause and induce shame, leading people to retreat into isolation. Reciprocal exchange facilitates benefits for people while avoiding shame and obligation, allowing trust and friendship to flourish. The greater the trust, the more it nurtures the growth of reciprocal exchange.

Although many participants had experienced their families as sites of generosity and help, most KWRU members had experienced difficulty with kin ties.[12] While negotiated exchange might offer a promise of support, James describes it as lending itself to one-time exchanges in relatively short order: "You know, I hate asking people that look for favors when they do a favor, you know what I mean." Reciprocal exchange may provide a longer-term exchange relationship during which social ties may be strengthened and trust increased when the reciprocity materializes. As Molm argues, "The kinds of resources that are usually associated with social capital and acquired through network ties—such as social support, information about opportunities, informal kinds of assistance—are most typically acquired . . . through reciprocal or generalized forms of exchange, not negotiated exchange."[13] Therefore, social capital develops from reciprocal exchange more than from negotiated exchange, and for James and many other KWRU members, more from KWRU than from extended family. Reciprocity needs to foster a level of trust instead of a negative sense of obligation, to effectively transform support into social capital.

Conflicted Feelings

Paloma describes the help she's gotten in her life as "enormous . . . from a plate of food to a house." When she thinks about it, she says, "I think I'm fortunate, like I'm one of those rare few people who can truly say that my life hasn't been easy, but I've been blessed. . . . I've been truly blessed." But she also thinks getting help from others is "harder than anything else in life." As Rosa tells me, "I mean, I won't deny it. I'm happy when I get the help, you know. I mean, I thank God most of the time when I do get the help, you know, but I don't know. Sometimes I sit down and I'll be like, 'I got the help from them, why can't I do this on my own?'" She's living with a KWRU member and she and her four youngest children would probably be homeless otherwise. Jessie also tells me that it feels good to know help is there if she needs it, but "it makes you feel bad sometimes to have to always have somebody help you." She and her four children would be homeless if she couldn't live in KWRU housing, so she has little choice but to accept help.

Help is a complicated issue for those who struggle to get by on a daily basis, as I described in chapter 2. The participants need and often depend on assistance from others, and they are grateful for it. Yet it's difficult to ask for help, as getting help implies indebtedness, part of a norm of reciprocity. That means that helping others should lead to receiving help as well, yet sometimes others fall short of reciprocal expectations and people feel used and taken advantage of.

While only James refers to what researchers see as the distinction between *negotiated exchange* versus *reciprocal exchange*, others also mention their dislike for instrumental relationships. But KWRU members who treat reciprocity in an instrumental way do so in the context of their relationship to the *organization*. They give within the organization (going to rallies or giving time at the office) to get something back (assistance). Their relationships with other members have less of a sense of instrumentality and more of a sense of trust. Outside KWRU, participants more often describe feeling taken advantage of or being under an obligation they cannot repay when they receive support.

As described above, members of KWRU feel positive about their involvement with the group; reciprocity effectively transforms social support from an organization into social capital in which they can continue to invest. But like participants outside the organization, most KWRU members feel a degree of shame and pride when in dire circumstances and needing help from others; it challenges the view that they should "go it alone," and most expressed that view at some time. Further, as I'll explain later in this chapter, *former* members of the group exist—not everyone maintains their commitment to the organization. Even among those involved in current group activities, not everyone sees the social ties that KWRU membership can provide in a positive light.

Lina, a soft-spoken African American mother of two young boys, tells me she got involved with KWRU because she was homeless. She has mixed feelings about her involvement but feels obligated because the organization is providing her with housing. I ask her what they ask her to do in return for a place to stay. She says, "Just go marching and go to places, with the union. . . . I feel good because they helped me. Sometimes like, sometimes when I have to do something like that I be mad or whatever but I know that they helped me get a place so I got to try to give back." Lina experiences positive emotions when she obeys reciprocity norms, but she also sees KWRU's exchange practices as obligations. Giving of her time sometimes makes her feel resentful of the burden, but she also feels good about herself and glad to be repaying the help she received.

When I last speak with her, Lina is adhering to KWRU's reciprocity norms. But others share her ambivalence for a number of reasons. Some members complain about others not obeying reciprocity norms, illustrating the importance of these norms and others' reactions to violations. Dora is a Latina in her forties, an active member of KWRU. She speaks about people who come to the KWRU office for help. KWRU expects that in exchange such people will give time back to the group in the future. Dora says, "And then you give it to them all. You find them shelter, food . . . money, clothing and everything, and then when you need 'em to do a protest . . . they hiding. It's like we always tell 'em . . . 'We expect you to help. . . .'" Dora, who has allowed KWRU members to share her home on more than one occasion, resents others' violations of the norms of reciprocity. Reciprocity implies mutual *aid* but also mutual *obligations*. She applauds the role that KWRU can play and its goals, but feels the drain on the group's collective resources when people who receive help do not do their part as she thinks they should. She wants members to obey the norms of reciprocity because she understands that KWRU depends on them.

However, this exchange may not always work efficiently, and members become frustrated when they feel they're giving of their time but not contributing in a way that makes a difference. Some perceive going to the KWRU office to give their time as senseless busywork. Naomi has been a member for the past few months when she tells me, "As much as they want us to come down there, they really don't be having anything for us to do down there." Rebecca tells me when she has gone, including on a bitterly cold day, "Nobody's there. . . . I was freezing too. I was so mad. But it was like, 'That's cool,' you know. Me and my old man just walked home."[14] I found that if there isn't much going on, KWRU leaders and activists still expect members, especially those currently receiving housing assistance from KWRU, to show their faces at the office and at rallies. I visited the office at times and found many people volunteering and there wasn't anything for most of them to do, though they did often spend time there and socialize. This led some members, like Rebecca and Naomi, to stop bothering to travel to the office; KWRU withdrew the temporary housing help the two women had received. Members made substantial sacrifices to get to the KWRU office because most did not have cars, and the sense of not being useful bred resentment.

"I Feel Like I Did a Good Deed Today"

Members cite the nature of KWRU as an organization of poor people as a factor that eases their difficulties with reciprocity. They describe finding it easier to ask for help when the request is directed to those who have experienced hardship themselves. Colleen says, "They've all done it too. . . . And they've been in that same situation and I know that they wouldn't think twice about it." Yet this can be its own challenge, as Colleen also wants to avoid asking those currently struggling. She says, "I think I'd never approach them or ask them for it. . . . Because I look at them as being in the same situation in some way. I don't want to do that." On the one hand, this hesitation reflects Colleen's understanding of how difficult it is to give for those with few resources. On the other hand, KWRU's model, in which she participates, is based in part on those with few resources sharing what little they have with one another.

Walter, a KWRU member for ten years, explains, "You know, society place[s] so much shame on those who are impoverished . . . [that] you feel like it's your fault. You feel less human for that . . . and so you live a life of shame. . . . Initially you have a tremendous amount of pride, and so, you try to avoid having to ask people for things. . . . But then after a while it becomes necessary, you got kids and stuff like that." The common belief in individualism and agency Walter describes exists in tension with asking for help. He states, "It becomes easier when you're part of [the KWRU] network because you're kind of mutually kind of helping each other, so you kind of get rid of that shame, because it's like you're all helping each other." He says now he feels differently about asking for help: "The support of a network is a mutual help. . . . It's clear that we're relying on each other. . . . It's to support each other, for a cause. And, you know for improving our lives and improving the lives of this country. . . . So it's a whole different type of feeling." Asking for help in the context of KWRU mitigates self-blame.

Carmen, Cate, Paloma, Amanda, Alice, and Jessie all specifically say they feel good when they help others. Carmen tells me about a time she helped a neighbor navigate available help with her utilities, and "it felt so good." Cate says when she helps someone else, "I feel like I did a good deed today." Paloma says, "It's a wonderful thing to do. . . . Because you're making changes in people's lives that you can't, you know, words can't express." Amanda says, "I think it's very fulfilling and, I mean that's what life is all about. . . . Everybody is inseparably connected to each other and, you know, we really can't live in a world alone and by ourselves. . . . Other human beings are as important as I am." Alice tells me giving help to others can be good "because sometimes you figure you were in that situation and somebody helped you out." Although these participants were all KWRU members, their comments addressed their feelings about giving help in general, not specifically within KWRU.

KWRU member Jessie tells me people come to her when they need help, and she seems profoundly ambivalent about having given it. She describes taking in a cousin who ran up bills and ate her food and resisted pitching in on child care, but she says that she doesn't refuse people she cares about who ask to stay with her: "I don't like turning anyone down because I know that I've been, you know, been there. . . . Because I know how it feels not to have somewhere to sleep or nowhere you're gonna sleep at night." Jessie feels her help is reciprocated in the organization, leading her to evaluate the pros and cons of giving help differently within the organization than outside it.

Shy, a member of KWRU who attends virtually all the rallies that occur during my research period, is not embarrassed to ask for help. When I ask her how comfortable she feels asking for help, she tells me, "Real comfortable. I ain't got no problem askin' nobody for nothin' . . . 'cause my Mommy taught, a closed mouth never get fed. Okay? So if I need somethin', I'm gonna ask. I ain't ashamed of it because everybody need it. . . . I'll ask you for a dollar in a minute. Never had a problem." I also ask Shy how comfortable she felt giving people help; her response illustrates that she viewed giving help as an investment in future help: "I don't have no problem because I know I might need that dollar back soon. . . . Yeah, you better help because you don't know, you never, never, never know when you gonna need somethin.'"

Shy is also very conscious of making investments in future help when it comes to her KWRU involvement. Shy's always direct, someone who hugs me at every interview and is quick to make a joke—and laugh at them. She specifically picked her pseudonym for its irony. She says when she was deciding to get involved she thought, "I know I'm gonna need these people. I'm fightin' for homelessness and I'm [going to] be homeless in about another year or so. So, let me stick with these people and see about it. So I can have their help so they can be there for me when we tryin' to fight to keep my place. . . . To be honest, that's what made me stay with 'em 'cause I knew what my predicament was about to be." Shy directly and explicitly connects her choice to be involved in KWRU to her anticipated need for the organization's help in the future. And her investment paid off, because as she faced homelessness, she knew she could turn to KWRU for help. They responded to her predicament by providing her a space in a Human Rights House.

When Reciprocity Falls Short

"Everybody Ain't for This"

Membership in KWRU adds another layer of complexity to norms of reciprocity; within the context of the group, reciprocity comes to be about more than paying people back for help. Members must be willing to commit resources to KWRU in order to draw assistance from the organization. While participants generally fulfill KWRU's norms of reciprocity and thereby build social capital through ties to the organization, at times people violate these norms and consequently lose access to what could be a valuable source of social capital.[15] For these members, the burdens become excessive and reciprocity doesn't make social support into social capital.[16]

Rebecca is one member I meet soon after she joins KWRU and who isn't a member by the time my research concludes, because she violates reciprocity norms. Her negative feelings about reciprocity predate her KWRU membership; she explains to me that she has helped many people, and it's been difficult for her to ask for help as she has been turned down in the past: "I ask for help and then I get screwed over. That's why I knew from when I was growing up, you know, you just don't ask people for help. . . . Because they won't help you. . . . I can't count on it." Rebecca describes having asked her sister for help and being rebuffed, the same sister who tried to wrest custody of her son from her. Her experience causes her to hold back, which ultimately makes it impossible for her to continue to get help through KWRU.[17]

Rebecca has two children and a common law husband; they are living together in a KWRU house when I meet her. A life in poverty means that dental problems were resolved by pulling teeth, which makes her look older than her thirty-three years, though her wide eyes and blond hair pulled tight into a high ponytail mitigate the appearance of older age. She longs for dentures to help make her feel more confident in interacting with others and frequently mentions how life will be different "when I have my teeth."[18] She expects reciprocity to function better within KWRU than outside it; in an interview she describes her expectation of housemates in the Human Rights House. One housemate is insisting her food be separate even though everyone else in the house shares. Rebecca says, "It's ridiculous [that she doesn't share] when we're all in the same predicament." Rebecca objects to anyone opting out of the exchange relationship, although KWRU does not specifically require such pooling.

At our second interview a little over a month later, Rebecca has been told by KWRU leaders that she must vacate the house they have been letting her live in for the past six months, and she isn't sure why. KWRU leaders claim it was due to a loud commotion in the house when the father of Naomi's children arrived unexpectedly and began causing trouble, and Rebecca and her husband stepped in to intervene, leading to a loud argument, but no one seems to believe this explanation. Rebecca believes that race was an important factor—that help is being withdrawn because she's white. I found no evidence of KWRU withholding help from people based on race, and Naomi, who must leave at the same time, is African American.[19] Helen was also white, and she did not cite race as a factor in her decision to withdraw from the group; I believe she would have told this white researcher if she felt marginalized because she is white.[20]

Rebecca also admits that some activists have accused her of having a drug problem, and KWRU explicitly prohibits drug use.[21] She has repeatedly offered to take a drug test, and she claims they took her up on it once and the drug test was negative. She also readily admits that she doesn't go to everything the organization requests she go to, because when she has gone she feels unappreciated. Like Naomi, she feels that adhering to such requests doesn't necessarily make a significant contribution, so it seems meaningless to her.

Given the importance of reciprocity norms in KWRU, I am convinced that KWRU withdrew aid from Rebecca[22] in part because of her reluctance to fulfill these norms.[23] While longtime members might fulfill reciprocity norms by opening their homes to homeless members, in general direct reciprocity did not fulfill KWRU membership requirements. Certainly sharing food with her housemates did not compensate for failing to show up as requested while living in a KWRU house. Members I interviewed made it clear to me—unsolicited—that reciprocity was an important aspect of KWRU membership.

Curiously, Rebecca shares the perspective of many other KWRU members I interviewed when she says at her first interview, "I want to help out, you know . . . because these people helped me when I needed help . . . and I want to give back. I really do. I want to give back to them." However, as noted above, she went to the office at times, an hour's walk away, and found no one there. "So I stopped going." Although she's staying in a Human Rights House—cramped and temporary, but better than living on the streets—she tells me at our second interview, "Because you know I'm here for help. I'm not getting any. So I don't feel that I'm getting help. I don't like the position I'm in so I don't like it. . . . I can't count on it." She says, "I wanted to stay part of it . . . because I think what they do is a great thing. . . . But you know what? . . . How I see it, they come here, they don't come around for . . . such a long time . . . and then they come around screaming things at you." Perhaps Rebecca's focus on direct reciprocity, as evidenced by her emphasis on sharing food with housemates, makes it difficult for her to understand the idea of generalized reciprocity. She wants to feel appreciated and needed at the office or at rallies because she wants to feel confident she's fulfilled an obligation directly.

At the very end of our interview, Rebecca tells me she would "still be part of the organization. . . . I'll still help out any way I can. Anytime they ever need anything, I'll do it." Helen too speaks to me with affection for KWRU's founder, even after relinquishing most of her KWRU activity. This continued goodwill toward the organization (the founder remains its most prominent member—Helen's affection in part suggests admiration for the founder's aims) demonstrates the positive effect it has on members' lives. Even when aspects of the connection are frustrating, members feel emotionally tied to KWRU.

The Unpredictable Payoff of Unwritten Norms

Rebecca's description of the reasons KWRU asks her to leave the Human Rights House actually points to another aspect of KWRU's reciprocity norms: as with most social norms, they are not laid out in entirely explicit terms. This is what makes them implicit norms rather than explicit policies; while leaders had asked Rebecca to attend certain rallies, they never explicitly told her that she might lose her housing if she did not. Unlike most membership organizations, KWRU cannot promise certain benefits in exchange for dues in a certain amount. While KWRU provides an impressive level of support for its members, the form and level of that support are necessarily unpredictable. Given that unpredictability, it would be difficult to make expectations of members specific and written.

In Rebecca's case, the unwritten nature of the norms really fails both sides. Rebecca doesn't seem to understand what motivated KWRU's frustration and KWRU leaders don't seem to understand why she fails to do her part. I believe it is a failure of communication, in which the mutual expectations are not clear to either party. One activist's comments to me during an interview more than a year earlier seem to foreshadow what happened to Rebecca:

> We never ask anybody to leave [the organization]. Now different points in time we figured out it was in our best interest to have people leave, but we set things up in place so that they would leave. We stopped giving them certain resources and stuff that they was using us for. And once we stopped giving them certain resources that they was using us for they tend to be like "fuck it, I'm out of here. What the fuck I'm a stay around here for and ain't getting no resources."

When I ask what situations would prompt KWRU to do this, this activist tells me they would withhold resources from people who were "shady . . . worrying about themselves . . . trying to not add to this process but hurt this process . . . [doing] all kinds of shit that stopped us from having to do the work we had to do. But go back and try to fix these problems and deal with this petty bullshit. . . . We feel . . . this is for everybody, but everybody ain't for this, you know what I mean?"

"It Doesn't Go Anywhere"

Most members of KWRU and certainly most active KWRU members feel positive about their involvement and connections with other members of the group and are very well aware of the resources membership makes available. I described Helen's ambivalence about the role of individual agency in chapter 1. The persistence of opposing viewpoints for her may reflect her past involvement with KWRU. Still a nominal member, Helen has basically relinquished the productivity of a strong tie with KWRU by choosing to stop fulfilling reciprocity norms. Helen has gone from being a very active member of KWRU to being a member in name only. If she no longer had a need for the type of help that KWRU provides, this separation from the group might have different implications. But Helen lives in a poor neighborhood in a house that is literally falling apart, the sink detached and hanging by a thread from the bathroom wall with no running water. She and her common law husband have nine children, seven of whom live with them, and they struggle to pay for even the most basic necessities. Helen works intermittently, but her work schedule is inconsistent and so her income is unpredictable. She does not receive cash assistance through welfare, although she has in the past.

Helen tells me she first got involved with KWRU in the early 1990s, and stayed with the group for five years: "I just . . . I don't know what changed, but . . . they did everything too late, then you sit there and then they tell you to move here and there." Helen considers KWRU's reciprocity requirements a poor investment. While she does say that she received support in exchange for her efforts, she came to resent what she perceived as an imbalance. She also notes that she could spend her time in other ways: "No, I'm tired . . . and I'm working. I got other things to do." I ask her what she learned from her involvement in KWRU and she says:

> It made me think about doing everything on my own because that's the only way it's gonna get done. That's the way I feel. I even told them that. . . . Why would I want to work with people that's gonna keep me down there instead of putting me up where I want to be? . . . There's people out there that really wants to get homes and stuff, and they act like they can help 'em, but they really can't. . . . It looks like it doesn't go anywhere.

Helen experienced the group as demanding more of her than it provided in turn, as relatively powerless against larger forces, and as unable to eliminate poverty. Indeed, social capital has its limits, and the bonding social capital KWRU provides does not facilitate mobility.[24] She has repudiated the collective and stopped investing her time with KWRU.[25] Sadly, Helen lives in conditions that are among the worst I observed, and rather than improve since she reduced her KWRU involvement, they have worsened. She has not found a source of social capital to replace KWRU and without social capital, her quality of life has deteriorated.

As Helen's situation reveals, reciprocity can curtail KWRU membership and therefore impede social capital. Sometimes participants fear their own inability to fulfill reciprocity norms and therefore shy away from asking for or accepting help.[26] Sometimes others have neglected to reciprocate, causing them to opt out of this reciprocal-exchange network to avoid being taken advantage of in the future. When people avoid reciprocity, they may protect their meager resources but they will find themselves alone, with no one to turn to in times of trouble. Helen does not openly regret severing her ties to KWRU, but my observation was that her circumstances deteriorated because of that detachment. Rebecca and Naomi both lose their housing because they fail to fulfill reciprocity norms. All three of these women lack familial ties to go to draw for housing or free child care, which is why they turned to KWRU in the first place, and why dissolving their connection to it makes them so vulnerable. KWRU members typically lack kin ties on whom to rely for social capital.

The fact that KWRU's model failed some members points to the difficulty of the organization's endeavor—stretching minimal resources across many members to let everyone survive—rather than to the limits of the model. The contribution KWRU makes to members' lives is in fact remarkable in light of the challenges. As Becky says, at KWRU "We have all been through the same thing. Each and every single one of us has been through hell and back again. And every one of us have our own stories."

Conclusion

Membership in KWRU does not provide strong employment networks or financial capital, and in that way the organization does not aid members in getting out of poverty. However, KWRU helps members build bonding social capital, which allows members to survive and eases some of the worst consequences of their dire poverty. The limits of reciprocity and social capital point to structural inequality too powerful for individuals to overcome, even with the strongest commitment to reciprocity possible. Social capital is a way to mitigate the worst effects of poverty and reciprocity is a way to make social ties productive of resources to aid survival, but social capital cannot eliminate systemic poverty or erase structured inequality.

In spite of this, reciprocity norms are surprisingly effective within KWRU. Most members speak about reciprocity in a positive way and most fulfill reciprocity norms in a way that both keeps the organization functioning and maintains their membership. Participants speak to me freely about KWRU activities, describe them as valuable, and seem to have a sense of pride at doing their part for a group that has become the safety net they previously lacked.

This chapter also lays bare the central fact of poverty, especially the level of deep vulnerability that KWRU members experience—it is a profound lack of resources: a lack of money, time, and services. KWRU's ability to prevent homelessness for its members as a result of the organization's system of reciprocity is a significant achievement; its ability to produce a good return on the investment of time and other resources for so many desperately poor people is also an extraordinary accomplishment. Reciprocity is a practical tool to mitigate the devastating effects of this lack of resources. Its limitations—the fact that reciprocity requirements push some people out and make it impossible for those who stay to develop mobility strategies that might, especially in the context of other systemic reforms, help them get out of poverty—point to the structural nature of poverty and inequality.

Cate reciprocates for the small demonstration KWRU staged for her, described at the beginning of chapter 3, by letting new members stay with her, traveling for the group, distributing food in poor Philadelphia neighborhoods, and recruiting new members. CC works in the KWRU office helping those who come in for assistance, goes to rallies and demonstrations, and travels to international meetings with the organization in return for the housing assistance KWRU gives her. Rebecca does not give of her time as KWRU expects and finds herself evicted from a KWRU house. For these women and others, the benefits available through the social ties described in chapter 3 come at a considerable cost, but in general members find that the group's reciprocity norms and pooling of resources make the investment worthwhile. KWRU's existence depends on these norms. Chapter 5 discusses how this receiving and giving of assistance lays the foundation for social ties. In fulfilling the organization's norms of reciprocity, KWRU members transform social support into social capital and build sustainable ties.

5

Our Strength Is in Our Unity

Sustainable Social Ties

When I'm down in my life that I really need people to back
me up, I have an organization full of them. And they [have]
shown me that in several times of my life.
—Paloma, 28, KWRU member for nine years

Jessie, who has been a member of KWRU for about four years, and Cate,
a member for close to five years, met through KWRU, and now Cate
is godmother to one of Jessie's children, while Cate's adult son Max is
godfather to another of Jessie's children. Jessie tells me, "I look at [Cate]
as another mom," and says she feels close to Cate and Max "because of
the fact that they took to me the way that they did. They welcomed me
right in like if I was family. Right off. No one else ever did that for me,
not even family. . . . So for some stranger to do that to me made me feel
that, you know, I have lots of love for them." Jessie tells me:

> Like not too long ago . . . I don't have a dryer, I have a washer. . . . And
> they were winter clothes in the summertime, so I was just trying to catch
> up with the laundry. So I washed all the laundry and I had like a big trash
> bag full of wet clothes. I throw them all in my car. I took 'em to [Cate's]
> house. . . . She dries them for me, she folds them for me and puts them
> back in the bags and I just picked them up. So that's the relationship that
> I have with [Cate].

Social scientists have long documented the importance of social ties
such as the one Jessie and Cate share. Whether they focus on the power
of social networks to further employment opportunities, or on the
effectiveness of social capital for support and for leverage, researchers
agree that social ties matter, though they do not always reach the same

conclusions about who has what sorts of ties, and with whom. Carol Stack, in her seminal work *All Our Kin: Strategies for Survival in a Black Community* (1974), documents the depth of support social ties among kin and fictive kin (friends who refer to each other with kin titles like "cousin" and "sister," and often feel and act as though they are related) can provide. Her work has been immensely influential; an entire generation of sociologists and anthropologists has continued to explore the meanings and mechanisms of social support in various poor communities in the decades since *All Our Kin* appeared. Few find that such networks continue to exist. Yet KWRU members are living, decades after Stack's work appeared, in much the same way as her participants.

This chapter discusses the lasting social ties KWRU members build, relying on my KWRU interviews and observations. I call these *sustainable ties*, which occupy in some ways a middle ground between kin ties and disposable ties. Kin ties can be functionally permanent and extremely valuable. Those without such ties may turn to disposable ties, which dissolve quickly, for aid in times of desperation. While ties that dissolve in the course of months can also involve the language of familial ties, relative permanence makes sustainable ties closer to familial ties in a way that's valuable to members and extends beyond the friendships themselves.

This chapter discusses KWRU members' experiences of their own kin ties providing limited support, and their sense that ties within KWRU take the place of family—a perception that hinges in many ways on the sustainability of their ties. It gives an overview of the findings of Matthew Desmond about poor people who built ties to one another without kinship, but experienced them as disposable. It describes the kinds of help KWRU members give one another, and also discusses the limits of the ties they build with one another. It describes members' ties to the organization itself as an independent mechanism that facilitates their individual ties and in many ways supersedes them. The chapter concludes after describing the impressive longevity of KWRU ties.

The Limits of Kin Ties and the Kinship of KWRU Ties

KWRU members provide each other support as varied as loaning clothes for a funeral, babysitting for one another's children, speaking to doctors in the hospital when a member gets sick, and cooking for each other. Thus KWRU has come to be a substitute family, and members of KWRU mention fellow members with kinship terms.[1] Dora, a member for nearly five years, says, "[Amanda], I feel as I love her. She's part of my family, like, my sister." James says, "I got mad love for KWRU and KWRU family you know what I mean. People in KWRU I see them as like my brothers and sisters all the way around the board." Paloma, a KWRU member for nine years, typifies the attitude of members when she says: "They're family. Hell, fuck friends. You can choose your friends, you can't choose your family. They're family." While she chooses to be a member of KWRU, she feels that other members are her family, whether she would choose them individually or not.

Walter, father to three adult children and currently separated from his wife, tells me, "I feel close to my organization, my organization is like a family, you know. And, we rely on each other, a whole lot." Pauline, a member for nearly three years, moved from out of state to live with her father and then had a conflict with him; with no other family to turn to for support, she found herself homeless and came to KWRU. She tells me:

> My family wasn't talking to me. . . . And I'm like, well, I don't need them. I got the people in the organization. . . . So I told them about my family and how my family wasn't with me. How they turned their backs on me. . . . . And when my family didn't give me nowhere to stay they did, and I need somewhere to sleep for my kids, and they helped me get back on welfare and stuff. . . . When I came here they treated me like a family, like I was part of their little family.

At her first interview soon after she joined the organization, Rebecca tells me that KWRU has "done more for us than my family has ever done. Meaning my mom and my sister. Yeah, when I was a kid my sister did, but as soon as I got older . . . They could care less if I was homeless." Indeed, her family attempted to gain custody of her son because she had nowhere to live, rather than letting her move in with them.

Colleen, tells me, "I think to me KWRU is much stronger than my own family." She has been a member for six years. She is close to her sister emotionally, but her sister in unwell and awaiting sentencing on a criminal charge; she is in no position to help her, and neither are their parents. She has no extended family to rely on either. Members of KWRU come to court with another participant when her son has legal trouble. A member for nearly ten years, she says:

> If anything goes wrong in my life, it's KWRU. To me they have become my family. They became my life. They gave me everything, everything back. I mean . . . a person feels as though you don't know where to turn and you're backed up against the wall and you have nothing and you have children to take care of and your health is not that great and along comes an organization that says, "Look I will teach you step by step how to get your life situated."

Cate, Jessie, Walter, Pauline, Rebecca, Colleen, and Becky all describe KWRU as a substitute family as they confront difficulties in their lives. Some KWRU members have kin ties on whom to draw but find them inadequate to their needs. Stefanie lives with her parents and receives cash assistance, but has a very tight budget. She had no sources of social support other than her parents until she came to KWRU. She would like to be able to get food stamps, but the age of eligibility has just been raised from twenty-one to twenty-two, and the state makes age exceptions only for those living independently. To live independently, as she longs to do, she knows she'll need her own food stamps. She learns at her first visit to KWRU that they may be able to help her secure food stamps sooner than she could on her own. Stefanie goes to KWRU not because she has no other ties on whom to draw, but because she finds those ties inadequate. Most KWRU members, however, did not have Stefanie's relative advantages because they did not have kin ties who would provide them a stable place to live. Stefanie resembles the non-KWRU participants more than she resembles most KWRU members in the receipt of stable housing from kin, the single biggest difference between KWRU and non-KWRU participants' lives.[2] Yet Stefanie's decision to seek help from KWRU sets her apart from non-KWRU participants; she does not, in that respect, "stay to herself."

As evidenced by the near-universal experience of homelessness among KWRU participants, KWRU members often do not feel they have family members on whom they can rely. As others have documented, this is not an unusual experience among poor people.[3] What is unusual is having a meaningful, sustainable alternative like KWRU.

Walter also explains that KWRU can fill a void left by family unable to provide needed assistance:

> You show me a poor person, I'll show you a person who's isolated. And that's because they, a lot of bridges have been burned because they, in their effort to try to get back on their feet, they've asked for help, from the people that they are usually around, especially relatives. . . . Their relatives do the best they can, but they're not too far away from your predicament. They don't have very much resources or reserves, so they're teetering. . . . And so increasingly people have no other recourse but to rely on each other, to organize for it.

KWRU's sustainable ties arise from relationships built on a mutual understanding of helping one another, much like the best qualities of extended kin and fictive kin networks like those Stack documented in *All Our Kin*. Exchanges create the possibilities for lasting ties.[4] Reciprocity creates the opportunity for valuable social capital; Desmond found disposable ties in the absence of kin, which contrast with sustainable ties. Walter says, "The support of a network is a mutual help. It's clear that we're relying on each other, and it's to support each other." I ask Cheri Honkala, the founder of KWRU, about what kind of help she gets and she says:

> Anything, you know, from the car breaks down every other day kind of thing to help with food, help with keeping a utility on if it's gonna be shut off . . . every possible thing. I could not live day to day if I didn't have a community of wonderful people that help me get by day to day. . . . From housing to food to transportation, I mean, I just couldn't survive if it wasn't collectively.

Cheri has lived in her car, on the street, in Takeover Houses, Tent Cities, and has moved frequently as she gets evicted for nonpayment of rent. Currently she's living in an apartment but estimates she'll be evicted in the next couple of months. Researchers who recognize that kin support is far from universal sometimes wonder how those without it survive and theorize that resources gathered from social service and philanthropic organizations must fill the void. Indeed, study participants rely on a variety of public services as well, including food stamps, Medicaid, and cash public assistance for those who have not hit TANF time limits. Yet welfare reform's transformation of AFDC to TANF as part of the 1996 Personal Responsibility and Work Opportunity Reconciliation Act demonstrates the erosion of this public safety net. In discussing people who are poor or homeless and have no family on whom to rely, Walter tells me:

> Right now, there's the dismantling of the welfare state. You just had . . . services and all those kinds of things that you can rely on. . . . Those programs are diminishing. . . . Their other safety net is not there, and so they suffer. I see that people who are not part of a network, they're gonna have very difficult times. People who are part of organizations have come to understand that when you're suffering, the worst thing is to suffer by yourself. Or suffer alone. So if you're a part of a network, you're able to network, and your contributing to the network saves you.

I ask him, "And what about people who aren't part of a network? How do they manage?" He answers, "I think that they, they're gonna pursue, you know, what exists of human services, they're gonna pursue the underground economy, and they're gonna die, unless they fight." KWRU offers an alternative to disposable ties for people who do not have strong and supportive kin ties, and as such they offer a sustainable survival strategy. KWRU members have found in the organization a means of survival predicated on mutual aid.

Many researchers have documented the limits of kin networks for the poor, who must seek employment referrals, material assistance, or emotional help elsewhere due to their kin's reluctance or inability to help. Their kin may be struggling to survive and therefore without the ability or willingness to provide support. This deficiency compounds the struggles of the poor, when it occurs. And yet the struggles of the poor do not dissipate simply because there are no kin available to provide assistance. Rather, the lack of family members on whom to rely compounds their struggles. Faced with an increasingly threadbare safety net, KWRU study participants were as desperate as those other scholars studied, if not more so, but they were unusual in that they had found one another in KWRU.[5]

When Kin Ties Are Absent

I describe the ties I found between KWRU members as sustainable ties in comparison to Matthew Desmond's findings of disposable ties; he details the experiences and strategies of a set of poor individuals encountering a difficult crisis.[6] His ethnographic work provides a compelling illustration of what may happen when poor people do not rely on kin. After being evicted, those he studied often did rely on some limited help from family members, but they also faced obstacles in doing so.

> As a result, to meet their most pressing needs, evicted tenants often relied more on *disposable ties* formed with new acquaintances than on a stable network of reliable kin. They established new ties quickly and accelerated their intimacy. Virtual strangers became roommates and "sisters." Once a disposable tie was formed, all kinds of resources flowed through it. But these bonds often were brittle and fleeting, lasting only for short bursts. This strategy of forming, using, and burning disposable ties allowed families caught in a desperate situation to make it from one day to the next, but it also bred instability and fostered misgivings between peers.[7]

As Desmond argues, prior literature either asserted the importance of kin support or documented its absence: "There are no stations, then, between kin support and raw individualism, embeddedness and isolation. If kin support has been eroded in poor neighborhoods, then their residents must learn to get by on their own. Yet all the evidence indicates that this is next to impossible."[8] Rather than muddle through alone or piece together assistance from social service agencies, strategies doomed to failure because of their inadequacy to the task, the individuals he studied formed what he calls "disposable ties." In some ways the ties take on the characteristics of kin relationships, due to their intimacy and cooperative exchange nature. Yet in other ways they are quite different, because the intimacy is formed in an accelerated way and, as Desmond shows, the relationships are fleeting—indeed, this is what makes these ties disposable. Such ties provide real support in moments of crisis, enabling Desmond's informants to move forward from one day to the next. Yet when the fragile threads connecting people to their disposable ties break under the weight of heavy burdens, people move on to the next tenuous connections.

Just as Desmond posits that the existing literature has presented us with an apparent dichotomy of "embeddedness and isolation," his addition to the spectrum, while it adds nuances to the meaning of support and social ties, still leaves a theoretical and practical gap between extremes. He does note that disposable ties vary in their duration; sometimes they may last months or transform into weak ties to be activated later on, but typically they are much more fleeting. Their instability is a distinguishing characteristic, as he says:

> When tenuous but intense relationships between virtual strangers ended badly—or violently, as they sometimes did—they fostered deep misgivings between peers and neighbors, eroding community and network stability. The memory of having been used or mistreated by a disposable tie encouraged people to be suspicious of others. Relying on disposable ties, then, is both a response to and a source of social instability.[9]

Like Stack, who found that support from kin and fictive kin was crucial to survival, Desmond did ethnographic work; they make no claim as to the generalizability of their results. Yet many other researchers have reached similar conclusions as did Stack, and it is quite possible Desmond discovered a common pattern, made more widespread in an era of rising residential mobility and fractured families, particularly in the context of the reduced role of government paving the way for deindustrialization, high unemployment, and an increasingly restrictive public safety net. It would be unsurprising if many of those in the direst circumstances, without kin on whom to rely, use disposable ties in order to survive. Indeed, Desmond notes that previous researchers, going back to Elliot Liebow's 1967 *Tally's Corner*, found evidence of disposable ties, although none focused on such ties.[10] If disposable ties are common and their dissolution can often negate their value, the fact that poor people can build sustainable ties—which are more reliably valuable—is significant.

Mutual Support

We all rely on help from others, often from those closest to us; whether it's transportation to the airport, babysitting on date night, or cosigning a loan, stably middle-class people and those above them in the socio-economic hierarchy get lots of help. For those struggling on the bottom of the socioeconomic ladder, the assistance they get from social ties in paying bills or watching their kids can be crucial for survival, and sometimes provides the only glimmer of hope for upward mobility. KWRU actively seeks to create opportunities for members to develop ties with one another as part of its strategy to increase membership and stage protests with large numbers of people.[11] Labor organizers know well how effective sharing stories and developing relationships with others can be; KWRU uses the same strategy. Walter tells me, "Well, I mean, what we've done is . . . to personally engage people . . . and to put them in relationship to others, that have similar [problems], and . . . the first effect is to, to get them to know that they're not crying alone. And that there's other people who are prepared to do something. And so they tell their stories to each other." He explains to me, "And so, to have someone reach down and touch you and say . . . 'You are somebody, let me hear what you have to say, I mean, let me hear your story.' . . . The telling of untold stories. 'What's your story? What problems are you having?' What does that say? Not only do I want to acknowledge you, but it says I care. You know?" This active encouragement of relationships is part of KWRU's strategy for increasing membership, but it also creates a climate in which people establish trusting, supportive ties with one another.

KWRU participants describe a variety of types of help they receive from one another, and I observed others as well. One member lists ten members of KWRU she has authorized to pick up her children from school. She clicks her manicured nails on the table and pushes her long dark hair behind her shoulders and chuckles as she tells me, "I think my son is the only person in any preschool that has a list of like ten people that have authorization to pick him up . . . all people from the organization that I have, like, family relationships with."

Two study participants have been KWRU members for three and a half years and almost two years, respectively. They are living together in a KWRU house when we first speak. One tells me that they "share everything," including pooling their food stamps and cooking and eating meals together, offering something neither gets from their own immediate family members, companionship: her own children live with her husband, from whom she is separated, and her friend's only child is an adult who doesn't live with her. Members frequently cook for each other. One day in the midst of my research, one study participant cooks a meal for another member and insists on feeding me too. The member in attendance has diabetes and she cooks a healthy meal, aware it might be that other member's only complete meal for the day. She cooks for other members as part of KWRU practice.

Colleen describes to me the sorts of help KWRU members provide for one another: "baby sitting, [another study participant] sometimes helps me with that, and I help [her] as well. Money, if we're in a meeting with KWRU or we're doing something and others are around and they go to get something to eat or to drink and I didn't have money on me, somebody's always provided, you know. . . . Someone's always had something." Colleen says they "are pretty close. . . . Just because having a bond and being a mom and being in a similar situation." It undoubtedly strengthens their connection that they have children roughly the same age. And when I ask what makes her feel close to this friend, she describes the kind of friendship most people either long for or consider themselves fortunate to have:

> Similar experiences, and we share information, personal, you know, things that we're going through in our life without casting any judgment or offering advice. I think that's the best thing. . . . [We] have a lot of similar experiences and compare stories and compare situations that we're in, even recognize differences in them, but neither one of us say that, "You should have did this or should have did that."

Colleen lists four people "that I share the most personal crises with when I'm in an emotional state that isn't good." One is her sister, but the other three are all people she has met and formed ties with through KWRU. She says, "I view KWRU as a safe place for me . . . to be just who I am."

Research on social support has demonstrated the importance of resources available through social networks.[12] Kin and fictive kin provide a variety of kinds of assistance, ranging from free meals to child care to financial support to employment referrals. Without the aid of social networks, the low-wage workers and welfare-reliant women Edin and Lein studied could not have survived. Low-wage work isn't enough to live on.[13] Stack found a dense network of closely connected kin and fictive kin pooling resources to help one another weather the worst of life's storms. Domínguez and Watkins found that family members were crucial sources of support for some of their participants as well. They found, as I did, that younger women were more likely to live at home with their parents than older women were, and they benefited from the housing provided and from the opportunities for sharing expenses and emotional support. KWRU member participants found an alternative when none of these other sources supplied assistance.

The Limits of Social Ties among the Poor

Often, poor people who have any social capital have only bonding, not bridging, social capital, not least because of economic residential seg-regation.[14] KWRU study participants have bonding social capital but lack bridging capital. For them, the practical resources and emotional support they receive from their ties characterize their social capital. It both makes their survival possible and helps them avoid social isola-tion and self-blame. As described in chapters 3 and 4, there are former members who might have stayed with the organization and contin-ued to draw on its benefits if the ties they had built had offered more benefits. Rebecca is pushed out because of her failure to obey reciproc-ity norms, but she might have obeyed them if KWRU could provide bridging social capital to its members—and in fact the umbrella of the organization would provide cover so that members might extend help to some while receiving the benefits of bridging social capital from others.[15] Helen was active for five years before she left KWRU to embrace isolation as a strategy. She might have deemed her KWRU investment worthwhile if she had found bridging capital there. Or if she saw KWRU's activism actually yielding changes in poverty, she might not have judged it to "look like it doesn't go anywhere." The reciprocity requirements described in chapter 4 also limit the value of social ties, since they require members to draw heavily on thin resources.[16]

Portes notes that social capital has two elements: 1) the relationship that allows individuals to claim access to resources belonging to others in their networks, and 2) the amount and quality of those resources.[17] Even when those living in neighborhoods with concentrated poverty have strong social ties to others in their communities, those ties rarely lead to upward mobility. That is, they are bonding ties but not bridging ties. Stack found that such bonding ties were crucial to the survival of the participants in her study.[18] Indeed, as I found, bridging ties were absent, but bonding ties through KWRU saved members from homelessness. Without those ties, members would have been worse off in obvious and measurable ways, not limited to their housing situations, but including their access to assistance paying for utilities as well as help with child care, food, health care, and emotional well-being.

For KWRU members, the limits of poor people's networks contribute to their decision to seek assistance outside their kin networks. The help KWRU expects them to provide in turn for help received, or as investment for further help, also drains their resources of time and effort. However, as outlined in the previous chapter, generalized reciprocity within the group ameliorates the problem and many members maintain their involvement for years.

My findings support the importance of KWRU's social ties for its members. James tells me, "People always been helping me since like I got involved with KWRU in 1997. I done met different people in different relationships that allowed me to be able to function, me and my [immediate] family. From transportation stuff to money stuff to food stuff, to you name it, people that helped me over the last seven years."

At our first interview, Jessie is living in a KWRU house with other members. By our last interview, she is living alone with three of her children (the fourth lives most of the time with her ex-husband's sister)[19] in a house in another Philadelphia neighborhood, through a transitional housing program that provides housing for twelve months and helps the recipient to secure a Section 8 voucher. She recalls the mutual support available in the KWRU house positively:

I don't have anybody here that's gonna watch the girls [in the morning]. On [Hancock] Street, so many people on [Hancock] Street that I could leave the girls [a]sleep and be like, "Keep an eye on the girls. They're sleeping. I'm gonna go drop [my son] off." Here I have to get them up at that time. . . . Take him to school, come back to try to get them to go back to sleep.

Jessie also tells me if she ran out of food, another KWRU member "would give me her food stamps or some of her food stamps and I would go and buy some stuff, and then when I got mine I would give them back to her."

Shy provides a detailed account of the kind of relationship she's developed with another member who joined KWRU around the same time. They lived in a KWRU house together for a time. They don't anymore, but their tie has persisted. The tie she developed with her was rooted in their common KWRU membership, and has taken on qualities of sharing resources but also of meaningful friendship. As she describes:

> We always helped each other out. . . . We both were in the Human Rights House, what, I'm gonna go shopping and don't feed her and her daughter? You just can't, it's impossible because then my stamps gonna run out and what I'm gonna eat towards the end when [she] get her stamps? So, we really had no choice besides to become friends and make it work. . . . Now, everybody else in the world, I don't know [how] everybody else doin' it. . . . But me and my friends, we gonna make sure each, 'cause that's all we got. . . . You got to come together or you won't survive.

Along with Marie, another KWRU study participant, Shy and her former housemate pool resources and they provide each other friendship and emotional support. They receive their food stamps at different points each month; the three women take turns taking each other food shopping. Shy explains that each of the women has a different number assigned to them, which denotes when in the month they receive their monthly allotment of food stamps. She indicates that their shared KWRU housing facilitated their pooling of resources and substantively reduced their hardship.

The food stamp program likely makes assistance available at different points for bureaucratic reasons, but it has the effect of driving recipients to pool their stamps when they have social ties that make that possible. This sort of pooling of food stamps is common among participants and among poor people with functioning kin networks, and sharing food stamps and trading child care is more common than sharing money.[20]

KWRU as a Social Tie

KWRU is itself a valuable social tie for members.[21] While social ties are typically people, membership in KWRU functions as a social tie that provides social capital through the organization and through its members. As chapter 3 discussed, this social tie provides members with benefits crucial to survival. In his work Mario Luis Small discusses the value of organizations as resource brokers, both connecting people to other people and thereby fostering social ties and connecting them to other organizations, promoting the development of organizational ties that can provide access to yet more resources. Participating in organizations that effectively broker social capital improves well-being; opportunities to socialize can generate ties that produce social capital and decrease social isolation.[22] There are ways in which KWRU fits this model as broker, particularly in brokering social ties.[23] KWRU itself also serves as a tie for members, removing some of the emotional complications of reciprocity and collectivizing the benefits as well as the costs.

"The Organization Is with You"

Paloma doesn't describe any individual KWRU members as family; as stated above, she just says that all KWRU members are "family." Becky describes the support she could get from a single person she knows through KWRU, but instead of saying that her closest friend in the organization is her sister, she says, "to me my sisters and brothers are KWRU." She explains:

> It's a closeness that you get. . . . Don't get me wrong, everybody has fights and arguments. Just like families, families have fights and arguments. There isn't any family that doesn't. But at the same time if it comes down to it that you're having a problem, the organization is there. The organization is with you. If you're having a problem, they're having a problem.

Many extended families without this level of trust or loyalty might envy the feelings Becky describes. This intensity makes it possible for KWRU to meaningfully contribute to members' survival on thin resources. Thus, organization itself is a tie for its members, bringing its collective resources to bear on a difficulty a member confronts, and connecting people who would otherwise be strangers. As Becky describes, this connection can transcend conflicts between individual members, which strengthens its value for members.

Conflicts and Their Effects on Social Ties

An argument between adult siblings or parents and children typically eventually resolves, even when those conflicts are intense and severe. "Blood is thicker than water" goes the common saying, implying that the ties between kin are stronger, better buffered against the trials they face. But when conflicts and tensions strain ties that are weak to begin with, those ties can fray and dissolve. When disposable ties form quickly and readily, they lack the foundation of mutual understanding that accompanies long-term close ties. So when acquaintances with new, tenuous connections face conflict over money, relationships, or other issues, it's easy—and probably more rational—to walk away from the association than to try to repair it; there may not be anything of note to salvage. Desmond's observations show that the ties he found frequently dissolved in conflict rather than just melting away, because of exactly this equation.[24] By contrast, people invest extended amounts of time and energy into kin ties and long-term friendships, so for emotional as well as practical reasons, when such relationships encounter difficulties people are more likely to find their way to resolution and continuation.

Ties built in KWRU get their sustainability from their ability to weather conflict. I see members continue to support each other even in spite of a conflict over child care, because they are both members. I see members remain friendly even when one retreats from a food-sharing arrangement. Even rifts that dissolve individual ties do not dissolve the tie to the organization or cut off aid to either party. For example, a member has a falling out with the activist who had taken in her family, but they both remain tied to the organization. KWRU removes her from the home and places her in a KWRU Takeover House. Other members have personal conflicts with a leading activist, but they continue to receive help from the organization.

KWRU's Role in Preserving Ties

The durability of KWRU ties doesn't mean that KWRU membership automatically generates ties, though some members speak as though it does. Like all poor people, KWRU members have varied difficulties, some of which relate directly to poverty and some of which poverty only intensifies. This instability jeopardizes lasting, meaningful ties. But disposable ties dissolve easily. KWRU serves as a bridge to *replacement* ties to fill a void left when a rift arises, and as long as people maintain their commitment to KWRU, the rift with another member does not end KWRU's support. Members who have suffered a rift all keep getting help when they need it, so long as they retain a tie to the organization and continue to follow its reciprocity norms. This institutional tie is much less fragile than a tie between two human beings. Only breaking the tie to the organization itself ends the flow of help from KWRU. Neglecting KWRU's norms of reciprocity will end support, but a rift with a person will not.

Sometimes, KWRU intervenes when a rift could have ripple effects. One participant tells me that during an argument with another member, KWRU's founder, Cheri Honkala, pulled them aside and said she was going away on a trip soon and "she didn't want no problems or nothing while she was going away, so we talked. . . . We got straightened out." The founder felt that the rift might affect others and therefore called on them to exercise restraint—a role that an authority figure can play in a family but that no one plays when peers forge disposable ties.[25]

Ties That Last

The ties shared by members of KWRU are not disposable. While they lack the relative permanence of kin ties, they also lack the fleeting nature of the ties Desmond documents and with it, many of their downsides. Disposable ties may in fact be an indispensable resource for the poor, but *sustainable ties* provide many of the same benefits with fewer of the drawbacks for those who cannot rely on kin.

Beyond lasting kin ties and fleeting disposable ties, there are in fact sustainable nonkin ties. The existence of these *sustainable ties* provides clues about other ways in which people form and use social ties and advances our understanding of the ways in which people cope with poverty. Just as knowledge about ties among extended families and fictive kin showed how some of the poorest stretched and pooled their resources to jump over holes in the safety net, knowledge about disposable ties between near-strangers illuminated the gravity of the need people without kin have and the strategies they may use to bridge gaps in assistance in order to survive. The existence of sustainable ties suggests the variety of situations the poor face in the United States. The poor are not a monolithic group and they have differing needs for and access to social ties. Sustainable ties suggest that an organization that supports new relationships provides a better context for forming social ties with near-strangers than exist without the aid of such an institution. Organizations can provide a literal space for new friendship, as KWRU provides at its office, its rallies, and its houses, as well as create the conditions that foster mutual trust and exchange, and such ties can provide practical benefits as well as meaningful emotional support.[26]

As discussed in the previous chapter, norms of reciprocity, the notion that people are obligated to help others because they've been helped, function as currency within the context of KWRU. Members could never pay dues; the organization depends on the time and resources that members provide to satisfy the norms of reciprocity established by the group. With the reciprocal obligations they fulfill and KWRU itself providing a binding mechanism, the members I speak with have generally been active in the group for a long period. Some enjoy close friendships with people they meet in KWRU—friendships that last for years—and rely on each other for child care and ongoing emotional support.

All the KWRU members I interview speak about mutual aid and obligations. I found that most members of KWRU feel positive about the sustainable ties they build in KWRU—about their involvement and connections with other members of the group. They are very well aware of the resources to which membership in the group gives them access. As described in previous chapters, *former* members of the group exist—not everyone maintains their commitment to the organization. Sustainable ties may not always be sustained. They can be broken, but they have more resilience than disposable ties and do not depend on kinship. For some, the burdens of membership are too great. Members who leave the group show the consequences of forgoing or forsaking sustainable ties. As described in chapter 4, Helen spent five years as a very active member of KWRU, but has since become a member in name only. Her house has no running water. She struggles to pay for even the most basic necessities on an unpredictable income. She reports no social ties consistently available to her. Even among those involved in current group activities, not everyone sees the social ties that come from KWRU in a positive light. But KWRU offers a very unusual resource for poor people, one that contributes to survival in vital ways.

Helen decided she was better off fighting her battles alone. Yet her conditions have worsened since dissolving her KWRU membership. I can only speculate that her life might be better if she had maintained her membership and the access to social capital it offered. KWRU provides a source of sustainable ties to those who remain involved. Like Rebecca, whose involvement ended because she did not fulfill KWRU's reciprocity requirements, Helen severed the sustainable ties she had through KWRU. In dissolving their connection to KWRU, these women also relinquished the possibility of continued ties with other members that could be strengthened by shared group membership.

KWRU's leaders recognize the importance of sustainable ties and seek to foster relationships between members as a way to build the organization. Walter tells me that coming together with others to build such ties can improve self-esteem, because he values "being out there and realizing that my crying is not a cry by itself. There's other people crying too. And by putting myself in relationship to other people, I gather strength. . . . There's no way that we can exist without each other." For KWRU leaders the possibility of a powerful social movement lies in this sense of shared struggle, but for members it also provides emotional benefits. One member met and all-but-legally adopted a homeless youth through a KWRU connection. While this is unusual, most members take the emotional side of the ties built through KWRU seriously. Carmen, a member for about four years, also emphasizes the emotional resonance of a shared sense of struggle, saying that she and other KWRU members "got nothin' but love, it's like, 'cause everybody's like for the same thing, everybody's coming from the same place, you know, everybody's been homeless one time or another, so everybody knows that feeling. So that's . . . we can all . . . we all connect like that."

The common experience of poverty, coupled with spending time together through that shared struggle, has the profound ability to create feelings of warmth, camaraderie, and love. Mutual experiences of suffering are a starting point, but when people live together and begin to depend on one another for practical and emotional needs, a deeper bond may develop. Shy tells me, "I just really met [my former KWRU housemate] in the last two years and we just became close because when we came off the bus [tour], we both lived here. So, that's how [we] became real close, because we needed each other . . . in order to survive." She continues, "I just learned to love her. . . . By me and her livin' here. And our struggles together and us bein' there made me close to her." Not only do sustainable ties outlive disposable ties but they can last a long time, with many KWRU members maintaining their membership for years.

Conclusion

KWRU provides an opportunity for people to develop lasting relationships with other members, and many do form meaningful friendships that extend beyond the group's activities, sharing resources and acting in capacities usually filled by kin. By protecting members' investment in one another even when friendships fracture, KWRU makes it possible to build such ties. A context characterized by the neoliberal disappearance of a public safety net amplifies the value of sustainable ties.

I would consider it striking if people built ties that lasted four or five years through KWRU, given that disposable ties often dissolve in months. But a decade after my original research I reconnect with several KWRU members and find that some of the ties that were already deep and long-held in 2003–2006 still persist. KWRU bolsters and strengthens otherwise thin and fragile bonds between people who start off as strangers. It provides a safe place for them to not stay to themselves, and by functioning as a tie it ensures that members can invest time in helping one another. If individuals disappear from the group, those to whom they were linked do not lose the benefits of that social bond, for the tie is really to the organization. Individuals can be replaced, with KWRU as the mediator and voucher for new individuals.[27] KWRU fosters trusting ties, but it also provides a means for the ties to work even when trust between individuals is absent. Poor individuals develop ties to the group and through the group to other individuals, but the organization acts to strengthen a tenuous strand between them, and the ties become better able to bear the heavy burdens they face, more likely to withstand swift winds of crisis, and therefore more likely to be sustainable. Of course, my research could not be used to suggest that everyone who seeks help from KWRU creates a sustained tie with it or other members. Indeed I saw the organization's ties and the members' ties dissolve at times. I selected participants who were still tied to the group as opposed to those whose connections had dissolved, with the exception perhaps of Helen, whose tie had all but dissolved when we spoke, so dissolution is not something I studied comprehensively. Yet the sustainability of some of the social ties between KWRU members distinguishes them sharply from ties between people in poverty other research has described.

Desmond explains that in his work, "The environment most conducive to producing disposable ties was that which gathered together people with pressing needs."[28] This certainly characterizes KWRU and its members, yet the organization renders those ties sustainable rather than disposable. Desmond notes that institutions geared to the poor were often sites of disposable tie formation: "Welfare offices, food pantries, job centers, Alcoholics Anonymous clubs, methadone clinics, even the waiting areas of eviction court—disposable ties regularly were initiated in such venues."[29] KWRU is both similar to and different from these sorts of institutions. Because KWRU requires something of its members rather than simply providing them with services, it creates social ties in which it is embedded as an organization,[30] thereby strengthening the tenuous bonds between new acquaintances. It also actively seeks to create opportunities for them to develop ties with one another.

As Walter says, KWRU members' strength is in their unity. Poor people have very little individually. But as a group KWRU members have built an organization with wider possibilities, and they have been able to do so because so many of the members invest so much of their meager resources in the organization and in one another. As this book's conclusion describes, a number of insights from my research can improve the lives of the poor, through public policies and social service program design.

Conclusion

Creating Change on the Outskirts of Hope

In the richest nation on Earth, far too many children are still born into poverty, far too few have a fair shot to escape it, and Americans of all races and backgrounds experience wages and incomes that aren't rising, making it harder to share in the opportunities a growing economy provides. That does not mean, as some suggest, abandoning the War on Poverty. . . . Instead, it means we must redouble our efforts to make sure our economy works for every working American. It means helping our businesses create new jobs with stronger wages and benefits, expanding access to education and health care, rebuilding those communities on the outskirts of hope, and constructing new ladders of opportunity for our people to climb.

—President Barack Obama, White House 2014b[1]

KWRU was founded in 1991. Over the eighteen years that followed, members engaged in countless protests and helped hundreds of individuals and families who came to the office, desperate for assistance navigating an increasingly complicated public support system. Members held sit-ins, marched on picket lines, set up tent cities, and toured the country by bus to spread their message and show their members poverty's reach. They sang together, prayed together, cooked together. They mourned the loss of longtime members to cancer, AIDS, and drug addiction. They housed homeless families in Human Rights Houses and Takeover Houses. Foundation funding allowed them to purchase some Human Rights Houses and rent others, while Takeover Houses were their extralegal response to the juxtaposed reality of thousands of homeless families in Philadelphia and thousands of vacant, abandoned homes.

Neoliberalism has been a growing fact of life in the nation and around the world since before this distinctive organization was founded. KWRU exists in opposition to a society that, as Silva describes, has economic and emotional spheres that are "mutually confirming," that tend to isolate the poor and blame them for their poverty, even as barriers to upward mobility have mounted.[2] It makes people feel responsible for their own success, but also for their own happiness, even as it isolates them and therefore makes social connection that could bring happiness all the more elusive. KWRU provides an alternative, though limited resources constrain the aid it can offer. In 2009 the organization lost its large foundation funding and its dedicated office space on North 5th Street. But its founder, director, and other key activists continued their efforts in other ways, and it is stunning that ties built through the organization were sustained through this crisis (and as they made clear to me in 2014–2016, those ties sustained *them* through this crisis). The need KWRU has served has certainly persisted; to cite one metric, the number of food stamp recipients in the United States rose by about 10 million between 2007 and 2009—reflecting consequences of the Great Recession—feeding one in eight Americans and nearly one in four children. In Philadelphia there was a 14 percent increase in the number of recipients, so that in 2009 26 percent of the population was receiving benefits under SNAP (the Supplemental Nutritional Assistance Program).[3] In 2013 SNAP usage hit a high of 47.6 million families nationwide. While it fell to 45.8 million in 2015, this number still represents a large increase over prior decades.[4]

In 2014, eight years after concluding my research, I connect with several organization leaders to talk about what's changed for the group. I learn that in 2009 KWRU effectively merged with the PPEHRC, an organization it spearheaded over a decade earlier. PPEHRC (called "P-Perk" by its members) works on political advocacy and shares KWRU's goals of ending poverty. Rather than focusing only on helping individuals and growing membership, they aim to educate the poor about human rights and become politically engaged. "This is our life," a member tells me, of the continuing efforts.

In 2014 they are planning the U.S. Social Forum for 2015, a gathering of social justice activists aiming to build a broad movement.[5] Galen Tyler, who had been the director of KWRU, invites me to come to a planning event for the Forum, and I make my way to an office in Center City, Philadelphia, on a bright August day. Another organization has provided PPEHRC and others planning the 2015 U.S. Social Forum the use of its space, including large conference rooms. About seventy-five people representing over twenty organizations gather for an all-day People's Movement Assembly to discuss the problems they see in the world and what kind of future they envision.

I walk in and see Amanda, who smiles broadly and gives me a hug. While members of various groups, including people of every age, from their early twenties to their seventies (and one grandfather who's brought his elementary-school-aged grandson), discuss the possibilities for things as diverse as rallying against corporate personhood and universal access to clean, safe water in light of recent threats from hydraulic fracturing and corporate pollution, I notice several long-time members of KWRU. During small group discussions, I look over and see two KWRU members I remember from a decade earlier, talking and laughing. One member, a woman I interviewed over a decade earlier, has come today to watch another's children while she joins in the discussion—a sign of a tie that has been successfully sustained, as the two women have been connected through KWRU for two decades. Cheri Honkala and Galen Tyler speak to the larger group about the day's agenda.

I notice the scar in the middle of a member's chest, peeking up from her gray v-neck T-shirt, a reminder of the heart surgery she had many years ago, when another member took the role of next of kin and spoke to doctors on her behalf. I ask her how she's doing and she says, "I'm trying to keep my health." I ask about her heart, and she says it's okay. As she tells me, "It's hard," and references the coming anniversary of another member's death due to cancer in 2008; they were very close. She says that now she and another participant both live near the PPEHRC office, and invites me to come by and visit her home and see the office.

One member regales me with updates on various members lost, some to drug addiction, some to their improved situations. When I ask about some, she says, "gone," with a wave of her hand as if to show me they flew away; they don't feel they need KWRU anymore. She tells me the organization is still helping a participant I remember well, who's bounced from one housing program to another, still waiting, perhaps in vain, for a Section 8 voucher. Paloma, James, Amanda, and Cate are still living in poverty in Philadelphia and still supporting one another.

In 2015 I speak with eminent photographer Harvey Finkle, who has been photographing the organization since its inception—one of his photographs appears on the cover of this book—and he tells me that Becky visited other members at the Tent City held in September 2015 during the papal visit to Philadelphia. Another member tells me via Facebook that she has moved away, to a state in the South as she had hoped a decade earlier, but she retains a connection to someone else in the group and continues to believe in the organization's work. In 2016 I learn about another participant, still involved: PPHERC helped her daughter get permanent housing. Marisol is working full-time but remains involved, as does Marie, who has stable housing. Carmen, Colleen, Jessie, Pauline, and Shy are also still members. PPHERC even has some connection to Helen, and the organization sends her children presents. At least fifteen of the twenty-five KWRU study participants are still involved or connected to the organization on some level.

The Social Forum occurs some months after the 2014 event, on rainy June days in 2015. At the opening ceremony, Cheri Honkala introduces a woman and her three children. The woman was recently laid off and the family was evicted. One of the children has cancer. In response to the applause when she says PPEHRC has housed this family, Cheri insists, "But it's not our job." PPEHRC's thirty Takeover Houses and the Human Rights Houses they are able to maintain keep this and many other families off the street. But Cheri maintains the message that the responsibility lies with society, not an organization like PPEHRC, to assume that burden.

On the third day of the four-day social forum, I walk to a fund-raiser in West Kensington from the nearby public transit stop. The weeds grow wild in this urban area, reaching tall between broken pieces of concrete. Just as municipal neglect of the physical environment allows such weeds to flourish, so does the abandonment of the community allow problems to grow and fester. Vacant lot after vacant lot, lack of street lights, and deserted streets are just the most visible representations of the neglect this community faces. At the fund-raiser one study participant gives a brief speech, in which she says she felt "very lucky to have such an extended family, not only my personal family . . . but also my movement family," referring to KWRU and PPEHRC, to help her. She continues, "People forget that the work that we do does burn you out, it does demoralize. But when we come together and figure it out for each other, that is the best."

In early 2016 I get more details on the study participants who were members of KWRU, over breakfast with Cheri and Galen. They confirm what one member said to me in 2014, that some study participants are no longer involved. They also note that participants who have hit their five-year lifetime limit on welfare, a restriction instituted as part of welfare reform two decades ago, are less involved in KWRU than they used to be. They also mention participants who are stably housed and employed. This achievement owes no small part to the ties members built through KWRU, which they continue to maintain to this day. Members who were homeless in 2003 now assist new homeless members, as more established members did then, opening their homes and letting activists raid their pantries for food to give to hungry newcomers. They cook food in their own kitchens to bring to rallies. Cheri and Galen describe these individuals as "soldiers for life." PPEHRC recognizes their contributions with gifts at Christmas and gives them access to free enriching summer camps for their children. A longtime member runs the camps with help from interns. Two members are no longer directly involved because they have moved out of Philadelphia, but they still consider themselves part of the network.

Members who've remained involved still have valuable social ties with one another, more than ten years after my research with KWRU began, which in some cases means they formed ties that span two decades through the organization. Some of these ties are extremely deep. Others are weak, yet still sustainable, and they provide resources newer, homeless members cannot offer.

The existing literature does not describe such *sustainable*, supportive ties among the poor outside of kinship. In describing the realities poor people face as they struggle to survive, it addresses reliance on kin, reliance on social services, the existence of disposable ties, and ties based on mutual alliance with an institution such as a day care center.[6] Like the KWRU study participants, many poor people do not have a dense network of closely connected and supportive kin in which members pool resources and help one another survive; even those who do may have reasons to need additional support. Social services may be inadequate, for example due to limits on available assistance, or undesirable, for such reasons as accompanying stigma or a perception that social service workers pity their clients. Disposable relationships are rife with potential problems that arise from misunderstandings, limits on resources, arguments over money, lovers' quarrels, and competing demands from other disposable ties. A day care center such as those Small studied may offer nonkin ties with fewer problems than disposable ties; such ties share some characteristics with the ties I found in KWRU, though they lack the sustainability of KWRU-built ties.

In KWRU, members find assistance as well as the obligation to reciprocate the help they receive, and in so doing they develop sustainable social ties with others in the organization and with the organization itself. The fact that poor people without supportive kin can access and build social ties that last is an opportunity worth expanding and developing.

In the Introduction, I noted the privatization of risk to which other scholars have called our attention. Jacob Hacker asserted, "For decades, Americans and their government were committed to a powerful set of ideals—never wholly achieved, never without internal tension—that combined a commitment to economic security with a faith in economic opportunity." He states, "Today that message is starkly different: *You are on your own.*"[7] Individualism has a long history in the United States; since the 1970s neoliberalism has made it stronger than ever before. Putnam declares that Americans "like to think of ourselves as 'rugged individualists,'" even though "the wagon train, with its mutual aid among a community of pioneers" is just as accurate a symbol of our story, and identifies a swing between individualism and community throughout U.S. history that has stalled at the individualist pole in the past half century.[8] Yet recent research suggests belief in the American Dream may be waning. A poll on the American Dream conducted in 2015 finds that a majority of participants think the American Dream is suffering. They "see more severe obstacles to achieving the Dream today than ever before." At the same time, researchers note, "For all their pessimism and division, most people are surprisingly upbeat about their personal lives. Perhaps paradoxically, a majority of Americans also believe that hard work and elbow grease are still enough for ordinary citizens to realize the Dream ... that hard work is more important than luck or where [i.e., in what position on the social ladder] you were born."[9]

Without structural changes and curbs to neoliberalism, the responses of the poor to their situations may make the best out of their own bad situations, but will not change the structural causes of their position in an economy designed to perpetuate inequality and poverty. Privatization elevates profit over the best interests of the populace and creates situations that serve to strengthen the aims of neoliberalism; for example, mass incarceration is one way society deals with surplus populations, those who are unable to be absorbed into the formal labor market.[10]

Thomas Edsall writes that the focus on individual responsibility works with "rapid technological advance, the internationalization of commerce and the demise of the paternalistic or loyalty-based workplace to exacerbate inequality. ... Collective action on behalf of the poor requires a shared belief in the obligation of the state to secure the well-being of the citizenry."[11] As Beck and Hacker note, this is exactly what the privatization of risk has undermined.[12] Given this, it seems unlikely the poor would work together—we've all lost our notion of the collective, of the responsibilities of the state in the neoliberal golden age of individualism. Yet KWRU/PPEHRC does demand recentering responsibilities of risk on the state, aiming for more fundamental change. And they simultaneously work to foster ties between poor people to enable immediate survival.

This book provides evidence that social ties matter, and that social isolation is a natural outgrowth of neoliberal ideas. It's very difficult to empower poor people to overcome all the barriers to building social ties in a neoliberal context. But doing so can bring meaningful benefits to poor people's lives, including ensuring their survival, providing a sense of community, reducing self-blame, and building trust between people, which in turn can allow people to build more social capital. Reciprocity is burdensome for those with the least resources, whether economic, emotional, or otherwise. But social capital is not built without it. It depends on reciprocity to grow and flourish. Social capital is only capital when it's a resource people can draw on and invest in; otherwise the social support that sometimes is mistaken for it is not renewable. Organizations can play a key role in connecting poor people with one another and providing the context in which trust can grow and reciprocity can develop.

While the Great Recession changed in small ways the public rhetoric about the causes of poverty, and the years since have seen inequality enter the lexicon in ways scholars of stratification and poverty have long hoped, insecurity, instability, and shame continue to characterize the lives of the poor.[13] Even as our society struggles to come to terms with what offsetting the worst consequences of neoliberalism for those most economically deprived might require, neoliberalization continues apace, the privatization of risk continues, and people, including the poor themselves, continue to blame the poor for being poor—part of an atmosphere that discourages social ties. The policies I recommend are meant to be realistic endeavors given the ideological and political climate in U.S. society; I do not mean to suggest them in place of a shift away from individualism, risk privatization, and neoliberalism. Rather, given that we aren't making that shift, at least in meaningful ways, the interventions I propose are meant to improve the lives of the poor. They do not address the underlying structural causes for the plight faced by the people in this book or others like them, but they do address some of the consequences.

As it stands today, KWRU/PPEHRC has a more limited ability to foster sustainable ties than it had when I did my research. It is my hope that they will someday gain substantial funding again, for with it KWRU could provide more support to people who otherwise fall through holes in the public and private safety nets. This concluding chapter discusses this proposal and others that have the potential to remake the reality of being poor in America in light of the key findings of my research. If we are to heed the lofty ideals of luminaries like Pope Francis, who has said, "The dignity of each human person and the pursuit of the common good are concerns which ought to shape all economic policies,"[14] the proposals below offer some key steps.

Crucial Aspects of the KWRU Model

This book has shown that there's something in between the individual choices people make and the actions they take on the one hand and the faceless intangible "structure" that limits their agency on the other:

community.[15] Whereas KWRU envisions community as an agent of political change, it also, in the context of the organization, aids the struggle to survive in crucial ways. By offering an alternative to the neighborhood-specific community on which poverty-related research has frequently focused, KWRU has been able at times to overpower the isolating influence of individualistic ideology. Poor people subscribe to the achievement ideology, believing their own hard work and reasoned decisions will better their situations. They pursue, or aspire to pursue, human capital investment in the form of education. Their individualistic focus leads them to avoid developing connections with potential social ties, as do other reasons; they often opt to stay to themselves. The most proximal potential sources of ties are their neighbors, but they frequently denigrate their neighbors as dangerous or otherwise unappealing as social ties; they stigmatize them in much the same way politicians and others stigmatize all poor people. Pervasive distrust causes many participants to consider no one a close confidant, sometimes even among family members. They fear gossip and others' judgment. And they fear new friends would ask for help. Failing to meet reciprocal demands has emotional consequences, and fulfilling them might strain resources, with no guarantee of a return.

Study participants who are not members of KWRU have less experience with homelessness than do KWRU participants; this often reflects their use of free housing from kin or housing subsidies through agencies, like Carole's housing provided by DHS. A lack of these kinds of stable and willingly available supports from kin ties generally leads members to go to KWRU for help; kin ties often prevent the dire situations that lead potential members to KWRU. When they do go to KWRU, members get substantial practical support, as well as the opportunity to develop a new perspective on avoidance of social ties; they sometimes even begin to question individualistic strategies in favor of collective ones. In exchange for the support they get, they give of their time and energy, volunteering for the organization and joining protests and rallies. The more they give, the more they are likely to get, and the exchange cultivates trust and social ties between members and the organization, even as the cost proves higher than some are willing to pay; it also occasions meaningful friendships among members. Crucially, the ties some make, both with each other and the organization, have sustained for decades.

KWRU is truly distinctive, but I believe social service agencies can replicate its model, providing aid that would augment and exceed the existing private safety net. My findings reveal the significant effects of the weakening of the public safety net. Most of the people I interviewed had been homeless, and some of the most effective support KWRU provides consists of helping members to secure a hold on one of the remaining threads of that net. Consequently, my findings reveal key areas of need for policy reform.

Building sustainable ties exacts a high cost for KWRU members. However, this very cost brings benefits: unlike the one-way support social service agencies offer, the reciprocal exchange of help within KWRU fosters relationships among members and between members and activists. The social capital those relationships provide yields instrumental support that proves key for survival, particularly in the context of weak or absent kin ties. While the poor cannot escape poverty with a simple recipe of either avoiding or developing social ties, the social ties available to KWRU members yield more rewards than they impose in costs.

One reason KWRU offers unique benefits in this regard is that it requires an investment from members; it places them in a position to draw on support from ties, but also to give back as a mechanism to invest in future support, creating the mutuality necessary for social capital to develop. KWRU membership does not automatically generate lasting ties, because, like all poor people, KWRU members' lives are made more difficult by economic instability, and this endangers their sustainable ties. Yet many members maintain ties for years, in contrast to disposable ties that dissolve in months, generally over personal rifts.[16] When a rift develops between individual members, KWRU can foster replacement ties to fill the void; as long as people maintain their commitment to KWRU, personal rifts do not end KWRU's support. So long as members maintain their tie to the organization itself, the flow of help from KWRU continues. This is a meaningful distinction from social support not based in an organization.

Policy Interventions: Directions for Social Service Agencies

Social service agencies serve a crucial role; even if policy makers made work pay and fulfilled the promise of the public safety net, we'd need a private safety net. This need also puts tremendous pressure on social ties. Agencies that strengthen the private safety net could provide meaningful benefits, and KWRU represents a distinctive model that would make such a task possible. Particularly for poor people like many participants in this study, who lack kin willing and able to provide the kind of assistance many of us take for granted, private nonfamily support is invaluable. I propose that social service agencies would benefit from taking KWRU as a model to make key changes. Many are private philanthropic organizations or nonprofits that receive a combination of public and private funding. They have long been a lifeline for poor people in the United States, providing indispensable support in soup kitchens, food banks, and opportunities to receive adult education, yet there are ways to increase the value of their services.

KWRU's model offers valuable insight. Poor people would have a better chance of surviving—and thriving—if they could pursue human capital investment, build sustainable ties, and access services that provided them the broad and deep support necessary to address varied aspects of their struggles. While most programs they access provide individual services such as job training, GED test preparation, or parenting classes, there are programs that provide a variety of services as a bundle, in one location and with useful coordination. (I recruited some non-KWRU participants through such a program.)[17] Such programs also have the potential to create community.[18] If such programs required reciprocity from the clients they served, as KWRU/PPEHRC does from its members, those clients would feel the power of their personal investment and overcome shame at asking for help, instead viewing it as a draw on their own investment. And by requiring reciprocity to the organization for the benefit of its members, they could sidestep the situation in which lack of trust complicates reciprocal demands. As in KWRU, the organization would essentially insure the investment. As the KWRU model suggests, keeping such reciprocity demands manageable is key; if the burden is too great, it will hinder rather than foster sustainable ties.

Supporting Sustainable Ties

While I found some ambivalence about the ties participants built through KWRU, Carmen's comment typifies the reward of sustainable ties: "We have to look out for each other, we have to help each other, because . . . I ain't doing it by myself, you know what I mean? Like it took a whole group to do it with me. A group of people that I didn't know. And they just opened their arms and just embraced me."

Like KWRU, social service agencies can provide a literal space for new ties to develop and, as noted above, a safe place for people to not stay to themselves.[19] We meet and make friends at school and work; shared time at an agency also allows people to make friends by providing a place. By requiring people to volunteer, a social service agency would require them to be present in a shared space that would allow them to forge ties. KWRU also fosters trusting ties; such ties can provide tangible benefits as well as emotional support.[20] As Small argues, the day care centers he studied "created access to social support by increasing trust [and] by *formally* institutionalizing obligations."[21] Social service agencies could take my findings and his as a way to foster trusting ties.

As noted in chapter 5, participating in organizations that allow people to build social capital improves their lives.[22] KWRU provides members access to resources through social ties with other members, but it could do more, especially by brokering resources with organizational ties, with adequate funding. As Small and Allard assert, the role of organizations in poor people's social ties is "particularly notable in the context of a decentralized safety net that depends on local organizations for the delivery of services to populations in need."[23]

Using Reciprocity

By requiring reciprocity, agencies could not only foster relationships, they could lessen their own burden and thereby be able to help more clients. They would mitigate clients' reluctance to developing ties and chip away at individualism as well. By developing social capital they would serve a greater number of people by offsetting some of their costs. Those with social network members who are able to provide child care or share housing might then be less in need of subsidies. The private safety net of social ties has historically helped fill the gap left by an inadequate welfare system, a system made more inadequate by welfare reform; agencies that strengthen the private safety net could confer real benefits.

As noted in chapter 4, KWRU members often felt pressured to spend time at the office even when they felt there was nothing for them to do that would directly contribute to the group's mission. If agencies kept track of how many people they needed on given days and times, they might make better use of volunteer hours than KWRU did.

My findings also suggest the downside of reciprocity requirements, but they point the way to managing this downside. Rebecca is not comfortable fulfilling KWRU's reciprocity requirements, as she feels she is getting shortchanged. As she tells me, "I'm here for help. I'm not getting any. So I don't feel that I'm getting help. I don't like the position I'm in." A social service agency could make more specific promises of compensation for time given and thereby prevent cases like Rebecca's. KWRU avoids some of the downsides of reciprocal obligations: members are not dependent on singular, resource-poor individuals for help but on the relatively better resources of a group; and what they provide in exchange is their time rather than their scarce limited funds. An agency could further mitigate these downsides.

In addition, Gutiérrez and Lewis describe the benefits of peer-to-peer interactions in the empowerment-based intervention they describe, noting that it "enhance[s] self-esteem, further[s] a sense of belonging, and break[s] down isolation while increasing mutual assistance."[24] I would argue that therefore such reciprocity from clients would help people feel invested and facilitate the building of social capital. Based on the finding of Gutiérrez and Lewis that confidence, consciousness, and connection are the most important aspects of empowerment, it would also support empowerment.

Providing Support Navigating Available Programs

KWRU offers valuable services to its members, such as helping people figure out how to navigate available programs—from learning what exists to determining their eligibility to knowing how to apply. Some social service agencies offer this kind of support; many more should. As I found, this support allows recipients to feel empowered. By facilitating their receipt of benefits, social service agencies could assist them in practical and significant ways. KWRU has served as a liaison for people, one they feel is on their side, in contrast to the way participants felt about welfare caseworkers. Savannah sums up what I heard from nearly everyone who participated in the study when she said that caseworkers "act like they're giving that money out of their pockets."

Social service agencies would do well to facilitate peer relationships that provide this sort of advice. Learning navigation skills from people who share life experiences with recipients is itself a valuable asset, making those getting the help feel less alone and stigmatized, particularly as they learn about the widespread conditions of poverty. Paloma, a long-term passionate activist in KWRU, says: "How can it be my fault or their fault if every town, the same situation's over and over and over again?" As I found, intended beneficiaries may avoid social service agencies in part because of a sense of being pitied; emulating KWRU's practice of peer assistance to guide recipients of help in finding support would reduce this problem.

Supporting Human Capital Investment

While ties built within KWRU do sometimes involve conflict and strife, participants are generally willing to navigate these conflicts to build relationships. Much of the ambivalence that drove people to limit their investment in sustainable ties, once built, stemmed from the difficulty of investing in human capital while maintaining such ties, as Helen opted to prioritize work over KWRU membership. A social service agency, funded appropriately, could mitigate this problem.[25] A person like Helen, who mostly dissolved her tie to KWRU after five years, might be more motivated to maintain a connection to a social service agency that took KWRU as a model.

By keeping volunteer hours reasonable, compatible with support recipients' work and education schedules and child care needs, and by providing opportunities that satisfy TANF work requirements, agencies could foster the simultaneous building of human capital and social capital. Human capital investment alone won't be sufficient for people like the participants in this study to escape poverty, but they almost certainly will not do so without it. To the extent that success and stability remain out of reach, in the right context sustainable ties can at least reverse their isolation and position them more strongly for security and mobility.

Unfortunately, increasing the effectiveness of this proposal requires more fundamental changes to society. While some policy makers point to a gap between skilled and unskilled workers, or between those with college degrees and those without, this focus on human capital is limited. Hacker and Pierson note that "skill-based technological change" is the most dominant explanation for trends in inequality in the United States.[26] There has been a shift to more knowledge-based employment over the past few decades and human capital does matter.[27] However, human capital investment isn't a foolproof method of escaping poverty. It's only one piece of the puzzle. Even when focusing on the early educational years, research finds much greater out-of-school effects than in-school effects.[28] But regardless of educational opportunity, the fact remains that someone needs to be at the bottom; even if everyone had access to good-quality education and everyone pursued and completed higher education successfully, some people would still be on the losing end of the inequality equation.

In spite of these limitations, by requiring clients to provide services that fit well with their skills, interests, and abilities, agencies could strengthen their service to clients. An exchange of services could offer the benefits of social capital that KWRU offers only in isolation from and in opposition to human capital, enabling agencies to support human capital in a new way.

Policy Interventions: Changes in State Support

Key differences between the poor and nonpoor suggest obvious interventions: an infusion of cash through expanded assistance programs and tax credits like the Earned Income Tax Credit (EITC), access to quality higher education, living wage jobs, housing stability, and family members willing and able to help shoulder life's unexpected burdens all would help the poor escape poverty. While poor people blame themselves for their own poverty, research reveals that the effects of deindustrialization and mass incarceration leave government programs the only way for some people to survive. The difference in measured needs of the poor and nonpoor provide the impetus for many of the more common proposals and existing programs. As I'll describe below, my specific findings point to key ways of improving and expanding such programs.

Putnam points out a major barrier to state support: "While large majorities favor pragmatic steps to limit inequality of condition, we are also philosophical conservatives, suspicious of the ability of government to redress inequality and convinced that responsibility for an individual's well-being rests chiefly with him or her."[29] At the same time, as he notes, "95 percent of us say that 'everyone in America should have equal opportunity to get ahead'—a level of consensus that is virtually never reached in contentious contemporary America."[30] It may seem contradictory: Americans "expect individuals to take care of themselves, but they accept that government help may be needed to address concrete barriers to pursuing opportunity."[31] History and the evidence from societies with a better social safety net suggest that government can provide the social services and public safety net that benefit the public good and that a just society demands.

While Page and Jacobs note that "Americans are simultaneously suspicious of government in the abstract" and support individualist ideology, we also care about inequality and are "supportive of concrete government help in the face of real-world challenges. [We] turn to government to maintain or expand opportunities for individuals to pursue the American Dream and to provide minimal economic security for those who are left behind."[32] Americans support government aid for education, job assistance, health care insurance, and disability—and believe that the government should spend "whatever is necessary" to ensure that all children can go to really good public schools. This finding crosses party lines, with a majority of people who identify as Republicans and a majority of people who identify as Democrats favoring this spending, paid for with tax dollars.

Edin and Shaefer make compelling recommendations in their book *$2.00 a Day: Living on Almost Nothing in America*, specifically noting the importance of reducing poverty stigma by integrating the poor into society.[33] They argue for increased work opportunity, higher wages, more affordable housing, and emergency help when poor families face urgent crises. They argue for jobs that recall those provided by the Works Progress Administration in the 1930s. Such initiatives would fly in the face of neoliberalism. But just as people often come to KWRU/PPEHRC believing in individualism but by building sustainable ties in the group begin to subscribe to the organization's rhetoric, achieving these initiatives might ultimately undermine the American belief in neoliberalism. Just as the implementation of marriage equality undermines opposition to it, perhaps people can witness the good that results from publicly funded employment opportunities and then begin to let go of their belief in neoliberalism. Restoring the safety net would work to undo the neoliberal privatization of risk.

The story I have told in this book illustrates the fact that the private safety net KWRU members found works best when they use it to extend government support, such as helping one another navigate government bureaucracy to receive aid or sharing a voucher-supported home with homeless KWRU members. My suggestions are not meant to focus only on what individuals can do in terms of building social capital, or even what agencies can do to foster social capital. Social capital should not be the only means to basic survival, although it can increase the value of government programs such as I discuss below.

By offering recommendations for expanded benefits for poor families, I do not mean to imply that they will give everyone in America equal opportunity to get ahead. Indeed, these recommendations will fall far short of leveling the playing field. Rather, it is precisely because structural conditions make it so difficult to escape poverty and because the playing field is so skewed that I suggest interventions, grounded in my research findings, that will improve the situations of people like the participants in this study. Jobs that pay living wages would do much to reduce the absolute poverty level, as would a minimum wage tied to inflation, affordable and universal health care, free and public pre-K, and free college education. But even these ambitious proposals remain responses to an inequitable system—not a panacea for its problems but a patch for its most dire consequences. These changes are no substitute for meaningful policy changes, but nonetheless will make the lives of the poor better than they are without them.

Housing

One area in which KWRU has provided a unique benefit is housing. Two related factors set KWRU members apart from the non-KWRU participants: a history of homelessness and a lack of kin ties. The non-KWRU participants are slightly better off than the KWRU participants by some measures and help provided by kin ties generally makes the crucial difference. Kin support prevents them from experiencing the most dire circumstances of poverty. Many receive housing free of charge from kin, which fills one of the most crucial and expensive basic needs of the poor; ten out of twenty-five are living with their parents when we speak, and one has reduced rent through a family friend. The elimination of a cost that tends to consume the largest share of people's budgets puts these participants at an advantage compared to those participants without the benefit of such assistance. The experiences of participants who live with family rent-free illustrate how invaluable housing assistance can be to those without such resources.

Meanwhile, nearly all the KWRU participants have experienced homelessness, a history shared by a minority of non-KWRU participants. Several KWRU participants are effectively homeless at the time of their interview, their temporary status in KWRU housing the only factor keeping them from being wholly unhoused. While most non-KWRU participants report both minor and significant aid from kin members, most KWRU participants report the absence of productive, supportive family ties. KWRU fills a void, providing instrumental support others get from relatives and offering the possibility of developing sustained ties with other members for emotional support, friendship, and a sense of family and community previously missing from their lives.

Expansion of housing subsidies would go a long way toward stabilizing the poor who lack access to safe, stable, affordable housing. Since 2009 the program known as "rapid re-housing" has received attention; its aim is to put homeless families directly into permanent housing, bypassing shelters. Families receive short-term housing subsidies and within a few months have to start paying their new rents independently. It does seem to be a viable solution for some—such as recently downwardly mobile individuals, including workers suffering from their first bout of unemployment in the Great Recession. But for those in deeper and longer-term poverty, without better-paying jobs or long-term financial assistance such as permanent housing subsidies, it may create the sort of churning welfare reform did, where the hardest to serve ended up back on the rolls. Thus people could end up back at shelters.[34] Providing universal housing vouchers would help everyone.[35]

Grants to provide working adults with funds for moving costs and security deposits would enable those who might be able to pay for their own housing costs on a monthly basis to secure housing. Safe and decent housing for everyone is a crucial component of making the American Dream—that anyone can succeed with enough effort—a reality. Without it the poor will continue to be unable to make the investment in human capital that the Dream demands.

Housing policies that have worked to deconcentrate poverty with the goal of improving the lives of those who move to mixed-income communities are one way to better the opportunities of poor people. Though they haven't been widespread enough to reduce concentrated poverty, they may provide opportunities to build bridging ties and access to better-resourced public schools where they are implemented. Yet these are opportunity-enhancement efforts that allow individual families to make changes as individual families, improving individual lives, not strengthening communities. And unfortunately, programs that move people out from poor communities also tend to weaken their social networks.[36] Even in these efforts, "the neoliberal economic agenda had worked against building communities in favor of rugged individualism."[37] Residential mobility means moving away from established ties with those who live nearby—something not every poor person can do, as this study demonstrates. But when people are fortunate enough to have found bonding social capital through social ties in their local communities, it is a tragedy to have to leave those social ties behind.

It is a common refrain that shelters do not have enough beds. But there are also homeless families who the shelter system cannot house, space limitations aside. In chapter 3 I noted that CC escaped domestic abuse but could not regain custody of her children without a place to live; her welfare payments were woefully inadequate. As I noted in chapter 3, she tells me, "I don't have decent housing, that's why I don't have my kids with me. That's why I'm here at Kensington Welfare Rights. 'Cause I get $158 every two weeks. Where can I live for $158?" KWRU provided much-needed temporary housing for her while she hopefully awaited a Section 8 voucher and sought to regain custody of her children. Similarly, in 2014 KWRU director Galen Tyler tells me about a family that came to KWRU for housing help, a mother and a fifteen-year-old son. Barred from bringing her son to a women's shelter because he was older than twelve, she could not imagine sending her child alone to a men's shelter. And as Galen says, "When you're dealing with homelessness, the last thing you want to do is split up your family." KWRU's Human Rights Houses and Takeover Houses filled gaps such as these. Since the completion of my research they have lost their large foundation funding, which has weakened their ability to offer shelter. The government and private foundations would do well to support KWRU and other organizations to fill local needs for families the shelter system cannot accommodate.

Housing is a meaningful benefit. On a practical level, it's fundamental to most other aspects of life. Supplying housing better positions people to address issues of mental illness and addiction.[38] Withholding housing until beneficiaries have addressed these other problems is a recipe for failure. Without a safe and consistent place to call home, children lack the stability they need to succeed in school and adults may falter at work. But the provision of housing allows people to focus on education and on building social ties for reasons other than needed housing. It frees those who need it from dangerous domestic violence and others from relying on negative ties, such as the exploitative experience of Alyssa, who lived for a time with family members but had to turn over all her WIC, much of her wages, and purchase food for the household. When I ask her if there were ever a time when she didn't have a place to live, she says, poignantly, "I've had places to stay. But not a home to live in."

Child Care

My research also reveals that child care is a clear and unavoidable need. While some poor people lack children and therefore have no such need, and children age out of the need for full-time child care (two factors that do not apply to housing),[39] poor parents require safe, affordable, and accessible child care in order to work outside the home or take advantage of educational opportunities. Parents also need child care in order to search and interview for jobs. Child care that works with nonstandard hours and inconsistent working hours is a clear need as well; most day care centers are still structured around a model of a 9 to 5 parental workday and a five-day week, when in fact parents may work any number of other possible hours, including fluctuating working hours, split shifts, and overnight shifts. Parents with fluctuating work schedules often do not know their work schedules much in advance.[40]

Many study participants have children too young to attend school, or children who are adolescents or young adults. Those with small children who are able to enroll their children in local Head Start programs, like Leslie and Kia, can work outside the home and attend school. Other participants, like Mandy and Karen, lack both access to child care they can afford and kin who might watch their children, which limits their ability to work or pursue an education. Child care support from network members isn't guaranteed; some simply have no one to rely on to watch their children.[41]

The simplest way to get child care to the greatest number of kids possible is to expand universal and public options. In Pennsylvania, kindergarten is not state-mandated, and where it is available, it is not always full-day.[42] A first step would be to fully fund public elementary education to make kindergarten universal and full-day throughout the country. Expanding prekindergarten programs—to universal, free programs similar to kindergarten—would be ideal. Long-term paid parental leave that is universally available, as exists in other countries, could be taken by the poor and nonpoor alike, reducing the poor's need for welfare's stigmatized cash assistance targeted only to low-income people. Elementary schools could provide after school supervisory care, with or without academic enrichment or extracurricular activities, freeing parents of young school-aged children to work full-time without concern for their children's safety.

The Poverty Threshold, Minimum Wage, and Welfare Payments

The poverty threshold, which many social scientists argue is arbitrarily low,[43] is not something full-time, year-round minimum wage workers can cross without funds beyond their wages, nor can welfare recipients. Minimum wage has not kept pace with inflation over time, and the purchasing power of the minimum wage has declined substantially since the 1980s.[44] As a White House Fact Sheet describes it, "In real terms, the minimum wage is worth less today than it was at the beginning of

1950."[45] The minimum wage of $7.25 per hour translates to $15,080 per year for forty hours of work per week, fifty-two weeks per year, less than the poverty threshold for a family of only two persons in the forty-eight contiguous states.[46] So a mother with just one child working a minimum wage job full-time, year-round, is below the poverty line. A higher minimum wage, indexed to inflation, would do a lot to lift workers out of poverty with employer funds.[47] In lieu of or in addition to that, an expanded Earned Income Tax Credit (EITC) would also make a meaningful difference in the life of the working poor.

Cash welfare payments are inadequate to pay for life's necessities as well.[48] Between 1970 and 1996 the value of average benefits declined substantially, and in 2016 TANF benefits do even less to alleviate poverty than they did in 1996.[49] Welfare reform (the Personal Responsibility and Work Opportunity Reconciliation Act) fundamentally changed welfare.[50] As the Center on Budget and Policy Priorities describes it:

> Cash assistance benefits for the nation's poorest families with children fell again in purchasing power in 2013 and are now at least 20 percent below their 1996 levels in 37 states, after adjusting for inflation. . . . These declines came on top of even larger declines in benefits over the preceding quarter-century; between 1970 and 1996, cash assistance benefit levels for poor families with children fell by more than 40 percent in real terms in two-thirds of the states. As of July 1, 2013, *every* state's benefits for a family of three with no other cash income were below *50 percent* of the federal poverty line, measured by the Department of Health and Human Services 2013 poverty guidelines. Benefits were below *30 percent* of the poverty line in most states. And, the TANF benefit level for a family of three with no other cash income is less than the Fair Market Rent for a two-bedroom apartment in every state, nationwide.[51] In fact, in 25 states, TANF benefits cover less than *half* of the Fair Market Rent. When SNAP benefits (the Supplemental Nutrition Assistance Program, formerly known as food stamps) are added to TANF family grants, families with no other income are still below the poverty line.[52]

The majority of study participants do not receive TANF,[53] often surviving only on food stamps and assistance from kin or other social ties; their homelessness reflects the low level of survival they experience.

Earned Income Tax Credit

Both Republican and Democratic administrations have expanded the EITC since the 1990s. It was originally based on a proposal of the conservative economist Milton Friedman, and it has replaced welfare (TANF) as the largest antipoverty program in the United States.[54] As others have proposed, the EITC reduces the material hardship of the working poor in meaningful ways.[55] The EITC is a politically popular program as well;[56] voters see it as rewarding work, as opposed to cash assistance only available to jobless people, which people view as rewarding laziness, or increases in the minimum wage, which some worry will depress employment rates or engender resentment among employers. Importantly, this program is popular precisely because it fits with the achievement ideology; if hard work leads to success, we should seek to make hard work pay off in measurable ways. And the EITC is not as stigmatized as welfare receipt is.[57] While the EITC doesn't aid mobility or provide long-term security, it does lessen immediate hardship.[58]

Education

Most Americans think education is the great equalizer, the thing that creates a level playing field to permit all with adequate motivation to succeed,[59] and participants seek education to improve their lives, hoping it will pay off in the way they imagine. Only two participants have a degree beyond a high school diploma, and Kia, Jasmine, and Bianca, who have completed certificate programs, have been unable to find jobs in their chosen fields. Most of the study participants currently pursuing education are preparing for their GED exams. Data suggest that a high school diploma or GED is insufficient to prepare the poor for a life out of poverty.[60] And the GED and standard diploma are not equivalent; while GED holders usually fare better than high school dropouts, they do not fare as well as those with a high school diploma.[61]

My research suggests that the models Katherine Newman proposed in her book *No Shame in My Game: The Working Poor in the Inner City*, which link students' education formally to job opportunities through expanded apprenticeship programs and vocational education that provides training employers value, would improve the lives of the poor.[62]

This model would address the credentialing problem in which a more educated population leads to increased educational requirements for even the most menial positions, a problem Dominique identified when she applied for a custodial job and was turned away because she lacked a high school diploma.

Others have taken up the question of how to make investments in human capital more productive for the poor. Participants' lives certainly reflected the fact that these investments have minimal payoff in the current structural context. My findings demonstrate that the belief in human capital, and the time and energy it requires, constrains the poor's access to social capital. In a structural context where social capital provides poor people more immediate and tangible benefits than does human capital, this is a dismal and unfair reality. In a better world where human capital investments would pay off for more than a tiny segment of the poor, they should still have the opportunity to invest in social capital at the same time.

If the goal is long-term financial self-sufficiency, those receiving welfare would be better served by a relaxing of work requirements while pursuing four-year college degrees.[63] While college is not the answer for everyone, making it completely inaccessible to welfare recipients doesn't make sense. As it stands now, recipients can count up to twelve months of vocational education while on welfare, but depending on the state, sometimes have to combine education with twenty to forty hours of work per week to meet welfare work requirements and maintain benefits.[64] "Women with a college degree are not only more likely to work; they also earn more than women without this credential."[65] For some welfare recipients a bachelor's degree could mean the end of poverty.[66]

Both degree-granting and vocational programs for adults might grow more accessible to students by allowing them to develop and use social ties as well. Parents could agree to watch each other's children while taking turns in classes. Programs could be the sites for such parents to meet one another and thereby create the opportunity for them to build social capital, even facilitating babysitting co-ops. Beyond providing the physical space for such ties to grow, a degree-granting program could also offer modest credits for hours worked in child care for fellow students. Various colleges and universities already serving nontraditional college students have offices and centers that could administer such programs.

Funding PPEHRC

PPEHRC's weakened ability to continue KWRU's practice of providing temporary legal housing to members (Human Rights Houses) has widened a hole in Philadelphia's threadbare safety net, though they do have some Human Rights Houses and they continue to engage in squatting in abandoned houses (Takeover Houses). KWRU has provided useful services in an effective manner, including temporary housing to people who the shelter system cannot accommodate. Funding PPHERC at the level required to support a stronger establishment of the Human Rights Houses would make a material difference to many in Philadelphia. Funding it better than it was before would allow it to live up to the ideals outlined in my section on directions for social services agencies. For example, the organization needs to have such strict requirements of reciprocity from its members largely because its organizational resources are so scant. More support would give KWRU more security to offer a buffer to those members who need it most, even when they have little to offer in return. There are practical reasons why those who don't reciprocate sufficiently are pushed out of the organization; adequate funding would allow for a more lenient policy, including warnings and reciprocity exemptions when warranted.

There is a notable precedent for funding organizations like KWRU. As part of the War on Poverty, the Economic Opportunity Act of 1964[67] created the Office of Economic Opportunity, which allowed community groups to receive public funds to provide assistance at the local level.[68] Community Action Agencies are nonprofit private and public organizations established under the Economic Opportunity Act of 1964 and funded through the Community Services Block Grant. Robert Beezat argues:

> One of the most significant successes of the first years of the War on Poverty was the strong emphasis on organizing and empowering people in

poor communities to take control of many aspects of their lives (education, job opportunities and training, crime control, health care, and legal issues, to name a few).

The original intent of the War on Poverty was not only to create safety net programs. It was to identify, train, and nurture the leaders and residents in low-income communities to mobilize and take control of their own destinies.

That kind of work was undertaken by local Community Action Agencies (CAAs) and it was so effective that it threatened the existing power structures.[69]

Today there are approximately a thousand Community Action Agencies.[70] These organizations seek to reduce poverty, promote financial security among the poor, and revitalize communities. They offer broad services to poor people to promote these goals, under their Community Services Block Grants.[71] Although Barack Obama proposed cutting funding for this program in 2011 and again in 2014, in spite of his own history as a community organizer who worked with groups like them,[72] according to publicly available information from the Administration for Children and Families the cuts were not implemented.[73]

The large grants that allowed KWRU to operate Human Rights Houses so effectively came from the Ford Foundation. KWRU lost its funding in 2009, the same year that the foundation changed its strategy to a business-minded approach that demanded proof of program results in a short period of time.[74] In June 2015, however, the Ford Foundation announced that inequality—"We are talking about inequality in all its forms—in influence, access, agency, resources, and respect"—would be the focus of its funding. The foundation's website references inequality's role in most social ills and the way in which it weakens economic growth and undermines social cohesion, pledging sharp increases from previous funding. Darren Walker, the new president of the foundation, has pledged to return Ford to its prior role as a supporter of organizations that address inequality in a way that recognizes that change takes time. Perhaps in this context, PPEHRC will regain its large foundation funding to accompany the very small grants it has been able to gather recently. Many more major funders need to get into this line of work.

Conclusion

This research focuses on social ties, but beyond microsociological mechanisms, the need for macroeconomic policy changes remains greater than ever. Reviewing Robert Putnam's policy recommendations in his 2015 *Our Kids: The American Dream in Crisis,* which include expanding and protecting antipoverty programs in general and the EITC specifically, funding child care and parental leave, and a number of policy changes related to education, Jill Lepore writes, "All of these ideas are admirable, many are excellent, none are new, and, at least at the federal level, few are achievable. The American political imagination has become as narrow as the gap between rich and poor is wide." I disagree with Lepore's assessment of these policies' achievability. Some interventions are less likely than others, to be sure, but research documents that the American public does want government intervention in these realms, and recent history demonstrates that in fact they are realistic. For example, in 2014 journalist Sandra Shea discussed her reaction to recent suggestions of raising the minimum wage:

> "Raise the minimum wage? Never going to happen." Fortunately, I was wrong. In the past year, the national conversation has shifted dramatically and quickly. Following President Obama's 2013 State of the Union address, seven states and the District of Columbia have raised their own minimum wages, and more than 30 states are debating the issue. Just last week, [Philadelphia] Mayor Nutter raised the wage that companies doing business with the city must pay their workers, to $12 an hour. Obama has recently proposed an expansion of the earned income tax credit that targets low-income workers. And nine states have introduced bills that would expand or create the earned income tax credit for their residents.

Rather than assuming that policies to reduce inequality and ameliorate the worst effects of dire poverty are unrealistic, we can aim high and hope and work for meaningful change.

KWRU/PPEHRC rightly insists that safe, affordable housing is a human right. Without it, the poor cannot build stable lives. And the costs to society of homelessness are enormous; as with health promotion and disease prevention, proactive intervention is less expensive than attending to untreated consequences. Housing subsidies are a better choice for society than dealing with the direct and indirect effects of homelessness.[75] Study participants' lives reveal the absolute necessity of housing subsidies and child care subsidies as the foundation for the kind of possibility for mobility that everyone in the United States believes should be universal. If we link the education and training available to the poor to jobs that pay a living wage, we might begin to have the society many argue we already do, in which hard work pays off for most people.

As the privatization of public support persists, social ties will continue to shape the poor's ability to survive. Kin ties will be crucial for some poor people; disposable ties will undoubtedly play a large role as well, both for those without kin available and for those who have only limited kin support. People like Diva, Jasmine, and Leslie exemplify how invaluable kin ties can be. However, the existence of kin ties does not necessarily mean deep and productive support from those ties, as the cases of Kia, Alyssa, and Betty suggest. As the need for a private safety net endures and perhaps grows, competing possibilities are equally likely: social ties may be forced to bear heavier burdens and therefore fray more frequently, multiplying the need for disposable ties, in order to replace ever-disappearing ones, or they may adapt to new circumstances and become more sustainable, particularly if organizations like KWRU become more prevalent as a means to help people cope with poverty.[76] Doing research in Philadelphia for a 2014 story, Sandra Shea found that "many of those who help are struggling themselves. While working on this report, we found strong networks and communities of low-income people helping each other. We found generosity and kindness where people could ill afford to be generous, and few reasons to be kind."[77]

Such observations suggest the possibility that organizations such as KWRU can grow, and in this way can make the poor better able to pool their resources to help one another. Members who leave the group, such as Helen, show the effect of forgoing or forsaking these ties. Sustainable ties can be broken, but they have more resilience than do disposable ties and do not depend on kinship. As such, they offer a source of support to poor people who would otherwise lack social support. KWRU may not be replicable; founded and run by a charismatic figure with the skill to get foundation funding and to whip up passionate outrage among members at protests, KWRU is unusual in important respects. Yet the variety of social ties helps us understand how social ties function among poor people and illustrates the range of ways in which people cope with poverty; extended kin ties, disposable ties, and sustainable ties are all elements of the survival strategies of the poor. To the extent that other KWRUs surface and develop over time, they will provide an important piece of the patchwork of help on which the poor rely, a piece different from what social service agencies offer and from family assistance limited to those with strong and productive kin ties. Rather, it is a sort of communal assistance to which people living in poverty can contribute and on which they can draw. These ties provide a source of social support similar to what disposable ties offer, but have greater stability. Certainly, organizations like KWRU alone cannot solve the problems of the poor, but they can help provide a productive, collective response to increasing poverty and the deepening challenges to survival.

Research Design, Methods, and Data Analysis

This book is based on in-depth, semi-structured interviews as well as some ethnographic participant observation. I conducted participant observation at social service programs, the KWRU office, and KWRU rallies and protests, where I recruited participants, and in the neighborhoods associated with the organizations and in which the participants reside. But this is better understood as an interview study rather than an ethnography, one reason detailed biographies do not appear.

The questions I explored revolve in part around identity, stigma, and self-worth, and are therefore sensitive, making them suited to qualitative methods. Such research depends on trust and rapport to get the most sincere answers possible, and in-depth conversations create this foundation. My research aimed to explore meanings and processes, another characteristic making qualitative work most appropriate.

In selecting participants, designing my interview guide and analyzing the data, I considered factors such as race, age, history of welfare receipt, experience of homelessness, and number of children. I focused on women, since the majority of means-tested social programs are targeted to children of unmarried mothers, though I interviewed two men in KWRU who were key leaders of the group and who seemed to influence other members as well as the direction of the organization.

I chose program sites in neighborhoods that vary in their degree of poverty concentration, allowing me to observe poor participants who live in high-poverty neighborhoods as well as those who reside in lower-poverty neighborhoods, though I didn't find any meaningful differences between them. Their individual economic situations played a larger role than did the poverty level of their residential neighborhoods.

I conducted all my research in Philadelphia.[1] Philadelphia can be divided into various regions or neighborhoods. At the time of data collection,[2] the Philadelphia City Planning Commission divided Philadelphia into twelve regions for planning purposes, and I conducted data collection in ten of the twelve regions.[3] The Philadelphia Neighborhood Information System sorts Philadelphia into 69 neighborhoods; I conducted research in 26 neighborhoods.[4]

According to the 2000 U.S. Census (via the cartographic modeling laboratory at the University of Pennsylvania), the lowest poverty rate was in the northeast and northwest sections of the city; the west and lower north neighborhoods have the highest concentrations of poverty.[5]

Site and Sample Selection

I began collecting data in November 2003 and did my final interview in March 2006. The map included in this appendix shows the location of the KWRU office and where KWRU participants resided. KWRU was located in the West Kensington area of the city and high poverty neighborhoods surrounded it. KWRU/PPEHRC members live all over the city and their sense of community comes from the organization, not the neighborhood. Some study participants, especially KWRU members, lived near the office in West Kensington, but others lived in West Philadelphia, the upper northeast, and elsewhere. Two KWRU participants lived in West and Southwest Philadelphia neighborhoods.

In addition to talking to members of KWRU, I recruited twenty women from various social programs around the city. I recruited these twenty participants from eleven[6] locations (eight different agencies), as described below:

- A Head Start in Pennsport, a neighborhood in South Philadelphia, yielded one participant (a parent of a student there);
- A Head Start in West Philadelphia yielded two participants (parents of students);
- A parenting class at a multiservice agency in West Kensington yielded two participants;
- An employment training/placement class at the same multiservice agency[7] in West Kensington yielded two participants;

- A GED preparation class managed by an agency in Fishtown and held in West Kensington[8] yielded one participant;
- A GED preparation class at an agency in West Kensington yielded one participant.
- This same agency had another location a few blocks away that yielded two participants,[9] both of whom are agency employees and former students/clients;
- An employment training and placement program in Germantown yielded two participants;
- An employment training/GED preparation class in South Philadelphia yielded three participants;
- A South Philadelphia satellite of a program designed to increase literacy and math skills, and aid clients attain GEDs if needed, yielded one participant; and
- Another satellite of this program, in Center City, yielded three participants.

The racial breakdown of this recruitment is as follows: seven African Americans came from three different agencies. Seven whites came from three different agencies (four locations). Six Latinas came from three different agencies (four locations). Those I recruited often lived near these agencies; however, at times this was not the case.[10] There is greater diversity in non-KWRU participants' residential locations; for example, non-KWRU participants but no KWRU participants lived in South Philadelphia and Germantown. But participants from both groups lived in Kensington, West Kensington, West Philadelphia, and the Northeast.

I recruited five additional non-KWRU participants by referral: two African Americans referred to me by two KWRU participants; one Latina I met through one KWRU participant and one Latina I met through one non-KWRU participant; and one white participant from a colleague of mine.[11] The figure in this appendix shows all agencies and participant residential locations. The tight clustering in West Kensington of agencies and participants may make it difficult to observe all dots distinctly. Additionally, only forty dots for the fifty participants appear visibly on the map: there are two locations representing three participants each; two locations representing two participants each; one KWRU house where there were two participants; two locations where participants lived so close to each other as to obscure the distinctive dots representing their residences; and finally, one participant lived outside Philadelphia.[12] Clearly, not all agencies or participants are located in the highest poverty neighborhoods. Many agencies and participants are in moderate poverty neighborhoods, and a few participants are even in low poverty neighborhoods.

Half the people I interviewed were members of KWRU and half were not. I was able to explore the distinct ways in which each group thought about poverty, the poor, ideal strategies, social ties, and reciprocity, and the way these modes of thought affected their actions. It permitted a focus on those poor who choose to associate with other poor people through an organization and a comparison with those who interact a good deal less with other poor people, aside from kin.

Without KWRU members in this study, it would have focused on the non-KWRU members—a set of low-income people who rely on a patchwork of government assistance, social services, low-wage work, and kin ties to survive, a story often told. The sample I gathered allowed me to investigate the opportunities provided by KWRU and their impact. The example of KWRU members revealed how much social ties among the poor differ, the importance of nonkin ties for a segment of the poor, and what allows nonkin ties to last over time. Without non-KWRU members in this study, I still would have found in KWRU a network of poor people relying on one another, but would not have realized the causes of isolation in people's lives and how impressive the accomplishments of the KWRU model are.

While Mario Luis Small examined both poor and nonpoor organizationally embedded people in his book *Unanticipated Gains: Origins of Network Inequality in Everyday Life*, all the participants I spoke with were poor, but their organizational embeddedness varied.[13] The KWRU sample covered a variety of levels of commitment, including those only peripherally involved as well as core activists, which allowed me to study the gradations of how these levels of commitment correlate with particular attitudes and actions. In addition, the Kensington Welfare Rights Union has always included many members who do not receive welfare but seek out help from KWRU in securing housing or help with utilities; thus, the membership includes many non–welfare recipients, which the name of the group might tend to obscure.

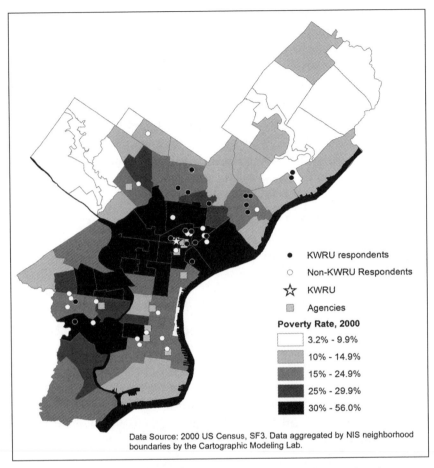

Legend:
- KWRU respondents (●)
- Non-KWRU Respondents (○)
- KWRU (☆)
- Agencies (▨)

Poverty Rate, 2000
- 3.2% - 9.9%
- 10% - 14.9%
- 15% - 24.9%
- 25% - 29.9%
- 30% - 56.0%

Data Source: 2000 US Census, SF3. Data aggregated by NIS neighborhood boundaries by the Cartographic Modeling Lab.

Map A.1. This map of Philadelphia from the Cartographic Modeling Lab at the University of Pennsylvania splits Philadelphia into sixty-nine neighborhoods. The darker the gray, the higher the rate of poverty in the neighborhood.

Participants live in various neighborhoods: Kensington, West Kensington, Juniata, Olney, Logan, North Central, West Philadelphia, South Philadelphia, Point Breeze, and Germantown. This provides variety in participant geography as well as some variety in the poverty rates of participants' neighborhoods.

Originally I planned to interview three sets of people: KWRU members, social program users, and people who were isolated—those needing available services but not using them. After some data collection, when I was nearly done with my planned twenty KWRU interviews and had about five interviews each with people from other agencies and people who were "isolated," I began to recognize that the social program group and the isolated group were not very different from one another. This is partly a function of my recruitment methods. Using referrals from participants to other participants to find an "isolated" group meant, by definition, that the isolated participants were not very isolated; they had a relationship with at least one person, and that person was actively using a social service. However, as I discovered in my data collection and analysis, most participants actively sought to avoid social ties, even if they were not isolated from available services.

Participant Recruitment and Descriptions

When I began the research, I approached KWRU, first trying to reach the organization by phone and then via email. I received an email response from a student working with KWRU as part of a University of Pennsylvania organization called Empty the Shelters, a group of undergraduates who advocated for housing and were working with KWRU. We subsequently met and discussed my planned research. Following this meeting, the student allowed me to accompany her to the KWRU office, where I met another young woman who volunteered by helping KWRU with administrative duties. The two women compiled a list of members they thought might be interested in being interviewed and gave me the phone number of one KWRU activist, Paloma, telling me to discuss my research with her and see what she thought. I called Paloma and she invited me to meet with her in her North Philadelphia neighborhood.

When I met with Paloma a few days later, I came to a subway station in North Philly, ready with my interview guide and tape recorder, set to conduct my first interview. Instead, she and another member picked me up in a car. Paloma drove us all to the house of an elderly woman who couldn't speak English. As I described in chapter 3, I watched Paloma conduct KWRU business—securing a payment plan for a member that let her keep a crucial utility.

There were several more errands before Paloma took us all to her home—where she had taken in a new member and her family, amounting to six extra people in her household—and turned her attention to me. She asked me to tell her more about what I wanted to do, and I explained that I wished to interview members of KWRU, that I sought people of different races and different levels of involvement, and that I was looking mainly for women because many social services and public support programs target women and their children. She went over the list the volunteers had compiled and thought of a few more to add. She said she would talk to people first before giving me their phone numbers, but she thought people would be happy to participate. She and the member with her both agreed to be interviewed.

Soon after this meeting, I attended a protest rally KWRU held outside the mayor's office in City Hall, as described in the Preface. I met many KWRU activists there and reconnected with the members I had met before. Days later I did my first interview with a KWRU participant. I began spending days at the KWRU office, meeting more people on my list and getting better acquainted with those I had met at the protest. As I met and got to know members and told them about my research, I asked them if they wanted to participate. No one turned me down.

Much of my KWRU fieldwork consisted of attending rallies and protests around the city, but I also spent weeks just visiting the office. I did my first several KWRU interviews in the office with members who were there answering phones, helping out, and socializing. Soon I became a fixture at the office and the members who were regularly involved knew me by face and name. They began referring me to other members and frequently provided me with the telephone numbers of prospective interviewees so that I could contact them and request their participation. I also spent some time with key activists outside the office, following them around during the day as they helped people with immediate problems, visited the welfare office, and attended meetings and other events. I spent time at Paloma's home, went out to lunch with Paloma and her babysitter, and accompanied them in picking up Paloma's children from school. I recorded brief jottings by hand in a small notebook during observations and typed up these notes on my computer when I arrived home, expanding my jottings into fuller narratives.

I continued going to rallies and other events and met more members. Seventeen months after my first meeting with Paloma, I went to a public hearing at City Hall at which KWRU members were scheduled to speak. Those I already knew greeted me warmly and I introduced myself to the new faces, including one woman, Rebecca, who volunteered to be interviewed that week and told me she was living in a KWRU house. We scheduled the interview before she left that day, because she had no working phone. When I went to her house the following week, I met two other women who were living at the house as well and recruited them for this study. I attended another protest which led to my final two KWRU participants; an activist gave me the telephone number of a woman he thought might be interested, and she in turn connected me to another participant I had previously recruited but had been unable to schedule because her phone has been disconnected. Occasionally I met KWRU members who were more peripherally involved and dropped off the radar before I was able to conduct interviews with them, but no KWRU member I met refused to participate.

I began recruitment at social service agencies after conducting the majority of the KWRU interviews. I chose agencies in a few different ways: I conducted online searches and then called and/or emailed the agencies; I asked other researchers for recommendations; I got referrals to additional agencies from agency directors who had already helped me with recruitment; I called one agency I saw profiled in a free neighborhood newspaper; and I called a Head Start I happened to see near where I lived at the time. When I contacted agencies, I introduced myself, naming my university affiliation, explaining that I was a sociologist interviewing low-income people in Philadelphia, and asked if I might be permitted to visit and meet some students or clients to invite to participate in my research.

The most common way I recruited participants at programs was by obtaining permission from agency directors to address a group of students in a class (a parenting class, GED class, etc.). I typically said something similar to the script for my oral consent form, shown below. I then passed around a piece of paper and got the names and telephone numbers of people who thought they might be interested. At that stage I left it open, knowing that people might have questions or might want to think it over before committing to it. I had great success with this method, calling those who gave me contact information soon after meeting them, and reminding them who I was and what I was doing. They nearly always agreed to take part—and scheduled an interview—during that telephone conversation. However, of course many of those I addressed in classes did not sign up at all.

I also met participants through connections with agency directors, administrators, and employees. In some cases they gave me permission to approach people, as I did at Head Starts when parents dropped off or picked up their children. I introduced myself, told them about my research, asked them if they would be interested in being interviewed, got their telephone numbers, and sometimes scheduled the interviews right then. In other cases the agency workers introduced me to individuals who they thought met my criteria. Then one-on-one I was able to discuss the study with the potential participant and go from there.

I contacted many social service agencies to gain these modes of access to non-KWRU participants. Some agency administrators acted as gatekeepers rather than as facilitators. For example, at one agency I emailed and met in person with a very sympathetic administrator. She was enthusiastic about helping me with my research, proposed I post a flyer, and offered to ask GED instructors to solicit volunteers for me. I felt that potential participants would want to meet me before agreeing to take part, and she permitted me to visit one GED class, from which I recruited one participant. While I was not able to do further recruitment with this agency, another employee from it referred me to a director at another GED training program, which led to recruitment of four women from two satellites of the program around the city. In another case, late in data collection, an agency director who had helped me to recruit three participants from his agency referred me to another agency. My initial contact was quite promising and the individual indicated he could find me more participants than I would even need. We met in person and I believed the recruitment would move forward, but he stopped responding to my emails or phone calls without helping me recruit anyone.

I conducted interviews with fifty participants. I recruited twenty-five from KWRU and twenty from other agencies. The remaining five I met through other means as described above: four through other participants and one through a colleague. By definition none of these five people were completely isolated—they knew at least one other person who knew how to contact them, and who knew enough of their situation to think they'd be a good person for me to interview. Fully isolated people I would never meet unless I wandered through neighborhoods and knocked on doors (a tactic widely known to be inefficient and ineffective in recruiting participants for this type of study). Even then, those willing to be interviewed at length about sensitive and personal issues by a total stranger who knocked on their doors, would likely be less isolated, less suspicious of strangers, and more outgoing than the typical person. In short, it is virtually impossible to successfully recruit the most isolated people for this kind of study.[14] Those with something to hide may have been less likely to end up in my sample; people may have been afraid to talk to me if they were engaged in criminal activities, child abuse, welfare fraud, were victims of domestic violence, or were homeless. And yet, of course many participants were victims of domestic violence and had experienced homelessness; some told me they had sold drugs.

The non-KWRU stage of fieldwork did not go as smoothly as had my KWRU fieldwork, partially because there were fewer activities for me to observe or participate in and so I was unable to conduct participant observation to the same extent as I had been with KWRU. Therefore, I usually made requests for interviews before I was able to establish rapport or become acquainted with potential participants. Consequently, I had some refusals and many of those I met and told about my research did not sign up or give me their telephone numbers. There were a few who agreed and signed up but never scheduled an interview, or who later declined to be interviewed. I had to omit two participants from my sample when they participated in first interviews but refused to meet with me to finish the remainder. This was a particularly frustrating incident for a researcher; for example, one woman repeatedly agreed to meet with me and then was never available to schedule. After months of attempting to follow up she finally admitted she did not want to finish the interview. In retrospect I realize I would have been better off taking her hesitation as a refusal and moving on, both to save time and to spare her the discomfort she might have felt in rejecting me.

For both the KWRU and non-KWRU interviews, I confronted obstacles inherent in research focusing on those with unstable lives. Many participants lacked consistent phone service and sometimes lacked consistent housing. This of course made it more difficult to schedule or reschedule interviews. With no car, I traveled all around the city for my research on SEPTA, Philadelphia's public transportation system. This required additional time in the field, as I often traveled an hour or more, each way, to get to and from a participant's home for an interview, and I frequently had to do this more than once to conduct multiple interviews with participants. Yet most participants lacked a car too, and the time I invested provided me with additional information about their lives. Another feature of the somewhat unstable lives of the people I interviewed meant that at times I traveled great distances to people's houses and found them not there at all, sometimes even when I had called to confirm before making the trip. For one participant, it was only on the third occasion I traveled over an hour to her house that she was there for our appointment.

I interviewed two men in KWRU, but the rest of the people I interviewed were women. At the time of the interviews, participants ranged in age from eighteen to fifty-nine years old. As stated above, two participants are men and forty-eight are women. Of the fifty participants I interviewed, eighteen participants are African American, sixteen are white, and sixteen are Latina. KWRU does not keep official membership records that I can compare to the ages and races of participants, but my sample selection in terms of age and gender roughly represented those I saw at the office at multiple visits per week over a period of several months. I observed a more diverse group at rallies because members often brought their children, so children comprised a large percentage of those present at protests. In addition, there were frequently men at the protests who I did not regularly see at the office, usually boyfriends or husbands of female members. As for race, I did not meet many white participants in the course of participant observation with KWRU, but through networking with other members I was able to find white members to interview. I selected my sample nonrandomly, through contacts made during participant observation and through referrals from participants.

Racial and ethnic categories are of course complicated; seven of the participants told me they were bi- or multiracial and ethnic.[15] In those cases, I generally assigned the participants to the racial/ethnic category they told me they most identified with. For example, one white participant had a white mother and a Latino father. She was raised by her mother and did not know her father. She told me she "felt" more white than Latina and that she could pass as white. Three Latina participants (two sisters and their cousin) had Latina mothers and African American fathers. Again, they had been raised by their mothers and did not identify as African American. One African American participant had a white mother and an African American father; she was in contact with both parents and told me she identified more as African American because when people look at her, they see her as black rather than as white. Finally, two African Americans described themselves as having multiracial heritage; one told me she most identified as black, noting however that she'd normally call herself "mixed with a lot of stuff," including Latina, Native American, and Caucasian as well as African American. I classified the other multiracial participant as African American, because she noted that most people see her as black. However, she told me she sees herself as "other" and that is what she checks on forms that require a choice of racial/ethnic categories.

It is important to note that while the study sample was racially balanced, I did not select participants as a means to achieve representativeness. Indeed, the sample was small and not randomly selected. I cannot accurately report that, for example, 5 percent of all KWRU members violate reciprocity norms, that 50 percent of white KWRU members are activists, or that African Americans are more likely to be in GED programs than are Latinas.

In both the KWRU and non-KWRU participant recruitment, I encountered great difficulty in finding whites, which I felt was important to creating a sample that would provide a range of experiences and opinions. KWRU has white members, but they tend to be more peripherally involved and so I did not happen to meet them as casually and frequently as I met the Latina and African American members of the group. I required more direct assistance from other KWRU members in finding and recruiting KWRU whites than I did for the KWRU African Americans and Latinas. When it came to the non-KWRU participants I had serious difficulties; I'm not certain why this was the case but there are a number of possible explanations.[16] Whereas I easily recruited Latinas and African Americans at the first agencies I approached to find such participants, I had to contact many more agencies to recruit whites, often finding that agencies other researchers assured me had white clients when they had done research in prior years seemed no longer to have many. The two partial interviews I conducted but which are not included in my final sample, mentioned above, were both with whites—one from KWRU and one from a social program.

Data Collection, Management, and Analysis

I spent time at KWRU and the agency sites to see what was going on, observing interactions among clients/members and between clients and staff. I watched and listened as clients spoke with instructors and interacted with each other. I observed material around the sites: brochures, pamphlets, signs, and posters, and took samples with me when available. All this observation gave me a fuller picture of the context in which I found participants, though I had much more of it for KWRU than for the other agencies. I took notes on site when possible and then typed detailed field notes when I got home. My field notes helped me make sense of my data and aided me in designing my interview guide.

I read a description of the research to each participant before initiating the interview and I obtained oral consent (the text I read appears below). I gave each participant the option not to have me tape record the interviews, saying I could take notes instead. No one declined to be recorded, though some participants occasionally asked me to turn off the recorder to tell me something they wanted to stay private, a request I honored by excluding these comments from my research—as it happens, they were all tangential to the questions of this study.

In tape recorded interviews I asked participants about their life histories, including occupational, educational, and welfare experience. I asked them about their neighborhoods, their views on welfare and work, their opinions about what should be done about poverty, their self-images and experiences with stigma, their financial struggles, their perceptions of both the working and the nonworking poor, and what they thought other poor people's views are. I also talked to them about what kinds of help they receive, what kind of help they give to others, and their involvement with different groups and organizations. Some of the subjects explored in this book arose organically in the data analysis process. Reciprocity was not a topic I undertook to study in the research. However, it emerged inductively as an important theme in the analytic process when I discovered that all participants discussed the importance of mutual aid and obligations in their daily lives, and of the added complexities of reciprocity within KWRU. I was able to compare these data to responses from non-KWRU interviewees because asking about help given and received spoke to these questions. The interview guide is included below, as is a participant key, showing pseudonyms, ages, number of children, racial/ethnic classifications, experience being homeless, and KWRU membership.

Oral Consent

I obtained consent orally from all participants rather than requiring them to read and sign consent forms. I chose this as a method to further a more relaxed interview. The text I read to them is below:

> My name is Joanie Mazelis. I'm going out into different neighborhoods in Philadelphia and talking to people who know what it's like to deal with financial struggles. I think it's really important to talk to people, because we hear a lot about what people in government and the media think but not enough about what people experiencing difficulties think themselves. I want to know about your life, your opinions, and your experiences. I really think that talking with ordinary people about their lives is the best way to inform the public about how families cope with financial struggles.
>
> Everything people tell me is anonymous. I remove any identifying information like real names and addresses from the transcripts of the tapes of the interviews. No one will know who you are, but people will hear what you have to say. You are the teacher—the expert. There will be no formal interview or forms to fill out. Instead, we will talk and get to know each other today. I may want to talk to you another time if we don't have enough time today and I still have questions left I want to ask you. I'll make sure you have my phone number, too, so you can always let me know if you think of something you want to tell me about after we're done talking.
>
> I'll ask you about several different aspects of your experience, like how you got to where you are now, any struggles or difficulties you may have, issues that are important to you, and your plans and hopes for the future.

There may also be things I don't think to ask about that you might want to talk about, and that's fine.

I usually like to tape record the conversations I have with families so I can get the story right. If you want me to turn the recorder off for any reason, I can press the pause button. That way you can tell me things off the record. Some people prefer not to use the tape and ask me to take notes instead. Either option is fine with me, but I prefer to tape record so I can give you my full attention instead of taking notes. Also, if I tape record our conversations, I know I won't miss anything.

Do you want to choose a name you'd like to go by, and names for your children, so we can keep everything confidential? Or I can choose fake names for you if you want.

Although I have a limited budget, I give each person who agrees to talk to me something in return for the time they spend with me. I know your time is valuable. So I can give you $10 today. If we end up having to talk a lot more after today, I can try to pay you for that, too. I pay people at the beginning of our talks rather than at the end, so people will feel free to not answer a question or to stop the conversation for whatever reason. You may do this at any time during my conversation with you. Participation in this study is completely voluntary, and you can discontinue participation at any time.

Do you have any questions?

Do you agree to participate?

After obtaining consent, I began the interview. All names reported in the book are pseudonyms, chosen by participants, except in rare cases when they asked me to choose for them. At times I omitted or changed minor details to protect confidentiality, and I left out participant pseudonyms completely in places for the same reason. It should be noted that many KWRU members specifically asked that I refer to them by their real names, but professional concerns prevented me from doing so. Participants are justly proud of their words and seek refuge from the invisibility that characterizes the lives and ideas of the poor most of the time. KWRU activists frequently mentioned that they've been invisible for so long; they shared hopes that maybe this book would help them be less obscured. I hope that by telling their stories I have fulfilled their desires in part.

Interview Guide

I devised a semi-structured interview guide, arranged by general topics, and printed it in small font so it fit on two sides of a single sheet of paper, and brought a copy to each interview for reference. I generally covered the topics in the order they appear below, but at times participants jumped ahead to talk about their children or work, and when that happened, I allowed the conversation to flow naturally, noting for myself anything skipped or covered. For each topic, I had a basic question I usually asked as appears below. Italicized text within topic areas indicate items I kept in mind to note whether and when participants offered information that spoke to these issues; when they didn't spontaneously mention these, I followed up with additional questions to gather the information.

1. LIFE HISTORY: I usually like to start with a very basic and general question: tell me about yourself. [How did you get to where you are now? *If necessary to get full narrative—i.e. if participant gives one-word answers—ask:* Tell me the story of your life. *Probe for: relationship history: circumstances surrounding birth of children, what it's been like raising kids; residential history; educational history: how far went in school, where and for what (if specialized vo-tech or college); occupational history: what kind of employment, how consistent, stable, etc.; welfare history: history of unemployment, struggles, difficulties making ends meet, etc.*

2. NEIGHBORHOOD: What is your neighborhood like? What is it like living here? What are your neighbors like? *Probe for:* Do you think there's a lot of people who aren't working or who are on welfare? How do you feel about that? What do you think of your neighborhood? What is the best thing about it? What is the worst thing about it? Are most of your friends and relatives nearby? Do they live in other neighborhoods?

3. DAILY LIFE: Tell me what a typical day is like for you. [*If participant has partner:* For your spouse/boyfriend/ girlfriend, etc.?]

4. CHILDREN: [*If participant has children*] Tell me about each of your kids. What is life like for them? What is a typical day like?

What is school like for them? What do they do during the school year after school? What do they do during the summer? What do you enjoy most about them? What do you worry about most about them? What kinds of problems do they face?

5. PROBLEMS/BLESSINGS: Tell me the best thing in your life— what are you most satisfied with? What about the worst? If you could change one thing about your life (or more than one), what would it be? How would you change it?

6. HOPES/PLANS: What are your hopes/plans for the future [*Probe for both—aspirations and expectations are often very different*]? In your own life? What about for your kid(s)? What do you think your life will be like in one year? Five years? Way down the road? What about for your kid(s)? Do you think your situation will improve? If yes, how will that happen? If no, why not?

7. WORKING/WELFARE: We talked a little before about your work history [*If did not come up in response to question 1, ask now:* Have you ever worked outside of your home for pay? [*If participant has worked/is working:* What is it like working? Tell me about your work experiences. [*Probe all participants:* Even if you're not sure, what do you think it's like? Do you think there are a lot of jobs out there? What kinds of jobs?] [*If participant has received or is receiving welfare—or if did not come up in response to question 1, ask: Have you ever received welfare?*]: What's it like being on welfare? What do you think of welfare compared to working?] What do you think about people on welfare? What do you have in common with them? How are you different?

8. STRUGGLE: Tell me about what people you know do when times get tough and they are struggling to get by. How did they manage? Tell me about a time when it was like that for you. How did you/ do you manage? What was it like? How did it change you?

9. STIGMA: Everyone has been treated badly by others at some point because of one thing or another. Sometimes people have opinions about people who don't have that much money. What kinds of things have you heard said? Do you think those things are true? Have you ever felt that you were treated differently or unfairly compared to people who have more money? Tell me about that.

Tell me about a time you were treated badly because . . . [*pick relevant life history item based on previous responses, for example:* you didn't finish high school; you receive cash assistance; you use food stamps; someone thought you were poor, etc.]. How did you react? How has that affected you? Do you think people see you as poor? Do you think of yourself as poor?

10. SELF-ESTEEM: How do you feel about yourself as a person? What are some of the things you are good at? What are some of the things you would like to change?

11. POVERTY POLICY/GOVERNMENT HELP: How do you think some people end up with lots of money and some have very little? Do you think that's fair? Tell me more. What do you think the government should do about poverty and that kind of stuff? Do you think the government should help poor people? Whose fault is it if people are poor? What do you think about welfare? Why are people on welfare? [*If received/receiving welfare,* why did/do you receive welfare?] What should people who are struggling do? What do you think those people might think about those things? If the president were to ask you what the government should do, what advice would you give him?

12. PRACTICAL EVERYDAY HELP: A lot of people rely on help from others to get by. People tell me that sometimes their friends or family members help them out, either day-to-day or in an emergency [*for example,* if the kids get sick or a major appliance breaks]. What kinds of help have you gotten [*for example,* money, clothes, food, child care]? Who have you gotten help from? Tell me about a time when you got that kind of help. What was going on for you then? What was it like? How comfortable did you feel about asking for help? Tell me about a time when someone came to you for help. How did you feel about that?

13. INFORMATIONAL HELP: Sometimes we learn about things from people we know, like where to go to get things, which stores have good bargains, where good schools are, things about the neighborhood or the city, etc. Tell me about a time when someone helped you with information. What about a time when you helped someone else with information?

14. EMPLOYMENT HELP: Sometimes people we know help us get jobs. Has anyone ever told you about a job or helped you get a job? Have you ever done that for someone else? Tell me about that.

15. MANAGING; COMBINING/SHARING RESOURCES: How else do you manage? Have you pooled resources [money, food stamps, housing, transportation, etc.] with someone else to get by?

16. EMOTIONAL SUPPORT: Tell me about people who you are close to. How often do you see/talk to these people? What makes you feel close to them? What do you share? What do you do for each other? [Give help? Advice?]

17. ALL HELP [Recap—cover all bases]: Who helps you with practical things, like food, child care, and money? What about for emotional support? Who do you go to for information about things? What about if you needed a place to stay? Do you think you get all the help you need? Tell me about what it's like to get help from others. What is it like to give help to others?

18. COMMUNITY SERVICES: What kinds of help have you gotten from a community group or organization? Food? Shelter? Clothing? Medical? Dental? Children's services? Educational services? Any other kinds of services? Tell me about services you've needed but couldn't get. What about services that are available that you haven't taken advantage of? What other services would you like to have in your neighborhood?

19. GROUPS/ORGANIZATIONS: Are you involved in any groups [churches, voluntary organization, KWRU, etc.]? How did you get involved with that? How did you decide to join/go there? Tell me about the people you know from there. How has being involved with that group changed you?

20. Is there anything I didn't ask you about that you wanted to talk about? [*Also get any missing demographic information: age, educational level completed, etc.*] Thank you so much for helping me out with my research project!

Sample Descriptive Statistics

	Age*	Number of children**	Homeless ever
All participants (50)	32.5	2.68	32
KWRU (25)	37.3	3.48	23
Non-KWRU (25)	27.7	1.88	9
African Americans (18)	35.0	2.56	14
Whites (16)	34.2	3.25	9
Latinas (16)	28.0	2.25	8
KWRU African Americans (9)	40.2	3.00	9
KWRU Whites (8)	39.4	3.88	7
KWRU Latinas (8)	31.9	3.63	7
Non-KWRU African Americans (9)	29.8	2.11	5
Non-KWRU Whites (8)	29.0	2.63	3
Non-KWRU Latinas (8)	24.1	0.88	1

*Average, rounded to the nearest tenth.
** Average, rounded to the nearest hundredth.

Participant Key

Non KWRU Participants

Pseudonym, Age	Number of children	Race/Ethnicity	Homeless ever
Alyssa, 23	4	White	No
April, 25	2	African American	No
Bebe, 18	0	Latina	Yes
Betty, 31	1	Latina	No
Bianca, 30	3	White	No
Carole, 35	5	White	Yes
Denise, 25	3	African American	Yes
Diva, 24	2	White	Yes
Dominique, 44	4	White	No
Gail, 29	2	White	No
Inez, 28	1	Latina	No
Jasmine, 20	1	African American	No
Jen, 24	0	White	No
Karen, 40	2	African American	Yes
Kelly, 22	1	Latina	No
Kia, 26	3	African American	Yes
Kim, 44	3	African American	Yes
Leslie, 23	1	White	No
Mandy, 29	3	African American	Yes
Maria, 20	1	Latina	No
Nicole, 21	1	Latina	No
Nina, 24	1	African American	Yes
Polly, 21	1	Latina	No
Savannah, 32	1	Latina	No
Stacie, 35	1	African American	No

KWRU Participants

Pseudonym, Age	Number of children	Race/Ethnicity	Homeless ever
Alice, 47	7	White	No
Amanda, 41	2	White	Yes
Becky, 58	2	White	Yes
Carmen, 36	2	Latina	Yes
Cate, 43	3	Latina	Yes
CC, 44	4	African American	Yes
Colleen, 29	4	White	Yes
Dora, 43	5	Latina	Yes
Helen, 45	9	White	Yes
James, 34	5	African American	Yes
Jessie, 26	4	Latina	Yes
Lina, 22	2	African American	Yes
Marie, 42	3	African American	Yes
Marisol, 25	3	Latina	Yes
Maureen, 33	2	White	Yes
Naomi, 26	2	African American	Yes
Paloma, 28	3	Latina	Yes
Pauline, 41	4	African American	Yes
Rebecca, 33	2	White	Yes
Rosa, 33	7	Latina	Yes
Shy, 39	1	African American	Yes
Stefanie, 21	2	Latina	No
Tina, 29	3	White	Yes
Walter, 55	3	African American	Yes
Why, 59	3	African American	Yes

I conducted about half the interviews in one session and the other half in two or more sessions; five interviews required three or more visits. I interviewed all but one participant in person; one participant I interviewed exclusively via telephone due to her health limitations. I conducted over half the interviews in the participants' homes. I met with some of the rest of the participants in private rooms at the agencies where I recruited them. I interviewed five participants at the KWRU office. One KWRU member came to my office, and three KWRU activists I interviewed on the go—at restaurants, in their cars, or other locations as they went about their errands for the day. I conducted all interviews in locations of participants' choosing. In addition to the interviews, averaging 3.5 hours apiece, I also wrote field notes after each interview, visit to KWRU or agency, or telephone conversation, and I kept all email correspondence with social service agency employees as I recruited participants.

A professional transcription service transcribed all interviews, which I then coded using NVivo qualitative analysis software, a code-based theory building program, and I relied on inductive analysis and grounded theory techniques to code the data.[17] I read interview transcripts carefully and used the software to attach labels to text from interviews based on the theme or themes of the interview content in a process of open coding.[18] Then, within each theme I coded further, for more detail, so that patterns became apparent across interviews, in a process of axial coding.

The qualitative research this study used was well-suited to the research questions, due to the focus on feelings, meanings, and experiences of participants.[19] As noted above, I recruited a racially diverse sample not to achieve representativeness, but to maximize variability across the range of potential participants and responses. The study encompassed observations and questions about ideas and norms within KWRU and among nonmembers relying on social programs and services for assistance, and comparisons of the experiences of people with different attitudes, leading to theoretical insights. The findings reported follow Strauss and Corbin's model of qualitative analysis: "We are referring not to the quantifying of qualitative data but rather to a non-mathematical process of interpretation, carried out for the purpose of discovering concepts and relationships in raw data and then organizing these into a theoretical explanatory scheme."[20] In-depth interviews, which allowed themes to emerge inductively, also yielded theoretical saturation:[21] each participant provided insights, which added to my understanding of the mechanisms of social ties within KWRU and outside it, and participant observation and interview processes portrayed the range of different experiences, eventually producing only affirmation of previously recorded information. As Small states, "The strengths of qualitative work come from understanding *how* and *why*, not understanding *how many*."[22] The findings reported do not reference the frequencies of particular responses, as the meaning lies in the range of variability. Rather than aiming to present a representative account of social ties for the poor, this study describes a range of experiences with social ties among members of an antipoverty organization, contrasted with the experiences of nonmembers.[23]

Author's Note: The Writing Process

Completing data collection and initial coding didn't mean I was able to leap to writing this book. My first attempt was a hurried, roughly-thrown-together drafty tome with a great deal of interview excerpts and scant analysis. I mention this because I believe many academics, especially early in their careers, flounder with their writing, struggling with the imposter syndrome, lacking confidence in their abilities, ideas, and analyses. I am immensely proud of this book, but I have at times shared every one of these feelings.

In her book *Unequal Childhoods*, Annette Lareau reflects on her analytical and writing process: "The intellectual journey was not complete when we finished our visits with the families. In some ways, it had just begun. Because of the intensity of the research experience (as well as changes in my personal life), I followed the active period of field-work with a lull of reflection."[24] I followed a similar path.

In the summer of 2012, I reread drafts of chapters I had written in 2006 and started by making a list of all the arguments I thought I could make—everything I thought the book was "about."[25] With that starting point, I constructed a book prospectus, but I knew I needed to reanalyze my data to be sure the data supported the ideas I thought they did. I began reviewing interview transcripts, and in the summer and fall of 2013, I reread and recoded every interview transcript and all my field notes, using an updated version of the NVivo qualitative coding software I had used in 2006, saw my plans for the book shift, revised my prospectus, and began the work of drafting the chapters of the book.

Throughout 2013 and 2014, I read literature and presented seeds of ideas at conferences, where I got invaluable suggestions for directions of analysis and relevant literature, refined my arguments, and revised chapters. I completed a first draft of this book in November 2014, and the final draft in January 2016. For the benefit of any writer struggling to get words on the page, I will say my experience taught me that starting is the most important part, and writing is an iterative process.

NOTES

INTRODUCTION

1 Putnam 2015.

2 Section 8 is the commonly used name for the Housing Choice Voucher Program, funded by the government through the U.S. Department of Housing and Urban Development. A tenant with a Section 8 voucher can use it to rent housing and pay a portion of his or her income on rent (usually around 30 percent), with the government paying the balance of a fair market rent to the landlord. There are waiting lists for vouchers, and even when tenants receive them they must find a suitable property with a landlord who will accept the voucher and which will pass Section 8 inspection (U.S. Department of Housing and Urban Development 2013).

3 Lepore 2015. Even when we talk about how inequality has widened and life is beyond difficult for "the poor," it's not clear who or how many people in the United States we mean. As Shea (2014) notes, "While the accepted number of people in poverty is about 46 million, that number is based on a flawed system for measuring poverty. The current measure was created in the 1960s, based on food costs, which at that time comprised about a quarter of people's incomes. Today, food costs are about 6 percent, while housing and health-care costs have grown much larger. And those costs can vary widely from city to city."

4 McCall 2013; McCoy 2015.

5 Perriello 2013; Goldfarb and Boorstein 2013.

6 These have included Ted Cruz, Rand Paul, and Marco Rubio. During his time as speaker of the House, Republican John Boehner expressed similar sentiments.

7 Chozick 2015.

8 "Income and Wealth Inequality," Bernie 2016 campaign website, accessed August 5, 2015, https://berniesanders.com.

9 Baptist and Rehmann 2011; Blackmon 2015; Edelman 2012; Gould and Davis 2015; Gould et al. 2015; Jeroslow 2015; Kahne and Mabel 2010; Stiglitz 2012; Yellen 2006.

10 Gould and Davis 2015.

11 Danziger and Gottschalk 1994; Desmond 2015; Edin and Shaefer 2015; Fox et al. 2015; Gilbert 2011; Massey 2007; Putnam 2015; Shaefer et al. 2015.

12 Nixon 1969.

13 Stiglitz 2013.

14 Silva 2013: 18.

15 Silva 2013: 151.
16 Silva 2013: 151.
17 Silva 2013: 145.
18 Sennett and Cobb 1972: 255.
19 Hacker 2008: xii–xiii; see also Cooper 2014.
20 Skobba et al. 2015.
21 U.S. Department of Agriculture 2016b.
22 Harris and Zakari 2015.
23 Baptist and Rehmann 2011; Harris and Zakari 2015; Harvey 2005.
24 There have been some efforts to address the consequences of this, such as the
    Credit Card Accountability Responsibility and Disclosure Act of 2009 (CARD),
    restricting banks' ability to impose higher fees and interest rates. With no safety
    net, credit cards have become a too-common last resort that exacerbates the diffi-
    culties of those without financial resources and without a public or a private safety
    net to rely upon. Provisions of the CARD Act went into effect in February 2010.
    American consumers saved billions of dollars in fees as a result (Delamaide 2013).
    By February 2011, a year after the effective date of many provisions of CARD,
    there had been significant changes:
    • The long-standing practice of hiking interest rates on existing cardholder ac-
      counts has been dramatically curtailed.
    • The amount of late fees consumers are paying has been substantially reduced.
    • Overlimit fees have virtually disappeared in the credit card industry.
    • Consumers report that their credit card costs are clearer, but significant con-
      fusion remains. (consumerfinance.gov)
    The Consumer Financial Protection Bureau (CFPB) was created by the 2010
    Dodd-Frank Wall Street Reform and Consumer Protection Act, a response
    to the financial crisis of 2007 and 2008 and the Great Recession (Eaglesham
    2011, www.consumerfinance.gov), and is an independent government agency
    responsible for consumer protection in the financial sector. It's now responsible
    for administering changes due to CARD and has put for-profit colleges under
    scrutiny (Kamenetz 2015). But there has been pushback. Congress tried to
    defund the CFPB and to prevent it from moving forward by blocking confirma-
    tion of a director. Obama eventually installed a director via recess appointment
    in 2012.
25 Hacker 2008: 5.
26 "As private and public support erodes, workers and their families must bear a
    great burden. This is the essence of the Great Risk Shift. Through the cutback and
    restructuring of workplace benefits, employers are seeking to offload more and
    more of the risk once pooled under their auspices. Facing fiscal constraint and
    political opposition, public social programs have eroded even as the demands on
    them have risen" (Hacker 2008: 8).
27 Hacker and Pierson 2010: 4.
28 Cooper 2014: 38.

29 Edsall 2015; Hacker 2008; Hacker and Pierson 2010.

30 Alkon and Mares 2012; Beck 2000; Cooper 2014; Hacker and Pierson 2010; Harris and Zakari 2015; Harvey 2005; Silva 2013.

31 Cooper 2014; Silva 2013.

32 Gilbert 2011; McCall 2013; McCoy 2015; Page and Jacobs 2009; Putnam 2015.

33 Portes 1998: 12.

34 Warren, Thompson, and Saegert 2001: 1; see also Small 2009b for a review.

35 Menjívar 2000.

36 See Bourdieu 1986; Briggs 1998; Coleman 1988, 1990; Lin 2001b; Menjívar 2000; Portes 1998; Small 2009b; Warren, Thompson, and Saegert 2001.

37 Silva 2013: 14.

38 Putnam 2015: 206.

39 NWRU was a reincarnation of the National Welfare Rights Organization of the 1960s and 1970s.

40 Personal communication with Cheri Honkala.

41 Bunch 2014; Lubrano 2014; Shea 2014. Milwaukee, Wisconsin, and Detroit, Michigan, both top Philadelphia in the list of poorest cities, but their populations are approximately 600,000 and 700,000 respectively, compared to Philadelphia's 1.5 million (Kennedy 2015). See Edelman 2012 for a good explanation of the poverty line.

42 "Tapped Out: A Timeline of Philadelphia Poverty through the 21st Century."

43 Furstenberg et al. 1999; Stern Smallacombe 2006.

44 Bunch 2014.

45 Fairbanks 2009; U.S. Census Bureau n.d.

46 Binzen 1970; Edin and Kefalas 2005; Fairbanks 2009; Putnam 2015; Stern Smallacombe 2006.

47 Bunch 2014; Stern Smallacombe 2006.

48 Furstenberg et al. 1999; Goode and O'Brien 2006.

49 Fairbanks 2009: 5.

50 Stern Smallacombe 2006: 178.

51 Edin and Kefalas 2005; Putnam 2015.

52 The quotations defining KWRU and stating its goals were taken from the Kensington Welfare Rights Union's website, no longer in existence. Readers can visit the Poor People's Economic Human Rights campaign website, http://economichumanrights.org/, to learn about current activities of the group. For more on KWRU's and PPEHRC's history, see Baptist and Rehmann 2011; Bricker-Jenkins et al. 2007; Honkala et al. 1999; Jewell 2015.

53 As Jennifer Jewell states of KWRU and related organizations, "Those who are directly impacted by poverty, welfare recipients, the unemployed, and homeless, form the leadership base and decision-making body of the organization" (2015: 527).

54 The Poor People's Economic Human Rights Campaign has an active web presence (http://economichumanrights.org and www.facebook.com). Its website states:

The Poor People's Economic Human Rights Campaign is committed to unit-
ing the poor across color lines as the leadership base for a broad movement
to abolish poverty. We work to accomplish this through advancing economic
human rights as named in the universal declaration of human rights- such as
the rights to food, housing, health, education, communication and a living
wage job.

Their online mission statement includes:

The founding creed of the United States of America, which asserts our rights
to Life, Liberty, and the Pursuit of Happiness, inspired the formulation of
these human rights. Our government signed the UDHR [Universal Declaration of Human Rights] in 1948; its full implementation would mean that our
country would be living out the true meaning of its creed. This American
Dream is possible because our country is the richest and most powerful in
the world.

The Poor People's Economic Human Rights Campaign website, accessed August
4, 2015, http://economichumanrights.org.

55 See Bricker-Jenkins et al. 2007; Honkala et al. 1999; Jewell 2015.

56 "U.S. Social Forum Philadelphia: Another World Is Possible," accessed July 9,
2015, http://ussfphilly.org: "U.S. Social Forum in Philadelphia. Another World
is Possible; Another World is Necessary. The U.S. Social Forum taking place in
Philadelphia, June 25–28, 2015 is a convergence driven by the understanding that
people's movements are what create social change. It is an opportunity for re-
gional and issue-specific social justice projects to work toward broader unity. The
goal is to map out action plans for a cohesive movement and organize to be on the
offense against all forms of oppression."

57 "Projects of Survival," website of the Poor People's Economic Human Rights Campaign, accessed August 7, 2015, http://economichumanrights.org.

58 "Educationals," website of the Poor People's Economic Human Rights Campaign,
accessed August 7, 2015, http://economichumanrights.org.

59 "Movement Building," website of the Poor People's Economic Human Rights
Campaign, accessed August 7, 2015, http://economichumanrights.org.

60 "Movement Building," 2015.

61 See Lavee and Offer 2012; Levine 2013; Offer 2010, 2012b; Roschelle 1997.

62 Levine 2013.

63 Levine 2013: 183. Also see Lavee and Offer 2012; Offer 2010, 2012b; Roschelle 1997.

64 For example, see Appelbaum and Gebeloff 2012. As numerous other researchers have documented, faith in welfare reform is misplaced. As Jennifer Sherman
writes, "Welfare reform was created with the belief that the poor lack proper work
ethics and must be coerced into the labor force. . . . Welfare reform attempted
to push marriage as a solution . . . marriage is highly prioritized but nonetheless
does not protect families from poverty" (2009: 24). See also Newman 1999.

65 Sherman 2009.

66 Harknett 2006; Henly et al. 2005; Mazelis and Mykyta 2011; Offer 2012a, 2012b; Nelson 2005; Phan et al. 2009; Small 2009b.

67 See Marwell 2007; Sampson 2012; Small 2009b.

68 Small and Allard 2013: 10. They further state, "First, the ability of low-income individuals to acquire resources to avoid hardship is structured, mediated, facilitated, or undermined by the organizations in which they participate . . . Second, how people understand their circumstances may also be mediated by the organization in which they participate. . . . Third, how people avoid social isolation, develop their personal networks, and form social capital are shaped by their participation in local organizations" (2013: 10–11).

69 As Mario Luis Small states, "Some believe that social capital theory 'blames the victims' for their problems, since it could lead one to the conclusion that if only people bothered to network more effectively, then social inequality might be lowered. More important, critics maintain that the theory's focus on personal networks comes at the expense of the study of larger structural forces" (2009b: 10).

70 See Willis 1977.

71 Anderson 1999; Edin and Lein 1997; Lamont 2000; Newman 1999; Sherman 2009.

72 See Lareau 2003.

73 Margaret Nelson does this compellingly:

I neither mean to deny that Sarah and the other single mothers who constitute the subject of this book have to make choices within a "shared set of constraints," nor do I mean to deny that they might even overstate the degree to which they can make choices. At the same time, I do suggest that if we focus exclusively on those constraints, or on the resulting survival strategy as measured only by economic resources (or on the patterns of assistance received from others), we cannot fully understand the contours of Sarah's daily life. Her limited choices are not simply determined by difficult economic considerations, but rather are framed within, and equally shaped by, a set of complex, and contradictory, *social* concerns, which include commitment to whatever is taken to be self-sufficiency and to meeting the emotional needs that accompany her particular pattern of family life. (2005: 11)

74 Hacker and Pierson 2010: 103, emphasis in original.

75 For example, Desmond 2012; Domínguez and Watkins 2003; Hansen 2005; Nelson 2005; Small 2009b; Stack 1974.

76 Nelson 2005: 180–181.

77 Marwell and McQuarrie argue this as well. Social ties are not "an all-purpose antidote to a range of systemically generated problems (including poverty)" (2013: 140).

78 As the next chapter will indicate, recent research suggests that strivers pay a heavy price in terms of their health.

79 Desmond 2012.

80 For example, Stack 1974.

81 Desmond 2012.
82 Desmond 2012.

CHAPTER 1. KEEP WORKING TO BE WHAT YOU WANT

1 Shea 2014.
2 Edin and Lein 1997; Hays 2003; Sherman 2009.
3 Hays 2003, Newman 1999; Sherman 2009; Silva 2013.
4 Annette Lareau states: "Many Americans believe that this country is fundamentally *open*. They assume the society is best understood as a collection of individuals. They believe that people who demonstrate hard work, effort, and talent are likely to achieve upward mobility. Put differently, many Americans believe in the American Dream. . . . The extent to which life chances vary can be traced to differences in aspirations, talent, and hard work on the part of individuals" (2003: 235).
5 Hochschild 1995: xvii.
6 Hacker and Pierson 2010: 29.
7 "Failure is made more harsh by the third premise of the American dream—the belief that success results from actions and traits under one's own control" (Hochschild 1995: 30). In addition, the American Dream "is highly *individual*, in that it leads one to focus on people's behaviors rather than on economic processes, environmental constraints, or political structures as the causal explanation for social orderings" (Hochschild 1995: 36).
8 Hochschild 1995: 259.
9 Lareau states, "The outcomes individuals achieve over the course of their lifetime are seen as their own responsibility" (2003: 30). See also Esping-Anderson 1990; Stiglitz 2012.
10 Silva 2013: 109.
11 Silva 2013: 109.
12 Domínguez 2011; Kluegel and Smith 1986; Wilson 1996.
13 Putnam 2015: 31.
14 Bill Clinton's 1993 speech to the Democratic Leadership Council, cited in Hochschild 1995:18. Also see Lareau 2003: 7.
15 White House 2013.
16 Edin and Shaefer 2015; Fader 2013; Hansen 2005; Hochschild 1995; Kluegel and Smith 1986; Lareau 2003. As Karen Hansen states, "Mainstream U.S. culture celebrates the individual and views both success and failure as the result of individual endeavor" (2005: 5).
17 Gans 1995; Hays 2003; Hochschild 1995; Katz 1989; Levine 2013; Newman 1999; Reese 2005; Skocpol 1992.
18 My research had concluded when I learned Bebe was expecting her first child less than a year later. I brought her a baby gift that she happily accepted. Though in the past she had told me having a baby imposes economic costs on poor women, it's also clear that she felt she had little to lose. The opportunity costs of having a

child sooner than she planned do not resemble those of her middle-class counterparts.

19 Putnam 2015: 34; see also McCall 2013; Page and Jacobs 2009.

20 Macleod 2008: 3.

21 Bellah et al. 1985; Franklin 2005.

22 Weber 1905.

23 Hamblin 2015.

24 Macleod explains this tradeoff in *Ain't No Makin' It: Aspirations and Attainment in a Low-Income Neighborhood* (2008). The Brothers accept the achievement ideology, leading them to put forth effort. This does really improve their chances but isn't enough to overcome structural obstacles. But when they fall short they blame themselves. The Hallway Hangers reject the achievement ideology, limiting their own chances in addition to other barriers they face. But they also protect their self-esteem by doing so.

25 MacLeod 2008.

26 King 1968.

27 Anderson 1999; Bourgois 1995; Duneier 1992; Edin and Kefalas 2005; Fairbanks 2009; Lamont 2000; MacLeod 2008; Newman 1999; Sherman 2009.

28 Wilson 1996: 179–180.

29 Snow and Anderson 1993: 131.

30 Newman 1999.

31 Bourgois 1995: 54.

32 Duneier 1992.

33 Lamont 2000.

34 Research participant James represents an exception. A leader and activist with KWRU, he told me: "Society . . . they give you this false, this false pretense that you can become a millionaire. And have everybody working towards this illusion. . . . They have like you know dead-end jobs and penitentiary and the grave and all these things waiting for you instead of the American Dream." James takes us through the thought process surrounding common aspirations; when people don't achieve their goals, they blame themselves:

> When you got parents and everybody teaching you, you got to get good grades. . . . You got to go to college. You got to be the best. You got to work hard. When people tell you all those different things and then you're going to be successful you going to have . . . [a] piece of paper saying that you graduated from a good university. And you have a job that pays a real good salary where you are able to buy a house and pay for a car and take vacations and have money for school for your kids, then you're successful. Anything less than that you are a failure. And so when your parents are telling you, these are all the things that your grandparents and everybody telling you . . . they're all around you. These are the things that you got to do to be a success and then you don't meet any of those things, boom you're going to automatically think it's yourself, you're a failure. It's you.

35 Cohen 1997; Goldsmith 1998; Katz 1989.

36 See Katz 1989.

37 Bebe's mother is abusive; Bebe lives with this other family to escape her mother's violence. As her legal guardian, her mother finds her every time she enrolls in school and disenrolls her as a way to control her activities and limit her future prospects. Bebe's narratives of her mother's activities portray an unfit parent consumed with anger, regret, and even jealousy, who physically and emotionally abused her.

38 See Community Legal Services of Philadelphia, n.d.a., n.d.b., which includes information and links to fact sheets and other resources.

39 Bureau of Labor Statistics 2014; Crosby and Moncarz 2006a, 2006b; Heckman et al. 2011; Putnam 2015; Rumberger 2011; Sanchez 2012; Sum et al. 2012.

40 Newman 1999.

41 The store fired Jessie because she was accused of stealing. As she describes it, the circumstances were very peculiar—her drawer reconciled when she left for the day, but she was later told that it had been recounted and it didn't reconcile. Her argument that she would have had to be a fool to steal the amount of which she was accused seems very reasonable. One hundred dollars is enough that it's sure to get noticed but not enough to take her very far or even replace her poorly paid position.

42 Bureau of Labor Statistics 2014; Crosby and Moncarz 2006a, 2006b; Heckman et al. 2011; Putnam 2015; Rumberger 2011; Sanchez 2012; Sum et al. 2012.

43 See U.S. Department of Health and Human Services n.d.a.

44 Bound et al. 2010. See also DeParle 2012; Leonhardt 2005; New York Times 2012.

45 Shea 2014; Volsky 2014.

46 Hacker 2008.

47 Goodman 2010; Hamilton and Gueron 2002.

48 Bureau of Labor Statistics 2014; Crosby and Moncarz 2006a, 2006b; Heckman et al. 2011; Rumberger 2011; Sanchez 2012; Sum et al. 2012; Putnam 2015.

49 Sanchez 2012.

50 Anderson 2014; U.S. Department of Education 2011; Weise 2014a.

51 Anderson 2014; U.S. Department of Education 2011; Weise 2014a. In 2010 the Department of Education proposed basing restrictions on three metrics: two debt-to-income ratios and how frequently students fall behind on loans; the last of these was thrown out by a federal judge (Anderson 2014; Weise 2014a). In July 2015, the Education Department's rule requiring that colleges track graduates' performance in the labor market took effect, stipulating that career training programs that fall short will lose government funding—this translates into 1,400 programs enrolling 840,000 students, 99 percent of whom attend for-profit colleges (Grasgreen 2015). However, the final version of the rule stipulates that programs will be evaluated only on graduates' debt-to-earnings ratios, an evaluation that leaves out the percentage of borrowers defaulting on their student loans

and students who fail to complete their programs, taking on debt but gaining no human capital they can point to with a degree (Anderson 2014; Field 2014; Weise 2014b).

To qualify for Federal aid, the law requires that most for-profit programs and certificate programs at nonprofit and public institutions prepare students for gainful employment in a recognized occupation. Under the regulations introduced today, a program would be considered to lead to gainful employment if it meets at least one of the following three metrics: at least 35 percent of former students are repaying their loans (defined as reducing the loan balance by at least $1); the estimated annual loan payment of a typical graduate does not exceed 30 percent of his or her discretionary income; or the estimated annual loan payment of a typical graduate does not exceed 12 percent of his or her total earnings. While the regulations apply to occupational training programs at all types of institutions, for-profit programs are most likely to leave their students with unaffordable debts and poor employment prospects. (U.S. Department of Education 2011)

Field explains that "programs will fail if their graduates' student-loan debt payments exceed 12 percent of their income and 30 percent of their discretionary income. Programs whose graduates have debt-to-income ratios of 8 to 12 percent or debt-to-discretionary-income ratios of 20 to 30 percent will fall in 'the zone' and will have to warn students that the programs and, in turn, their students may become ineligible for aid. Programs that fail both debt-to-income tests twice in any three-year period or are in the zone for four consecutive years will be ineligible for aid" (Field 2014).

52 Institute for College Access & Success 2014.

53 Brown 2012.

54 Hotez 2014.

55 Mullainathan and Shafir 2013. See also Kristof 2015.

56 Kristof 2015.

57 High achievers from advantaged backgrounds exhibit the reverse; for them, greater success correlates with better health: "If you just go a little bit up the income/education ladder, these same traits are associated with slower aging and better health. The exact opposite correlation exists in advantaged kids: Self-control is associated with all sorts of positive health outcomes. Only in the disadvantaged communities does this paradox exist: good outcomes on the behavioral/educational/psychosocial side, but apparently at a cost to physical health" (Hamblin 2015).

58 Edin and Lein 1997; Newman 1999.

59 Edin and Lein 1997; Newman 1999.

60 Clampet-Lundquist 2004; Sherman 2009; Stack 1974.

61 See Centeno and Cohen 2012; Hochschild 1995; Piven and Cloward 1993. The poor blame the poor for their situations too.

62 Silva 2013: 25.

63 See also Gilbert 2011; Macleod 2008; *New York Times* 2005. Politicians and policy makers nonetheless argue that the poor will benefit if the government weakens assistance programs (Alkon and Mares 2012; Luxton 2010), and the poor have internalized these views (Gross and Rosenberger 2010; Luxton 2010).

CHAPTER 2. I STAY TO MYSELF

1 Levine found this as well; her participants kept others at arm's length, and considered few or no people to be their friends. She states, "Many of these same mothers reported past events in which they had risked relying on others and had gotten burned. Thus many mothers had developed their self-protective stance of preemptive distrust out of earlier experiences when they had placed trust in others whom they later deemed unworthy of that trust" (2013: 207).

2 Putnam 2000.

3 Silva (2013) found a lack of trust as well, often rooted in experiences of trust betrayed. Those she interviewed said they learned not to expect anything from anyone, after

> investing their time and energy in relationships and institutions, only to find that their efforts were one-sided . . . experiences of betrayal, within both the labor market and the institutions that frame their coming of age experiences, teach young working-class men and women that they are completely alone, responsible for their own fates and dependent on outside help only at their peril. They learn to approach others with suspicion and distrust. Many make a virtue out of necessity, equating self-reliance and atomic individualism with self-worth and dignity: if they had to survive on their own, then everyone else should too. In an era of short-term flexibility, constant flux, and hollow institutions, the transition to adulthood has been inverted; coming of age does not entail entry *into* social groups and institutions but rather the explicit rejection *of* them. (Silva 2013: 83–84)

Because I found this as well, I argue that self-reliance and individualism are more universally equated with self-worth; they are not limited to the experiences of young adults, nor need they include betrayal by institutions. The privatization of risk and the strength of individualism often prevent people from forming social ties even in the absence of experiences of betrayal.

4 Edin 2001; Hogan et al. 1993. As Menjívar states:

> People need a minimum of resources to help others; otherwise they simply have nothing to share. Thus our attention should shift from reifying the notion that immigrants achieve benefits through informal exchanges with relatives and friends toward examining the structure of opportunities that determines if immigrants will have the means (and what kind) to help one another in the first place. The assumption that extended social networks represent a "survival strategy" to ameliorate the effects of poverty needs to

be reexamined, perhaps even reversed, for the very conditions that informal networks supposedly mitigate may impede resource-strapped people from assisting one another. (2000:156)

5 Harknett 2006: 174; see also Domínguez and Watkins 2003; Menjívar 2000.

6 Desmond 2012.

7 Levine 2013.

8 Duneier 1999; Furstenberg et al. 1993; Zucchino 1997.

9 Portes 1998. Fader (2013) describes a respondent who reported avoiding all of the people from his neighborhood: "In poor communities, success such as his— even saving enough to live independently—is big news. In the context of a dense network of exchange, those who are doing well are expected to take care of those who are struggling. Spending time with his peers in Southwest Philly meant constantly negotiating requests for 'loans,' most of which could not realistically be repaid. Success became a lonely endeavor" (2013: 174).

10 Silva 2013: 17.

11 Domínguez and Watkins 2003; Hertz and Ferguson 1997; Lavee and Offer 2012; Nelson 2000, 2005; Offer et al. 2010.

12 Hansen (2005) and Nelson (2005) found this as well. As Nelson states, "As they rejected dependence, the women interviewed for this study . . . quickly aligned themselves with the morally *approved* traits of self-sufficiency and independence." Her participants talk about how they are self-sufficient and pride themselves on their independence. "These code words *self-sufficiency* and *independence* tap into deep values with widespread appeal and they become a theme in the lives of single mothers. . . . The need to demonstrate self-reliance, self-sufficiency, and independence, however, runs counter to the very real needs single mothers have: The material realities mean that they cannot get by without drawing on others for assistance with daily living and financial support and, occasionally, without drawing on the state" (2005: 56).

13 Hansen (2005) and Nelson (2005) found this same perspective among their participants. Hansen notes that people sometimes think that "relying too much on someone's assistance means becoming a burden, in effect becoming dependent" (2005: 173).

14 Similarly, as Nelson states, "Those who rely on state support do not view this practice as being incompatible with the exercise of independent agency in a tough situation. That is, while not holding themselves responsible for the circumstances in which they find themselves, the women express pride in the fact that they have actively sought to alleviate those circumstances. In so doing, they insist that 'dependence' on the state does not come at the expense of independence" (2005: 102).

15 Granovetter [1974] 1995.

16 Newman 1999; Smith 2007.

17 See, for example, Fader 2013.

18 Although there are social aspects to successful entrepreneurship as well. See Byers et al. 1998: 1–3:

The emphasis on rugged individualism is so prevalent in western culture that many of the lists of "characteristics of successful entrepreneurs" barely reflect that launching a start-up entails constant interaction with others. For example, five of the six characteristics of entrepreneurs identified in Timmons' [1994] review could just as easily be used for identifying which people are best suited for a solo activity that entails little or no interaction with others, such as racing a sailboat alone. Commitment, opportunity obsession, tolerance of risk, ambiguity and uncertainty, creativity, self-reliance, ability to adapt, and motivation to excel all seem to describe the kind of rugged individualist who struggles alone to win a contest under difficult circumstances. Only one of the categories identified by Timmons—leadership—refers to the social nature of entrepreneurship.

19 Bureau of Labor Statistics n.d. See also Sadeghi 2008.

20 Small Business Administration n.d.

21 Anderson 1990; Massey and Denton 1993; Offer 2012a; Wilson 1987, 2001.

22 Portes 1998; Putnam 2000, 2015; Wilson 1987.

23 Stack 1974: 125.

24 See also Edin and Lein 1997; Hansen 2005; Menjívar 2000; Nelson 2005.

25 Phan et al. cite work by Ross et al. (2001), noting that "neighborhood disorder increased mistrust among residents, an effect that was amplified by individuals' sense of powerlessness and thereby reinforced disadvantages already experienced by vulnerable individuals" (2009: 903).

26 "It is neighborhood socio-economic conditions that exacerbate individual disadvantage by reducing their participation in helping networks" (Phan et al. 2009: 909; see also Klinenberg 2002; Putnam 2015).

Participants' structural positions create the situations that lead to distrust and social withdrawal. As Levine states: "The stigma of the relative powerlessness of these structural positions leads some women to feel that they need to protect themselves in interactions with those who hold power over them. And even if interaction partners are peers, sometimes resources are so scarce that competition results and distrust is again protective" (2013: 210). Levine's documentation of poor people's variety of responses to their structural barriers reveals, like my own research, that structural position alone doesn't shape these responses.

27 "While close to three-quarters of those with above-average incomes in deprived neighborhoods continue to engage in helping within their non-kin network, only a little more than half of low-income respondents in the same neighborhoods do so" (Phan et al. 2009: 908).

28 Phan et al. also note, "Bandura (1982) and Wilson (1991) argued that individual experiences of unemployment or poverty, when combined with disorganized neighborhoods and fragmented social networks, lowered a resident's ability to help oneself or others" (2009: 904).

29 Edin and Kefalas noted that, "trust among residents of poor communities is astonishingly low—so low that most mothers we spoke with said they have no close friends, and many even distrust close kin" (2005: 34). Many researchers have found a pervasive culture of distrust (Fader 2013; Furstenberg 2001; Hannerz 1969; Levine 2013; Rainwater 1970; Seccombe 1999). See also Smith (2007) for an excellent discussion of the evidence available showing both high levels of distrust and reliance on trusted networks.

In her book, *Ain't No Trust*, Judith Levine states:
One of the key factors on which people base expectations about trustworthiness is whether they believe their interaction partners share their interests. Because of the women's disadvantaged structural position both in several of the contexts I study and more generally in U.S. society at large, their interests were often at odds with those of their interaction partners. . . . When the women were interacting with those who were in a more equal structural position . . . the likelihood that they would share interests was greater and thus the potential for trust was greater. However, their shared powerlessness in relation to the outside world, that is, their mutual relegation to the bottom of what I have called the U.S. stratification system, often meant that their interaction partners were scrambling to survive and hence could not be relied upon to take their interests to heart. The desperation that powerlessness creates means that everyone must be out for him- or herself at times. (2013: 40–41)

30 Silva 2013: 18.

31 Levine 2013: 205; see also Coleman 1988; Putnam 2000; Sampson 2000; Stack 1974. Levine states: "Much sociological work celebrates the bonding social capital that close ties with kin produce and, in particular, its value in the survival strategies of those in poverty. Indeed, many of the women interviewed prized such productive relationships. However, social interaction with family and friends was also a source of strain for women who learned the hard way that they could not trust everyone in their networks. As a result, some of these women withdrew from social life. This withdrawal isolated them and their children from the harms, but perhaps also the potential benefits, of social interaction" (2013: 216).

32 Edin and Kefalas 2005; Levine 2013; Smith 2007.

33 As Margaret Nelson notes, "If there is secrecy and concealment, it seems more often to involve hiding from others just how many times one has done without" (2000: 314).

34 U.S. Department of Justice 2005.

35 Sampson 2012.

36 U.S. Department of Justice 2005.

37 Go to U.S. Department of Justice n.d., choose "cities of 1,000,000 or over," choose "Philadelphia Police Dept" and "Violent crime rate" to view the data table.

38 Jacobs 1961.

39 These are common findings. See Appelbaum and Gebeloff 2012; Baptist and Rehmann 2011; Jewell 2015; Kristof 2015; Lamont and Fournier 1992; Sherman 2009; Silva 2013. As Silva states: "Many draw unforgiving boundaries against their family members and friends who cannot transform their selves—overcome addictions, save money, heal troubled relationships—through sheer determination alone. Just as neoliberalism teaches young people that they are solely responsible for their economic fortunes, the mood economy renders them responsible for their *emotional* fates. . . . The mood economy dovetails with neoliberalism by privatizing happiness" (Silva 2013: 21–22).

40 Hays 2003: 121. See also Sherman 2009.

41 Badger 2015; Ferdman 2015; Weissman 2015. In Missouri, a state legislator advanced a bill to limit what SNAP recipients can purchase, including banning the purchase of seafood or steak with SNAP benefits (Ferdman 2015). And a new law in Kansas now bans using assistance funds to see movies or visit swimming pools (Holley and Izadi 2015). These proposals are as misguided and paternalistic as those pushing work and marriage as answers to poverty; they stigmatize the poor by focusing on policing behavior rather than addressing needs.

42 Delaney 2015; see also Alvarez 2014; "Drug Testing for Welfare Recipients and Public Assistance," 2015; Robles 2013. Florida taxpayers spent $118,140 to reimburse people who tested negative for the cost of testing, which amounted to $45,780 more than the state saved on benefits denied to the 2.6 percent of applicants who tested positive (Davis 2012). The state of Florida has also spent hundreds of thousands of dollars to continue to fight to overturn the ruling in court.

43 Delaney 2010.

44 Goldsmith 1998; Nelson 2002, 2005; Udesky 1991.

45 Edin and Kefalas 2005.

46 For similar findings, see Burton et al. 1998; Cherlin et al. 2000; Lamont and Fournier 1992; Sherman 2009.

47 Supplemental Security Income, a program that pays benefits to disabled children and adults who have limited income and resources, and to senior citizens without disabilities who do not exceed financial limits (Social Security Administration, n.d.).

48 Catalan 2014. Sean Hannity made the same comparison (Media Matters Staff 2013). See also Lachman 2014.

49 The article reporting this statement from Corbett states, "There are currently five people looking for work for every job opening, according to the Department of Labor, and only 67 percent of the nearly 15 million unemployed receive benefits in the first place. For all the anecdotes about business owners having hiring trouble, there are job ads flatly stating that the unemployed need not apply. But suspicion of the unemployed, coupled with wariness of the deficit, has led to an epic holdup in Congress over reauthorizing benefits for people who've been jobless for six

months or longer. The benefits lapsed at the end of May, causing some 2.1 million so far to miss checks" (Delaney 2010; see also Bassett 2010).

50 Anderson 1976.

51 Snow and Anderson 1993.

52 Lamont and Fournier 1992; Seccombe 1999; Sherman 2009; Zucchino 1997.

53 Levin 2013.

54 Levin 2013; Weissman 2013.

55 Levin 2013. Levin argues there are far-reaching consequences: "If Linda Taylor had been seen as a suspect rather than a scapegoat, lives may have been saved. Prosecutors have great discretion in choosing what cases to bring—that's how the rate of welfare indictments could shoot up so dramatically in a single decade. When politicians and journalists whip the public into a frenzy about welfare fraud, the limitations of municipal budgets and judicial resources dictate that less attention be paid to everything else. Linda Taylor's story shows that there are real costs associated with this kind of panic, a moral climate in which stealing welfare money takes precedence over kidnapping and homicide."

56 Ferdman 2015; Levin 2013.

57 Levin 2013; Schnurer 2013.

58 Levin 2013.

59 Broughton 2001.

60 Broughton 2001: 109.

61 Lamont 1992: 11; see also Lamont and Fournier 1992; Sherman 2009.

62 Goldsmith 1998.

63 Sherman 2009: 112.

64 Burton et al. 1998; Cherlin et al. 2000.

65 Roschelle asserts that poverty makes people "less likely to participate in informal social support networks . . . as resources become more scarce, network participation disintegrates because of a lack of resources to exchange" (1997: 194); see also Anderson 1999; Nelson 2000, 2005; Offer 2012b; Phan et al. 2009; Sampson et al. 1999; Smith 2007.

66 Gouldner 1960; Uehara 1995.

67 Hansen 2004; Henly 2002; Hogan et al. 1993; Menjívar 2000; Nelson 2000, 2005; Offer et al. 2010; Phan et al. 1999; Uehara 1995.

68 Nelson 2005. Depending on the norms of a social network, people may reciprocate in nontraditional ways. Nelson notes: "Recall that the single mothers *do* have acute and unpredictable needs, and for the most part, limited material resources, time, and energy with which to make exchanges. This is not to imply that the women readily accepted unmitigated dependence" (2005: 80). Instead, her participants came up with ways to frame their behavior as fitting within the norms of reciprocity, and also did reciprocate as much as they could. Nelson (2000, 2005) also found that some of her participants defined their own reciprocation to include gratitude, loyalty, and giving satisfaction to those who provided aid (see

also Lavee and Offer 2012). I did not find participants to define reciprocity this broadly.

69 This dynamic may explain two interactions, similar to one another, that surprised me. One participant was unavailable to meet twice when I traveled more than an hour to get to her house. Twice I found I needed a restroom, and I observed children playing outside at nearby houses; at my request the children fetched an adult, and both times the adult permitted me inside. While my ease at gaining entry to strangers' houses to use their bathrooms is partly due to my appearance as a relatively young, short, white woman and the fact that people do not perceive me as a threat—a male fieldworker would have had more difficulty, as might a person of color, even in this Latino neighborhood—this points to the fact that people weren't especially mistrustful of strangers. However, as someone unfamiliar who mentioned traveling a long way to meet with someone, I was palpably unlikely to turn the interaction into a sustained relationship with reciprocal demands.

70 See Levine 2013; Portes 1998.

71 Offer (2012b) states: "Poverty may also lead people to voluntarily withdraw from social relationships if they feel that they will not be able to contribute to the network or fail to adequately reciprocate support, which will lead to the exhaustion of others' scarce resources" (797). See also Edin and Lein 1997; Hansen 2004; Nelson 2005.

72 When others see them as a net drain on resources, they often deny them assistance and exclude them from the network (Domínguez 2011; Domínguez and Watkins 2003; Mazelis 2015; Nelson 2005; Offer 2012a). Domínguez and Watkins (2003) demonstrate that many low-income African American women cannot rely on their families for anything and those relationships dissolve as a result. Menjívar (2000) documents that family social networks fragment under conditions of extreme deprivation as well. When kin have few resources, it is difficult for people to help each other, making kin support unreliable and inconsistent at best.

73 Judith Levine notes: "When women distrusted network members it was most often because they drained the women's households of resources or created disruptions in the women's lives. . . . The cuts in the social safety net, the erosion of wages at the bottom of the labor market, the burgeoning drug economy, and related forces created an environment in which not only the women were struggling but many of their network members were struggling as well. Shared hardship often led to situations in which some network members became a burden to others" (2013: 182).

74 Levine reached similar findings. She describes Lashawna who trusted and depended on her family for child care and other assistance, and Iliana, who had no one to trust (see Levine 2013: 180–181). Iliana lived with her mean grandmother who threatened to kick her out for not paying rent. There's a distinction between having no help, positive help based on trust, and negative help. Levine states:

Lashawna and Iliana represent two extremes among the women I interviewed. Some were embedded in social networks rich in support, while others faced very challenging lives all alone. . . . The women I interviewed provide evidence of both [social cohesion and support]. . . . Some had experienced abuse or rejection by their families. Some had been mistreated by friends who had exposed not only the women themselves but also their children to harm. These women learned to distrust others and retreated into a protective shell, shielding themselves and their children from those who might wreak havoc, but also blocking out any potential source of network-based help. (Levine 2013: 181–182)

75 Desmond 2012; Roschelle 1997; Smith 2007.

CHAPTER 3. THE ONLY WAY WE'RE GOING TO SURVIVE

1 KWRU leaders view social services and charity programs to aid the poor as addressing the symptoms of poverty, while they seek to address its causes. As a movement to end poverty, led by the poor for the poor, KWRU seeks to find ways to get out of poverty, and focuses on educating and organizing other poor people to join the organization.

2 "HUD House Occupied," 1999.

3 Feemster 2004.

4 Goldberg 2004.

5 Helen may be an exception to the rule that people join KWRU when they are desperate; she joined KWRU a number of years before I met her so I didn't personally observe her circumstances when she joined, though she also recounted to me that KWRU provided her financial assistance to get her heat turned back on after it had been shut off for nonpayment. It's also possible that the stigma of admitting hunger led her to mask her need, to them and to me.

6 Flores-Yeffal 2013; Roll and Steiner 2015; Seefeldt and Sandstrom 2015.

7 Harknett 2006; Hogan et al. 1990; Menjívar 2000; Offer 2012a.

8 Domínguez and Watkins 2003; Henly et al. 2005; Hogan et al. 1993; Hogan et al. 1990; Nelson 2000; Offer 2012a; Roschelle 1997.

9 Offer 2012a: 120.

10 Hansen 2005; Roschelle 1997.

11 Desmond 2012.

12 Offer states: "Going to charities and private social service agencies for material support provides an alternative source of assistance and may constitute a 'last-resort' strategy to which low-income women resort when the amount of support they can obtain from their personal networks is limited. Respondents with high levels of network support were found to be significantly less likely to use agency-based support compared to their socially disadvantaged counterparts" (2010: 297). I found this as well, and KWRU was often a last resort.

13 Edin and Lein 1997; Henly 2002; Hogan et al. 1993; Offer 2010; Roschelle 1997.

14 Offer 2010; Small 2009b. Small's study examined people, both poor and nonpoor, who were part of organizations (he terms them organizationally embedded), and found that organizations in poor neighborhoods were better situated to have ac-

cess to valuable resources than organizations in wealthier neighborhoods because of their ties to other organizations.

15 Small documents that child care centers served to connect people to social ties as well as to organizational ties, fostering friendships and also allowing them to gather resources from other organizations. Further, he found that the support they provided was more important for those most socially isolated: "People who have no close friends have everything to gain from having a support network of nonfriends to turn to in an emergency. . . . In these cases, having an extended support network may mean the difference between getting by and experiencing significant hardship" (2009b: 122–123).

16 Domínguez and Watkins (2003) also found people getting meaningful support from social service agencies.

17 An abandoned building in which KWRU members squat.

18 In July 2014, Debra Harrell allowed her nine-year-old daughter to play in a nearby park while she went to work. Another parent at the playground, realizing the child was unaccompanied, called the police. Harrell's daughter was taken into foster care and Harrell went to jail (Friedersdorf 2014). In March 2014, Shanesha Taylor left her two-year-old and six-month-old in her car while she went to a job interview. She had arranged child care, but the babysitter then failed to show. Taylor's decision is difficult to excuse, but she may have been weighing the possibility that canceling her job interview at the last minute would preclude rescheduling, the reality that she'd had very few such opportunities, and the fact that poverty can cause loss of custody as the law deems lack of housing or food to be neglect (McDonald 2014).

  While the Taylor case seems more likely to have endangered the children than the Harrell case due to the risk of hyperthermia in children left in cars, both cases involve low-income mothers without access to child care, attempting to fulfill obligations as wage-earning providers. Their arrests effectively criminalize poverty; they highlight the need for affordable, if not free, child care. Both Taylor and Harrell are African American. Perhaps Colleen's whiteness would have protected her from prison, had she chosen to leave her child unattended in order to keep her job.

19 "KWRU: Frequently Asked Questions," retrieved October 1, 2002, http://www.kwru.org/kwru/kwrufaq.html (site discontinued).

20 As described above, Carmen was an exception and she used the knowledge she learned in KWRU to benefit a neighbor.

21 See Edelman 2012; Gans 1995; Garin et al. 1994; Gilens 1999; Handler and Hasenfeld 1997; Jencks 1992; Katz 1983, 1986; Wilson 2000.

22 Edelman 2012; Mazelis and Gaughan 2015; Sherman 2013. Mazelis and Gaughan argue that high unemployment and Occupy Wall Street rhetoric mitigated the stigma, but it didn't eliminate it.

23 In some ways KWRU's practices fit with the empowerment-based intervention Gutiérrez and Lewis (1999) describe. They discuss the importance of building

confidence, consciousness, and connection among low-income women, and how self-efficacy can lead to collective efficacy.

24 Internalized oppression is when the oppressed believe the stereotypes about their group and use them against others in their group (David 2014).

25 Small 2009b: 84. See also Wellman 1979.

26 Granovetter 1973.

27 Briggs 1998; Putnam 2000; Small 2009b; Wellman 1979.

28 Briggs 1998; Domínguez and Watkins 2003; Henly et al. 2005; Menjívar 2000. Small 2004.

29 "Many low-income families have themselves become embedded in resource-poor networks, whose members may no longer have or have only limited resources to share" (Offer 2010: 285–286; see also Menjívar 2000; Roschelle 1997).

30 Briggs 1998; Granovetter 1973; Putnam 2000.

31 Putnam 2000: 317. As Levine notes, "Social capital is an input that, just like financial capital, can be invested to reap rewards." Levine continues, citing Sandra Susan Smith: "There has been much debate in the literature on whether low-income communities are best characterized as socially organized and rich in social capital or socially disorganized and devoid of social capital" (2013: 198), referencing the dialogue between Stack's *All Our Kin* and Roschelle's *No More Kin* over two decades later. See also Bourdieu 1986; Coleman 1988, 1990; Lin 2001a, 2001b; Portes 1998; Putnam 2000; Roschelle 1997; Sampson 2012; Sarkisian and Gerstel 2004; Small 2009b; Smith 2007; Stack 1974.

32 Massey and Denton 1993; Wilson 1987, 1996, 2001.

CHAPTER 4. WHAT GOES AROUND COMES AROUND

1 See, for example, Hansen 2005.

2 Only a few members had cars: James, Amanda, and Paloma during the early part of my research, and Jessie did for a time. Paloma's car broke down and she had no means to replace it.

3 Philadelphia's public transit fares are complicated and high; few KWRU members use the system enough to make weekly or monthly passes cost-effective, even if the substantial advance outlay was feasible for them. For single rides, tokens are cheaper than paying by cash, yet tokens can be hard to find and transfers cost extra. Some El stations have token vending machines, and some drugstores sell tokens. But token booths at El stops do not sell tokens. For those without tokens riding the bus, trolley, Broad Street Line, or Market-Frankford El, they must pay individual fares in dollar bills and coins.

4 Stack 1974: 29, 43.

5 This fits with the basic notion of generalized reciprocity, referred to by Phan and coauthors (2009) as network-generalized exchange: "*Network-generalized exchange* occurs when an individual provides resources to someone in their network and receives benefits from a different individual in that network at some other time (Ekeh 1974; Uehara 1990; Yamagishi & Cook 1993). Network-generalized exchange is more consistent with the notion of social capital as residing in the

structure of social relations, rather than in the characteristics of two individuals' mutual interactions (Coleman 1988)." Citing Gouldner (1960) and Uehara (1995), the authors state that network-generalized exchanges are based on norms of obligation rather than maximizing return and analyzing benefits and costs.

6   This is also called direct reciprocity or sometimes, balanced reciprocity, though the latter includes the notion that the repayment will be in relatively short order and equivalent to the benefit (see Hansen 2005; Nelson 2000, 2005; Offer 2012b; Phan et al. 2009; Sahlins 1972; Uehara 1990). Small cites Levi-Strauss (1969) in describing "generalized exchange systems, in which each person gives to or receives from any other without expecting direct reciprocity, provided there is sufficient solidarity in the whole" (2009b: 126). Small describes child care centers as similar to generalized exchange systems in that exchange needn't depend on closeness between two people, but also states that the system of exchange in child care centers "does not depend on the solidarity or cohesiveness of the group." Their formal relationship to the child care center stands in for the cohesion of a group with "strongly enforced informal norms" that provides mothers access to mutual support (126). My findings differ in that the system does depend on the cohesiveness of the group to an extent, and its strongly enforced informal norms.

7   And it's possible that generalized reciprocity is more positive than specific reciprocity. As Shira Offer (2012b) discusses, Uehara (1990) found: "Networks characterized by generalized reciprocity were substantially more supportive and had higher levels of solidarity than networks based on restricted exchanges" (Offer 2012b: 792). Hansen notes, "This system of reciprocity rests on a deeply rooted assumption of common goals, trust, and longevity of the relationships" (2005: 174). People believe it will all work out, as with balanced reciprocity, and also are not as worried about when they will pay back.

Offer also states:

The type of reciprocity most conducive to social integration and solidarity corresponds to what researchers typically refer to as *generalized* reciprocity. Generalized reciprocity is based on indirect multi-party exchanges, in which all parties depend on each other for benefits. The conditions and forms of return under generalized reciprocity are highly flexible and not stipulated in advance. Unlike restricted or balanced reciprocity, to use Sahlins' (1972) typology, generalized reciprocity does not require immediate return, return in the same domain, or even return from the same party (Ekeh, 1974; Yamagishi and Cook, 1993). Seinen and Schram (2006) suggested that people seek to build up a good reputation of "helpers" by reciprocating assistance to third parties they were not initially socially involved with and that this type of exchange (referred to as "indirect reciprocity") is used as a strategy for increasing the likelihood that they will be helped in the future. (2012b: 792)

8   Nelson heard the same from her participants: "What goes 'round comes 'round" (2005: 75).

9 As Levine states: "Equality between partners in an exchange promotes trust" (2013: 119). See also Molm et al. 2000. KWRU membership brings together people who are similarly situated, economically.

10 See Wellman 1999.

11 Molm 2010.

12 Other researchers have also found this difficulty with kin ties among their own participants. See Edin and Lein 1997; Harknett 2006; Henly et al. 2005; Menjívar 2000; Nelson 2000; Stack 1974.

13 Molm 2010: 126.

14 There were times I went to the office for a prescheduled appointment and also found no one there, the door locked.

15 Small notes, "Through mechanisms such as the threat of lost membership, organizations may enforce norms or practices that result in such consequences" (2009b: 18).

16 As Small states, "Participating in organizationally embedded networks may generate important disadvantages, or what social capital scholars have called 'negative social capital'"—giving up their leisure time. Further, he refers to "institutional coercion" when "people are forced, for the good of the organization and its members, to forgo at least some rudimentary rights, such as the right to refuse to represent the organization or the right to privacy about their contact information" (2009b: 187–188).

17 Levine acknowledges the difficulty of sorting out cause and effect in cases like Rebecca's: "It is difficult to determine the origin of these relationships among trust, distrust, and contributions to or drains on resources. We do not know whether the offer of resources builds trust (while draining resources builds distrust), or whether the temporal order is the reverse and those who place trust in others open the pathway to resource sharing. Perhaps it is a little bit of both" (2013: 197).

18 Carol Stack noted, "Dental care is equivalent in mediocrity to medical care. Few Blacks over the age of 25 have many of their original teeth. It is not uncommon to find people who had all their teeth pulled on their first visit to the dentist. Among young women this usually occurred when they were in their early twenties and covered by the same AFDC health benefits as their young children" (1974: 4). While Rebecca is white, not black, Stack's finding here is illustrative; needing dentures at a young age, and having to wait to get them, is a consequence of her poverty, and this obvious marker of her poverty exacerbates the stigma she already faces due to her poverty.

19 The Appendix discusses the racial composition of membership, but I never observed any correlation between racial identification and KWRU help.

20 This is not to say that race has no correlation with membership in KWRU. While the organization's founder is white, and seven of the other KWRU participants (including Helen) are white, I did find most of the members I encountered day to day to be African American or Latino, and I had to work harder to find most of the white KWRU members I interviewed.

21 This defies the stereotype that most poor people use drugs. If the stereotype were true, this rule would eliminate (or severely curtail) membership. It does suggest, though, that KWRU leadership believes that it is impossible to use drugs and be faithful to reciprocity requirements. Two participants admitted to occasional recreational use in interviews, though no one I met displayed any obvious signs of addiction. My belief is that the rule largely reflects a policy of eliminating people who cannot adhere to reciprocity requirements for any reason, including active drug addiction.

22 It also withdrew its aid from Naomi. Rebecca was more forthcoming with me about the entire sequence of events and her perspective on what the organization expected, but I think a similar dynamic may have been operating in relation to Naomi.

23 Nelson notes that "failure to abide by [rules] can result in being thrust out of a sustaining network" (2005: 77). As Offer argues, "Giving too little in return, or failing to reciprocate altogether, can thus induce dependency and eventually lead to exclusion from future exchanges, in that information about uncooperativeness spreads quickly in the network." (2012b: 793). In Offer's model of social fragmentation, Rebecca is an example of "*exclusion*": "*Exclusion* refers to the active prohibition of individuals who are (or are perceived to be) a burden on others to participate in the network. Those who are unwilling, unable, or have a limited ability to reciprocate tend to be excluded from participating in the network and accessing its resources" (2012b: 795).

24 I did meet with one member in 2015 who had gotten a job because of a connection made with a KWRU intern, but this was an exceptional case. Because it was unique, confidentiality concerns make it difficult to give additional details. But this was the only case that ever came to my attention of bridging capital offered through the organization that actually led to an improved life for a KWRU member.

25 In Offer's model of social fragmentation, Helen's is a case of *withdrawal:* "*Withdrawal* is the exemption of self from participation in the network. It is based on self-imposed restrictions that make individuals voluntarily disengage from their network" (2012b: 795).

26 As Offer (2012b) argues, citing Domínguez and Watkins 2003 and Nelson 2005, people also seek to avoid judgmental interactions and maintain their pride, which might cause them to limit their ties to others.

CHAPTER 5. OUR STRENGTH IS IN OUR UNITY

1 Nelson demonstrates how reciprocity and mutual obligation can create fictive kinship. However, she states, "If kinship terminology helps to bind individuals in trusting relationships, trust does not rely on the assertion of kinship alone. Perhaps even more important to the creation of trust (and the claiming of others as kin) is the assurance that those who live in similar circumstances will understand, and be sympathetic about, one's circumstances" (2005: 69; see also Nelson 2000).

2 Alyssa is the only non-KWRU participant who reports having paid rent to parents; she has also paid rent to her mother-in-law.

3 See, for example, Desmond 2012; Harknett 2006; Henly 2002; Henly et al. 2005; McDonald and Armstrong 2001; Smith 2007. Harknett demonstrated, using a large survey dataset, that support is not universally available to all who may need it, but she found that those without support from family were less likely to be employed and earned less money. Consequently, they were more likely to seek help from the public safety net. Henly, Danziger, and Offer's (2005) study came to the same conclusion, and they noted that the lack of family support makes it that much more difficult for people to leave welfare behind. McDonald and Armstrong discovered family support "to contemporary young African American mothers may be neither as abundant nor as ubiquitous today as past theorizing on the Black family intimated" (2001: 221). And Sandra Susan Smith (2005, 2007) found that having others in their networks doesn't mean those others will be forthcoming in providing assistance in finding employment.

4 Stack notes, "The process of exchange joins individuals in personal relationships" (1974: 43).

5 Desmond 2012; Harknett 2006; Henly 2002; Henly et al. 2005; McDonald and Armstrong 2001; Smith 2005, 2007.

6 Desmond 2012.

7 Desmond 2012: 1296–1297.

8 Desmond 2012: 1298.

9 Desmond 2012: 1322.

10 See Desmond 2012: 1322–1323. See also Menjívar 2000. She describes how people with limited resources may become overly indebted to network members, which results in tension or even dissolution.

11 As Mario Luis Small explains, building a friendship requires frequent interaction. He states: "People are more likely to form ties when they have opportunities to interact, when they do so frequently, when they are focused on some activity, when they are not competitors, and when they have reason to cooperate" (2009b: 15). He further explains, "Mothers so often make friends [through child care centers] because centers generate multiple opportunities and inducements for parents to interact. Through their rules and norms of interaction and their requests that parents help conduct many of their regular tasks and operations . . . centers created opportunities for friendships to form and even induced such networks inadvertently" (2009b: 51). In KWRU, it definitely was not about occasioning contact or even facilitating copresence and cooperation, but more concerted coreliance. KWRU members really need each other for survival as opposed to simply having to cooperate to accomplish a small task for the group.

Small asserts that people trust each other more as they encounter each other more often; they become familiar and trustworthy through such contact, because "centers represent a kind of safe space" (2009b: 184). He also notes, "But if centers created access to social support by increasing trust, they also did so by *formally* institutionalizing obligations" (2009b: 118, emphasis in original).

12 Domínguez 2011; Domínguez and Watkins 2003; Edin and Lein 1997; Mazelis 2015; Mazelis and Mykyta 2011; Menjívar 2000; Newman 1999; Stack 1974.

13 Edin and Lein 1997; Newman 1999; Sherman 2009.

14 Henly et al. 2005; Massey and Denton 1993; Wilson 1987, 1996.

15 Someone familiar with the biography of KWRU's founder, Cheri Honkala, may be surprised that KWRU does not provide bridging connections. The KWRU experience does not include using Cheri's ties for leverage for personal upward mobility. Cheri ran for vice president of the United States with Jill Stein in 2012 on the Green Party ticket and her son is a successful film actor and director. However, she herself continues to live in poverty and insecurity in a poor Philadelphia neighborhood, so even she isn't leveraging the ties she has to accomplish upward mobility for herself. KWRU members are not able to build bridging capital by virtue of being tied to KWRU. KWRU's mission is not about individuals rising from poverty, but ending poverty for all.

16 See also Mazelis 2015.

17 Portes 1998.

18 Stack 1974. See also Edin and Lein 1997; Mazelis and Mykyta 2011; Seccombe 1999.

19 Her ex-husband's sister has primary custody of her second child. She lost custody of him when he was a baby due to her drug use at the time. She has him on weekends, holidays, and summers.

20 Henly et al. 2005; Roschelle 1997; Sarkisian and Gerstel 2004.

21 For more on the importance of organizations for social ties for the poor, see Marwell 2007; Sampson 2012; Small 2009b; Small and Allard 2013. Small states, "While these ties are no substitute for informal social ties, they nonetheless often provide resources that informal social ties do not; they prove especially beneficial to resource-poor mothers, to socially isolated mothers, and to those mothers who only have connections to others deprived of resources. Mothers so deprived have much to gain through organizational ties" (2009b: 156), provided the organizations are themselves well-connected.

22 Small explains that, as brokers of social ties between people, organizations exhibit: "(a) many opportunities for (b) regular and (c) long-lasting interaction, (d) minimally competitive and (e) maximally cooperative institutional environments, and both (f) internal and (g) external motivations to maintain those opportunities and sustain those environments—particularly such practices that would likely contribute to organizational survival" (2009b: 21). In terms of organizational ties, "effective brokers will likely demonstrate (a) resource rich and (b) diverse organizational networks in which (c) transferring resources fulfills the objectives of multiple constituencies" (2009b: 21). Small also notes that there are four mechanisms of brokerage: storage, validation, referral, and collaboration (see Small 2009b: 152). Storage is when organizations have pamphlets and the like out for clients to see, conveying information. Validation is when centers tell other

organizations that patrons deserve the resource in question. Referral is when the center formally refers people to other organizations. Collaboration is when centers work with other groups to provide goods to parents. KWRU engaged in referrals and some storage, but not collaboration or validation in the sense Small describes.

23 Though KWRU is not as well-positioned to broker organizational ties as the organizations Small describes seem to be. Organizations can facilitate ties (Watkins-Hayes 2009), but not all organizations are the same; some engage in intensive efforts and others may not at all (Marwell 2007; Marwell and McQuarrie 2013).

24 Desmond 2012.

25 Organizations can often perform such roles of meaningful support for relationships. Small argues that the relationships parents built in the child care centers he studied were "an especially advantageous form of social capital, wherein mothers were saved from the more daunting obligations of standard intimate ties. . . . Organizations can institutionally perform much of the 'work' required to sustain strong friendships. When institutional conditions sustain a friendship, the burden of maintenance inevitably shifts" (2009b: 87). Small also states that centers provide what he describes as an advantage and a disadvantage: "a place to interact and institutionally set times for the parties to do so sustains the relationship without requiring much effort from the parties to maintain it. Thanks to the organization, the relationship both deepens week by week and remains within its bounds; without it, the relationship will likely wither" (2009b: 106).

26 Other researchers have found that neighborhood institutions such as child care centers can provide a similar mechanism for tie creation, brokering both social ties to occasion friendship and organizational ties to help clients gather resources (Small 2009b; see also Marwell 2007; Marwell and McQuarrie 2013; Small and Allard 2013: Watkins-Hayes 2009, 2013), though what is unique about KWRU is its reciprocity requirement, which is what creates the possibility for sustainability.

27 As Levine argues, people use what they can glean from past behaviors to decide if they should trust "based on direct interactions themselves, similar past experiences, or the experiences of others they knew" (2013: 40). Small (2009b) found that child care centers alleviated the need for such investigations; enrollment constituted a proxy showing their trustworthiness. KWRU membership functions in a similar way. In addition, generalized reciprocity within the organization means that KWRU will repay the help they give even if other members do not.

28 Desmond 2012: 1313.

29 Desmond 2012: 1313.

30 Small (2009b) argues for a perspective of organizational embeddedness to modify social capital theory, to avoid reducing lived realities to actors' choices. He rightly argues that choices and interactions are structured and contextual. As I found, while not everyone who has access to resources mobilizes those resources, and "actors differ in their ability and willingness to exercise agency to solve their problems" (Small 2009b: 155), these outcomes are also structurally influenced and

it would be a grave error to view these as wholly agentic decisions or choices. See also Small and Allard 2013. Small states:

> Organizational contexts may affect not only ties but also these resources—specifically, whether a person has access to them and whether she makes use of them, which scholars have called, respectively, *access to* and *mobilization of* social capital. Organizations affect the former by influencing whether people form ties to the people or organizations that possess the goods; they contribute to the latter to the extent that they enact, enforce, or encourage trust, pro-social norms, supportive services, information sharing, the provision of services, and the distribution of material goods. One must not neglect the importance of people's agency: some actors mobilize connections more effectively than others, and some will take greater advantage of the network resources available in a given organization. However, I suggest that mobilization does not depend solely on how willing a person is to use her ties; mobilization is mediated, and sometimes perpetrated, by organizations. (2009b: 18, emphasis in original)

See also Lin 1999, 2001a, 2001b; Marwell and McQuarrie 2013.

CONCLUSION

1 President Obama borrowed the phrase, "the outskirts of hope" from Lyndon Baines Johnson, who announced the War on Poverty in 1964 with a speech that included: "Unfortunately, many Americans live on the outskirts of hope—some because of their poverty, and some because of their color, and all too many because of both. Our task is to help replace their despair with opportunity." Lyndon B. Johnson, "Annual Message to the Congress on the State of the Union," January 8, 1964. Online by Gerhard Peters and John T. Woolley, The American Presidency Project, www.presidency.ucsb.edu.

2 Silva 2013: 98.

3 "Food Stamp Usage Across the Country—Interactive Map" 2009.

4 U.S. Department of Agriculture 2016a.

5 The U.S. Social Forum defines itself as "a movement building process. It is not a conference but it is a space to come up with the people's solutions to the economic and ecological crisis. The USSF is the next most important step in our struggle to build a powerful multi-racial, multi-sectoral, inter-generational, diverse, inclusive, internationalist movement that transforms this country and changes history" (U.S. Social Forum, "What Is the U.S. Social Forum?" accessed November 5, 2014, www.ussocialforum.net).

6 See Desmond 2012; Domínguez and Watkins 2003; Small 2009b; Stack 1974.

7 Hacker 2008: xvi, emphasis in original; see also Cooper 2014.

8 Putnam 2015: 206.

9 McCoy 2015.

10 See Derber and Magrass 2012, and Rehmann 2015 for the argument that neoliberalism creates a surplus population, people who are unemployed or underemployed.

11 Edsall 2015.

12 Beck 2000; Cooper 2014; Hacker 2004, 2008.

13 Sherman 2013.

14 Catholic Relief Securities, n.d.

15 See also Sampson 2012.

16 See Desmond 2012.

17 Programs that are multidimensional and comprehensive do well. In Jamie Fader's discussion of the Harlem Children's Zone (HCZ), she states, "The program includes parenting workshops, prekindergarten preparation, charter schools, college support, assistance programs for tenants who want to convert their city-owned buildings into co-ops, and recreation, arts, and health programs for community members" (2013: 225). Putnam's description of it provides a compelling argument for this holistic approach: "Begun in 1970, HCZ includes early childhood programs, after-school tutoring and extracurricular offerings, family, community, and health programs; college encouragement; foster-care-prevention programs; and many others" (2015: 254). Small and Allard (2013) note that while there is a dearth of information about the work of organizations within HCZ, providing a more holistic approach does seem promising. Sampson (2012) also argues for a holistic approach.

18 See Newman 1999. Some might say an organization should focus on one thing and do it well, but bundled services create community. Newman advocates a comprehensive approach, calling it a "saturation" model rather than a "dispersed" one. Small and Allard (2013) point out that most support services require people to interact with multiple bureaucracies and organizations, and the poor have to therefore navigate multiple services to get the help they need, which can be confusing and logistically onerous. It's a great argument for "one-stop shopping"—providing a bundle of services together. Watkins-Hayes states, "Organizational networks, specialized knowledge, and the ability to bundle resources" are what organizations can provide to clients (2013: 84). Such benefits are even more important to those with low income. Watkins-Hayes found that the middle-class women she studied had fewer connections to AIDS service organizations than the low-income women and fewer HIV-positive network members, making them more socially isolated from others facing the same difficulties, even though economically they were better off. She stated, "While middle-class women may exceed low-income women in their access to social capital in general, they tend to trail these women in terms of HIV-specific social capital" (2013: 98). This is similar to my finding that the non-KWRU participants have more family social capital, but the KWRU participants are less isolated from others like them and therefore have more emotional support to deal with their current difficulties.

19 Small argues that "studies of networks in other urban organizations—such as beauty salons, diners, schools, bathhouses, churches, and community colleges—confirm several of my propositions about how organizations condition personal networks" (Small 2009b: 179). My findings confirm Small's assertion that the power of organizations to condition personal networks is not unique to child care centers.

20 The fact that other researchers have found that individuals build ties through neighborhood institutions (Marwell 2007; Small 2009b; Watkins-Hayes 2009) reinforces my argument.

21 Small 2009b: 118, emphasis in original.

22 Small 2009b.

23 Small and Allard 2013: 8.

24 Gutiérrez and Lewis 1999: 22.

25 Small notes, "The state can, in fact, create conditions that generate social capital. Some have come to believe that social capital is impossible to shape, structure, or institutionalize, because they have conceived it as a largely informal process" (2009b: 190). I would also add to this that some policy makers and scholars have conceived of it as an agentic process as well, but this ignores the ways in which opportunities to develop meaningful and significant social capital are structured in often limiting ways.

26 Hacker and Pierson 2010: 34.

27 Krueger 2005; Putnam 2015.

28 Lemann (2015) argues:

> More than a hundred years ago, Frederick Jackson Turner proposed that state universities could replace the frontier as the means of offering opportunity to all Americans. Today most discussions of inequality and opportunity still focus on education as the best way to prevent, or even to reverse, class divisions. (This is why, for example, American philanthropists today are so intensely focused on funding charter schools—it's the expectation that they can create economic opportunities for their students that they otherwise wouldn't have.) One problem with this idea, appealing as it is, is that one of the most consistent findings in education research is that students' performance in school is far more closely correlated with what kind of home they come from—parental income, education, marital status, how they make use of time, and so on—than with anything that goes on in their school. That isn't to say that schools can't make a contribution to equal opportunity, but it has to be understood as commanding only a limited territory.

29 Putnam 2015: 32; see also McCall 2013; Page and Jacobs 2009.

30 Putnam 2015: 241.

31 Page and Jacobs 2009: 3.

32 Page and Jacobs 2009: 22.

33 Edin and Shaefer 2015.

34 Henderson 2015; National Alliance to End Homelessness 2015; Schulte 2013.

35 Desmond 2016.

36 Clampet-Lundquist 2004.

37 Roll and Steiner 2015: 568.

38 "Research has shown that supportive housing has positive effects on housing stability, employment, mental and physical health, and school attendance. People in supportive housing live more stable and productive lives"; "Cost studies in six different states and cities found that supportive housing results in tenants' decreased use of homeless shelters, hospitals, emergency rooms, jails and prisons" (Corporation for Supportive Housing. n.d.).

39 Of course, while we think of "child care" in terms of preschool ages, adolescents in low-income families also need safe and affordable after-school programs.

40 Lambert, Fugiel, and Henly 2014.

41 See also Roschelle 1997. And as Hansen notes, "State-supported services are important because not every parent has a network, and by themselves, informal networks are typically not enough to meet all the needs of parents and care for school-age children" (2005: 216).

42 Even "full-day" generally means 8:30 to 3, causing difficulty even for parents who work traditional 9 to 5 hours, let alone those who work noon to 8 or 4 to midnight.

43 Cauthen and Fass 2008; Edelman 2012; Fisher 1992.

44 The 1938 Fair Labor Standards Act (FLSA) established a minimum wage of 25 cents per hour (for covered workers), and "has been raised 22 separate times, in part to keep up with rising prices. Most recently, in July 2009, it was increased to $7.25 an hour. Because there have been some extended periods between these adjustments while inflation generally has increased, the real value (purchasing power) of the minimum wage has decreased substantially over time" (Elwell 2014: 1). The uniform federal minimum wage (unadjusted for inflation) has gone from $2.90/hour in 1979, to $3.10 in 1980, to $3.35 in 1981, to $3.80 in 1991, to $4.25 in 1992, to $4.75 in 1996, to $5.15 in 1997, to $5.85 in 2007, $6.55 in 2008, to $7.25 in 2009. Some states mandate higher than federal minimum wage laws, but there are a few states with minimum wage rates lower than the federal rate for workers not covered under the FLSA (U.S Department of Labor 2013; see also Elwell 2014; Mishel 2013; National Conference of State Legislatures 2016). There has recently been a push to increase the minimum wage markedly, with popular $10.10 per hour, or even $15 per hour, campaigns (Barro 2015). Over a dozen states have taken action to raise their minimum wages. In 2015, over half the states have a minimum wage above $7.25 per hour (U.S. Department of Labor 2015).

45 White House 2014a.

46 U.S. Department of Health and Human Services, n.d.c., It's less than the poverty threshold for a family of two in 2016 as well.

47 White House 2014a.

48 Floyd and Schott state, "TANF benefit levels are so low that they are not sufficient to provide family income above half of the poverty line in any state" (2013: 3),

and in a footnote to this the authors note: "The 2013 HHS poverty guideline for a family of three is about $1,628 per month in the 48 contiguous states and D.C.; Alaska and Hawaii have higher poverty levels." (See U.S. Department of Health and Human Services, n.d.b. In 2014 it's about $1,649 per month (U.S. Department of Health and Human Services, n.d.c. See also Falk 2014.

49 Floyd and Schott 2013.

50 As Shaefer and Edin note, "The Personal Responsibility and Work Opportunity Reconciliation Act (PRWORA) of 1996 ended the only cash entitlement program for poor families with children, Aid to Families with Dependent Children (AFDC), and replaced it with Temporary Assistance for Needy Families (TANF), a program that offers time-limited cash assistance and requires able-bodied recipients to participate in work-related activities" (2013: 250).

51 Footnote in original: "The Fair Market Rent is the U.S. Department of Housing and Urban Development's estimate of the amount needed to cover the rent and utility costs of a modest housing unit in a given local area" (Floyd and Schott 2013).

52 Floyd and Schott 2013, emphases in original. TANF's cash value is "so low that it doesn't bring a family's income even to half the poverty line in any state. In thirty-two states plus the District of Columbia, TANF benefits for a family of three with no other income are now below 30 percent of the poverty threshold. In sixteen states, the maximum payment is below 20 percent of the poverty line. And in one state, Mississippi, TANF benefits are so low they wouldn't even lift a family above the $2-a-day threshold" (Edin and Shaefer 2015: 170).

53 Mendenhall et al. state, "Welfare, as the United States knew it, ended in 1996. Temporary Assistance for Needy Families (TANF) replaced the entitlement program Aid to Families with Dependent Children. The new program imposed strict time limits and participation requirements on beneficiaries. Over the next 15 years, the number of families receiving such assistance plummeted from roughly 4.5 million in 1996 to 1.9 million in 2011" (2012: 368).

54 See Tach and Halpern-Meekin, who state, "The EITC was first enacted in 1975 as a small tax credit, worth several hundred dollars, to reimburse the social security taxes paid by low-income workers with children. It has expanded dramatically since then, most notably in the Tax Reform Act of 1986 and the Omnibus Reconciliation Acts of 1990 and 1993. The EITC expansion in 1993, phased in between 1994 and 1996, was used to fulfill President Clinton's promise to low-wage workers that "if you work, you should not be poor" (2014: 413). See also Newman 1999 for a discussion of the EITC's start.

55 Mendenhall et al. state: "In 1993, the Omnibus Budget Reconciliation Act (107 Stat. 433) roughly tripled the value of the means-tested benefit of the Earned Income Tax Credit (EITC), then a little-known program for low- and moderate-wage workers with dependent children. When the EITC began in 1975, the program only served 6.2 million families with dependent children. In 2011, it dwarfed

the old welfare system, serving around 26.2 million families, which received nearly $58.6 billion (US Department of the Treasury 2011). From 1995 to 2009, the EITC also transferred more money to individuals than did the Supplemental Nutrition Assistance Program (SNAP), the federal food-assistance program formerly known as the Food Stamp Program" (2012: 368). See also Edin and Shaefer 2015; Putnam 2015; Shaefer and Edin 2013.

56 Putnam 2015. See also Page and Jacobs, who state, "Large majorities of Americans favor raising the minimum wage and expanding the Earned Income Tax Credit, so that people who work hard will not be stuck in poverty. . . . Majorities of Americans say that government should make sure that no one goes without food, clothing, or shelter" (2009: 98).

57 Tach and Halpern-Meekin argue that "the EITC's lack of transparency, and its delivery in a refund check that includes money withheld from weekly paychecks, made the redistributive nature of this antipoverty program largely invisible and destigmatized relative to other cash transfers programs for low-income households" (2014: 433).

58 Mendenhall et al. note, citing the Center on Budget and Policy Priorities 2012: "In 2010, the EITC lifted roughly 6.3 million people out of poverty, including 3 million children. Without the EITC, one-quarter more children would live in poverty. The EITC program is also viewed as a vehicle that benefits communities, boosting local economies and decreasing crime rates by raising wages" (2012: 369). See also Center on Budget and Policy Priorities 2012.

59 Gilbert 2011.

60 Rumberger 2011. Also see Bureau of Labor Statistics 2014; Crosby and Moncarz 2006a, 2006b; Heckman et al. 2011; Putnam 2015; Sanchez 2012; Sum et al. 2012.

61 Sum et al. 2012. As Putnam states, "Much recent research has confirmed that the GED does not have the same value as a regular high school degree, either in terms of continuing on to college or in the labor market. Indeed, some research suggests that the GED adds very little compared to dropping out of high school and getting no degree at all" (2015: 184).

62 Newman (1999) talks in detail about some small pilot programs linking students with work opportunities, as well as Japanese and German models for connecting high school students with employers. For the non–college bound, knowing that the skills they're gaining in vocational high schools will actually lead to work is powerful. The programs she describes can serve as resource brokers, in Mario Luis Small's (2009b) terminology, brokering organizational ties and increasing the opportunity for the students to develop bridging capital. They would be sites not just for education, but also provide a bundle of services. See Newman's chapter 9, "What We Can Do for the Working Poor."

Putnam also notes the importance of "a vigorous system of vocational education, apprenticeship, and workforce training, both in and out of schools" (2015: 255), similar to what existed in the United States in the past. He relates the dismantling of this system to the "college for all" mantra, which draws attention and resources from secondary and postsecondary education in vocational skills, noting the success of such programs as Career Academies, whose participants earn 17 percent more than their nonacademy counterparts and have as great a likelihood of obtaining postsecondary degrees as their counterparts.

63 See American Association of University Women 2009.

64 Hamilton and Scrivener explain,

> The law limits the degree to which education and training count toward the participation rate. Specifically, hours in vocational training can count toward the participation requirement, but can only count toward all hours of participation for 12 months for a given recipient. After 12 months, a state can only count the hours in which a family member is participating in higher education toward the participation rate (counted as job skills training) if he or she is also participating for at least 20 hours per week in a "core" work activity, such as subsidized or unsubsidized employment or work experience. (2012: 2)

Schott (2015) details the work requirements of TANF:

> The 1996 law sets forth 12 categories of work activities that can count toward the work rates; the parameters for each activity are shaped by definitions set by post-DRA federal rules. Nine of these 12 categories are core categories that can count toward any hours of participation; participation in the three non-core categories can only count if the individual also participates in core activities for at least 20 hours per week (30 hours for two-parent families).
>
> The nine core activities are:
>
> Unsubsidized employment;
> Subsidized private-sector employment;
> Subsidized public-sector employment;
> Work experience;
> On-the-job training;
> Job search and job readiness assistance;
> Community service programs;
> Vocational educational training (for up to 12 months); and
> Providing child care services to an individual who is participating in a community service program.
>
> The three non-core activities are:
>
> • Job skills training directly related to employment;
> • Education directly related to employment;
> • Satisfactory attendance at secondary school or in a course of study leading to a GED.
>
> Federal law includes additional rules on when certain activities can count toward the federal work rate. For example, an individual's participation in job search or job readiness activities can only count for six weeks in a year (12 weeks in hard economic times) and for four consecutive weeks. In addi-

tion, no more than 30 percent of the families that a state counts toward its federal work rates may do so through participation in vocational educational training or, for parents under age 20, school attendance or education directly related to employment. (Under a special rule, secondary or GED-related school attendance or education directly related to employment can count as participation for parents under age 20 even if it would otherwise be a non-core activity that can only count after 20 hours per week of core participation.) (2015: 5)

65 See American Association of University Women 2009.

66 Hamilton and Scrivener state:

Notably, states can allow participation in postsecondary education and training regardless of whether it is countable toward the TANF participation standard. Moreover, even under the TANF standard, postsecondary education can often be counted as vocational training for up to a year and, even after that year, it can be counted when combined with 20 hours of work or work experience. The practices of some programs currently encouraging postsecondary education and training under TANF may provide specific ideas for TANF administrators. The Kentucky Ready to Work program, for example, facilitates access to higher education by using TANF resources to fund counselors at community colleges who help TANF recipients negotiate school, family, TANF, and work obligations. A significant share of the program's resources also goes toward engaging program participants in paid workstudy jobs while they pursue their education. As another example, the Arkansas Career Pathways Initiative is using TANF resources to fund support services (including child care and transportation), tutoring, and counseling for individuals attending certain community college programs, including some TANF recipients. (2012: 5)

67 The Act created the Office of Economic Opportunity (OEO), which used community action program (CAP) funds in part to fund local programs developed by community agencies themselves ("Economic Opportunity Act of 1964"). See also Levitan 1969.

68 See Cohen 2014; Fletcher 2005; Kornbluh 2007; Levitan 1969; Marcus 2006; Ralph 2014. As just one example, Laurence Ralph notes, "Major street gangs became recipients of private grants and public funds (most notably from President Johnson's War on Poverty) earmarked for community organizations, the development of social welfare programs, and profit-making commercial enterprises" (2014: 63).

69 Beezat (2014) further argues,

Combating poverty now and in the future should once again be built around poor people organizing to address the challenges that they see their families and communities up against every day. While government is unlikely to fund these kinds of efforts, non-partisan, private foundations should indeed support this type of grassroots organizing. If it works as well now as it did 50 years ago, it would force all of our elected officials, Democrats and Republicans, to listen to all of the people, not just those who have the money and organizational power to influence legislation. And the country as a whole would benefit.

70 Chaffin 2014; Community Action Partnership: The National Association 2015.

71 Chaffin 2014; U.S. Deparment of Health and Human Services n.d.d.

72 Holeywell 2013; Lifson 2011.

73 Chaffin and Hassett 2015.

74 Daniels 2015.

75 National Alliance to End Homelessness 2014.

76 Offer argues that her findings, which "highlight the double-edged sword of deprivation by demonstrating how those in greatest need for support are the least likely to have it available to them, call for establishing formal channels of support in the community [and show that] social service agencies and community-based organizations constitute an important alternative to family- and friends-based support networks" (2012a: 129; also see Domínguez and Watkins 2003, Small 2009b, Small and Allard 2013; Marwell 2007; Marwell and McQuarrie 2013; Watkins-Hayes 2009, 2013). Offer argues that nonprofits can "facilitate socializing and link low-income mothers to other mothers in the community and encourage them, through their ties with professionals and social service providers to general personal connections outside the community" (2012a: 130; see also Small 2009b).

77 Shea 2014.

APPENDIX

1 With the exception of one participant who lived with her parents in the suburbs of Philadelphia at the time of our interview.

2 2003–2006.

3 See Philadelphia City Planning Commission 2013 for the 18 districts as of April 2013. Based on these new divisions, I conducted research in 12 of the 18 regions.

4 See Cartographic Modeling Laboratory 2006b.

5 See Cartographic Modeling Laboratory 2006a. Users may select U.S. Census data as a category and then select poverty rate as an indicator for a graphic illustration of how poverty rates map onto the city.

6 Twelve agency locations (plus KWRU) appear on the map, due to mapping of the agency that manages a GED class that occurs elsewhere. I recruited no participants at that agency location but included it on the map nonetheless.

7 The parenting class and the employment class were in different buildings. Both locations are indicated on the map.

8 Both locations are shown on the map.

9 Both locations are shown on the map.

10 I met Bianca and Carole at a Center City agency but Bianca lived in South Philadelphia and Carole lived in West Philadelphia. I met Jasmine at a South Philadelphia agency but she lived in West Philadelphia.

11 The last participant in question was a young single mother and recent welfare recipient who had been a student in a class my colleague taught.

12 At the time I met her she lived in West Philadelphia, though by the time of our interview she was staying with her parents outside Philadelphia, in Chester County. Therefore, her residential location is not represented on the map in this appendix.

13 Small 2009b.

14 Lavee and Offer also note that their study likely excluded some even worse off: "All the women who participated in the study were recruited through governmental or private social service agencies, thus leaving out the most marginalized women. Hence, the extent of hardship and social isolation experienced by low-income women is likely to be more severe than what the findings of this study suggest" (2012: 390). And others, including participants in this study, rely on kin. Those who have others they can rely on, even in potentially burdensome exchanges, may be better off than those with no one to rely on but just as much need; it's possible that Stack (1974) and others (including me) who've found cooperative exchange networks, found people slightly more advantaged than an uncaptured group of poor people without the ability to be in such networks (see also Roschelle 1997).

15 All seven of them were non-KWRU participants.

16 This racial makeup probably reflects three relevant interactions between race and poverty. First, statistics suggest that there are fewer poor white people in Philadelphia than poor African Americans. Second, it's possible kin support is more available for whites, so they are less likely to turn to social programs for aid. Researchers have found kin more able to provide financial support among whites (Haxton and Harknett 2009; Henly et al. 2005; Hofferth 1984; Hogan et al. 1993; Lee and Aytac 1998; Mazelis and Mykyta 2011; Roschelle 1997; Sarkisian and Gerstel 2004, Sarkisian et al. 2007). Third, it is possible that the stigma of poverty affects whites differently than it does African Americans and Latinos, leading whites to avoid seeking assistance from an organization like KWRU. As described in chapter 1, the achievement ideology leads people to blame themselves rather than the social structure for their poverty; I suspect this may be particularly true for whites. While African Americans can legitimately point to historical and contemporary racial discrimination as a barrier to success (MacLeod 2008), poor whites have no such claim. Without language to discuss class-based systemic disadvantage, they may be more apt to blame themselves and internalize poverty stigma to a greater degree.

17 Berg and Lune 2012; Strauss and Corbin 1998.

18 Strauss and Corbin 1998.

19 Berg and Lune 2012; Strauss and Corbin 1998.

20 Strauss and Corbin 1998: 11.

21 Small 2009a.

22 Small 2008: 170; emphasis in original.

23 See Small 2006.

24 Lareau continues:

> Gradually, I began to analyze the data, mainly by reading, rereading, and reading again the field notes from the families (for each family, there was a chronologically arranged file of notes). For the interviews of the parents of the eighty-eight children, I coded the response data and then entered this information into a qualitative software program. For the twelve families, though, I proceeded the old-fashioned way: I read field notes, read the literature, talked to people, and reread the notes. I tried to link the bits and pieces of data to ideas; when the argument took shape, I looked for disconfirming evidence. In writing the book, I first considered organizing the chapters analytically, comparing all of the families with respect to one overarching theme. But ultimately, following the book *The Second Shift* by Arlie Hochschild, I chose to try to bring the families to life by devoting a separate chapter to each. I had begun the study interested in how children spend their time and in the nature of the interactions between families and institutions; those themes flourished in the book. Yet other, unexpected themes also emerged: particularly the role of language, the relative importance of kinship ties, the analogies of concerted cultivation and natural growth, and the limitations of social class in daily life. (2003: 273–274)

25 Wonderful advice from my friend and developmental editor extraordinaire Kate Epstein, which got me moving forward.

REFERENCES

Alkon, Alison Hope, and Teresa Marie Mares. 2012. "Food Sovereignty in U.S. Food Movements: Radical Visions and Neoliberal Constraints." *Agriculture and Human Values* 29(3): 347–359.

Allen, Tom. 2013. "Criticisms of Obamacare." September 27, www.blog.oup.com.

Alvarez, Lizette. 2014. "Court Strikes Down Drug Tests for Florida Welfare Applicants." December 3, www.nytimes.com.

American Association of University Women. 2009. "Breaking through Barriers for Women and Girls: Education and Training in Welfare/TANF." www.aauw.org.

Anderson, Elijah. 1976. *A Place on the Corner.* Chicago: University of Chicago Press.

———. 1990. *Streetwise: Race, Class, and Change in an Urban Community.* Chicago: University of Chicago Press.

———. 1999. *Code of the Street: Decency, Violence, and the Moral Life of the Inner City.* New York: W. W. Norton.

Anderson, Nick. 2014. "Obama Administration Offers Second Plan to Regulate Colleges with Career-Training Classes." March 13, www.washingtonpost.com.

Appelbaum, Binyamin, and Robert Gebeloff. 2012. "Even Critics of Safety Net Increasingly Depend on It." February 11, www.nytimes.com.

Badger, Emily. 2015. "The Double-Standard of Making the Poor Prove They're Worthy of Government Benefits." April 7, www.washingtonpost.com.

Bandura, Albert. 1982. "Self-Efficacy Mechanism in Human Agency." *American Psychologist* 37: 122–147.

Baptist, Willie, and Jan Rehmann. 2011. *Pedagogy of the Poor: Building the Movement to End Poverty.* New York: Teachers College Press.

Barro, John. 2015. "A $15 Minimum Wage. But Why Just for Fast-Food Workers?" July 28, www.nytimes.com.

Bassett, Laura. 2010. "Disturbing Job Ads: 'The Unemployed Will Not Be Considered.'" June 4, www.huffingtonpost.com.

Beck, Ulrich. 2000. *The Brave New World of Work.* Cambridge, U.K.: Polity Press.

Beezat, Robert. 2014. "A Forgotten Lesson of the War on Poverty." June 19, www.talkpoverty.org.

Bellah, Robert N., Richard Madsen, William M. Sullivan, Ann Swidler, and Steven M. Tipton. 1985. *Habits of the Heart: Individualism and Commitment in American Life.* Berkeley: University of California Press.

Berg, Bruce L., and Howard Lune. 2012. *Qualitative Research Methods for the Social Sciences*. 8th edition. Essex, U.K.: Pearson.

Binzen, Peter. 1970. *Whitetown, U.S.A.* New York: Random House.

Blackmon, Pamela. 2015. "Beyond Coincidence: How Neoliberal Policy Initiatives in the IMF and World Bank Affected U.S. Poverty Levels." Pp. 11–18 in *The Routledge Handbook of Poverty in the United States*, edited by Stephen Nathan Haymes, María Vidal de Haymes, and Reuben Jonathan Miller. New York: Routledge.

Blow, Charles M. 2014. "Paul Ryan, Culture and Poverty." March 21, www.nytimes.com.

Bound, John, Michael F. Lovenheim, and Sarah Turner. 2010. "Why Have College Completion Rates Declined? An Analysis of Changing Student Preparation and Collegiate Resources." *American Economic Journal: Applied Economics* 2(3): 129–157.

Bourdieu, Pierre. 1986. "The Forms of Capital." Pp. 241–58 in *Handbook of Theory and Research for the Sociology of Education*, edited by John G. Richardson. New York: Greenwood.

Bourgois, Philippe I. 1995. *In Search of Respect: Selling Crack in El Barrio*. New York: Cambridge University Press.

Bricker-Jenkins, Mary, Carrie Young, and Cheri Honkala. 2007. "Using Economic Human Rights in the Movement to End Poverty: The Kensington Welfare Rights Union and the Poor People's Economic Human Rights Campaign." Pp. 122–137 in *Challenges in Human Rights: A Social Work Perspective*, edited by Elisabeth Reichert. New York: Columbia University Press.

Briggs, Xavier de Souza. 1998. "Brown Kids in White Suburbs: Housing Mobility and the Many Faces of Social Capital." *Housing Policy Debate* 9: 177–221.

Broughton, Chad. 2001. "Reforming Poor Women: The Cultural Politics and Practices of Welfare Reform." Ph.D. dissertation, Department of Sociology, University of Chicago, Chicago.

Brown, Alyssa. 2012. "With Poverty Comes Depression, More than Other Illnesses." October 30, www.gallup.com.

Bunch, Will. 2014. "In Ruins: How Philadelphia Became the Poorest Big City in America." May 14, www.articles.philly.com.

Bureau of Labor Statistics. 2014. "Earnings and Unemployment Rates by Educational Attainment." www.bls.gov.

———. 2014. "Entrepreneurship and the U.S. Economy," www.bls.gov.

Burton, Linda, Andrew J. Cherlin, Judith Francis, Robin Jarrett, James Quane, Constance Williams, and N. Michelle Stem Cook. 1998. "What Welfare Recipients and the Fathers of Their Children Are Saying about Welfare Reform: A Report on 15 Focus Group Discussions in Baltimore, Boston, and Chicago." www.web.jhu.edu.

Byers, Tom, Heleen Kist, and Robert I. Sutton. 1998. "Characteristics of the Entrepreneur: Social Creatures, Not Solo Heroes." Pp. 1-1–1-6 in *The Technology Management Handbook*, edited by Richard C. Dorf. Boca Raton, Fl.: CRC Press.

"The CARD Act: One Year Later." 2011. February 22, www.consumerfinance.gov.

Cartographic Modeling Laboratory. 2006a. neighborhoodBase, www.cml.upenn.edu.

———. 2006b. Philadelphia Neighborhood Information System, www.cml.upenn.edu.

Catalan, Julissa. 2014. "Candidate Compares People Receiving Food Stamps to Wild Animals." *DiversityInc.* May 2, www.diversityinc.com.

Catholic Relief Services. n.d. "Pope Francis on Care for the Poor," www.crs.org.

Cauthen, Nancy K., and Sarah Fass. 2008. "Measuring Poverty in the United States." National Center for Children in Poverty, Columbia University Mailman School of Public Health, Department of Health Policy & Management. June, www.nccp.org.

Centeno, Miguel A., and Joseph N. Cohen. 2012. "The Arc of Neoliberalism." *Annual Review of Sociology* 38: 317–340.

Center on Budget and Policy Priorities. 2012. "Policy Basics: The Earned Income Tax Credit." Policy Basics Report. February 22, www.cbpp.org.

Chaffin, Jeannie. 2014. "The Role of Community Action in the War on Poverty." *U.S. Department of Health & Human Services. Administration for Children & Families.* June 5, www.acf.hhs.gov.

Chaffin, Jeannie L., and Seth Hassett. 2015. "CSBG Dear Colleague Letter FY 2015 3rd Quarter Allocations." *Administration for Children & Families. Office of Community Services. An Office of the Administration for Children & Families* April 15, www.acf.hhs.gov.

Cherlin, Andrew, Pamela Winston, Ronald Angel, Linda Burton, P. Lindsay Chase-Lansdale, Robert Moffitt, William Julius Wilson, Rebekah Levine Coley, and James Quane. 2000. "Welfare, Children & Families: A Three City Study: What Welfare Recipients Know about the New Rules and What They Have to Say about Them." Policy Brief 00–1, www.web.jhu.edu.

Chozick, Amy. 2015. "Hillary Clinton Blames Republicans for Promoting Inequality." July 13, www.nytimes.com.

Christoffersen, John. 2012. "Romney's '47%' Chosen as Year's Best Quote." December 14, www.usatoday.com.

Clampet-Lundquist, Susan. 2004. "Moving Over or Moving Up? Short-Term Gains and Losses for Relocated HOPE VI Families." *Journal of Policy Development and Research* 7 (1): 57–80.

Cohen, Jodi R. 1997. "Poverty: Talk, Identity, and Action (Nature of Poverty Revealed by the Conversations of the Poor)." *Qualitative Inquiry* 3 (1): 71–92.

Cohen, Rick. 2014. "Coming Full Circle: The War on Poverty's Invaluable Contribution to Today's Nonprofit Sector." *Nonprofit Quarterly: Promoting an Active and Engaged Democracy.* January 9, http://nonprofitquarterly.org.

Coleman, James S. 1988. "Social Capital in the Creation of Human Capital." *American Journal of Sociology* 94 Supplement: S95-S120.

———. 1990. *Foundations of Social Theory.* Cambridge, Mass.: Belknap.

Community Action Partnership: The National Association. 2015. "Community Action Partnership—About CAAs." Washington, D.C., www.communityactionpartnership.com.

Community Legal Services of Philadelphia. n.d.a. "Employment with a Criminal Record." www.clsphila.org.

———. n.d.b. "Legal Rights of People with Criminal Records: Employment." www. clsphila.org.

"Consumer Financial Protection Bureau." 2015. *Consumer Financial Protection Bureau*, www.consumerfinance.gov.

Cooper, Marianne. 2014. *Cut Adrift: Families in Insecure Times*. Berkeley: University of California Press.

Corporation for Supportive Housing. n.d. "Supportive Housing Facts: Evidence and Research." CSH: The Source for Housing Solutions, www.csh.org.

Crosby, Olivia, and Roger Moncarz. 2006a. "The 2004–14 Job Outlook for People Who Don't Have a Bachelor's Degree." Bureau of Labor Statistics. *Occupational Outlook Quarterly* 50 (3): 27–41, www.bls.gov.

———. 2006b. "The 2004–14 Job Outlook for People Who Don't Have a Bachelor's Degree." Bureau of Labor Statistics. *Occupational Outlook Quarterly* 50 (3): 42–57, www.bls.gov.

Daniels, Alex. 2015. "Ford Shifts Grant Making to Focus Entirely on Inequality." June 11, www.philanthropy.com.

Danziger, Sheldon, and Peter Gottschalk, eds. 1994. *Uneven Tides: Rising Inequality in America*. New York: Russell Sage Foundation.

David, E. J. R. 2014. *Internalized Oppression: The Psychology of Marginalized Groups*. New York: Springer Publishing.

Davis, Brittany Alana. 2012. "Florida Didn't Save Money by Drug Testing Welfare Recipients, Data Shows." April 18, www.tampabay.com.

Delamaide, Darrell. 2013. "Credit Cards Show How Regulatory Reform Can Work." October 8, www.usatoday.com.

Delaney, Arthur. 2010. "Tom Corbett Says the Unemployed Just 'Sit There.'" July 13, www.huffingtonpost.com.

———. 2015. "GOP's Big Government Welfare Reforms." May 27, www.huffingtonpost. com.

DeParle, Jason. 2012. "For Poor, Leap to College Often Ends in a Hard Fall." December 22, www.nytimes.com.

DeParle, Jason, and Robert Gebeloff. 2009. "Food Stamp Use Soars, and Stigma Fades." November 28, www.nytimes.com.

Derber, Charles, and Yale A. Magrass. 2012. *Surplus American: How the 1% Is Making Us Redundant*. New York: Routledge.

Desmond, Matthew. 2012. "Disposable Ties and the Urban Poor." *American Journal of Sociology* 117 (5): 1295–1335.

———. 2015. "Severe Deprivation in America: An Introduction." *Russell Sage Foundation Journal* 1 (2):1–11, www.rsfjournal.org.

———. 2016. *Evicted: Poverty and Profit in the American City*. New York: Crown.

Dietrich, Sharon M. 2010. "Fact Sheet: Employers' Rejection of People with Criminal Records Is Putting a Large Percentage of the Population Out of Work Unnecessarily." www.clsphila.org.

Domínguez, Silvia. 2011. *Getting Ahead: Social Mobility, Public Housing, and Immigrant Social Networks.* New York: NYU Press.

Domínguez, Silvia, and Celeste Watkins. 2003. "Creating Networks for Survival and Mobility: Social Capital among African-American and Latin-American Low-Income Mothers." *Social Problems* 50 (1): 111–135.

"Drug Testing for Welfare Recipients and Public Assistance." 2015. *National Conference of State Legislatures.* July 27, www.ncsl.org.

Duneier, Mitchell. 1992. *Slim's Table: Race, Respectability, and Masculinity.* Chicago: University of Chicago Press.

———. 1999. *Sidewalk.* New York: Farrar, Strauss and Giroux.

Eaglesham, Jean. 2011. "Warning Shot on Financial Protection." February 9, www.wsj.com.

"Economic Opportunity Act of 1964." PUBLIC LAW 88–452-AUG. 20, 1964, www.gpo.gov.

Edelman, Peter. 2012. *So Rich, So Poor: Why It's So Hard to End Poverty in America.* New York: New Press.

Edin, Kathryn. 2001. "More than Money: The Role of Assets in the Survival Strategies and Material Well-Being of the Poor." Pp. 206–31 in *Assets for the Poor: The Benefits of Spreading Asset Ownership,* edited by Thomas M. Shapiro and Edward N. Wolff. New York: Russell Sage Foundation.

Edin, Kathryn, and Maria Kefalas. 2005. *Promises I Can Keep: Why Poor Women Put Motherhood before Marriage.* Berkeley: University of California Press.

Edin, Kathryn, and Laura Lein. 1996. "Work, Welfare, and Single Mothers' Economic Survival Strategies." *American Sociological Review* 62 (2): 253–266.

———. 1997. *Making Ends Meet: How Single Mothers Survive Welfare and Low-Wage Work.* New York: Russell Sage Foundation.

Edin, Kathryn J., and H. Luke Shaefer. 2015. *$2.00 a Day: Living on Almost Nothing in America.* Boston: Houghton Mifflin Harcourt.

Edsall, Thomas B. 2015. "Why Don't the Poor Rise Up?" June 24, www.nytimes.com.

Ekeh, Peter Palmer. 1974. *Social Exchange Theory: The Two Traditions.* Cambridge: Harvard University Press.

Elwell, Craig K. 2014. "Inflation and the Real Minimum Wage: A Fact Sheet." Congressional Research Service. January 8, www.fas.org.

Esping-Anderson, G. 1990. *The Three Worlds of Welfare Capitalism.* Princeton: Princeton University Press.

Fader, Jamie J. 2013. *Falling Back: Incarceration and Transitions to Adulthood among Urban Youth.* New Brunswick: Rutgers University Press.

Fairbanks, Robert P. II. 2009. *How It Works: Recovering Citizens in Post-Welfare Philadelphia.* Chicago: University of Chicago Press.

Falk, Gene. 2014. "Temporary Assistance for Needy Families (TANF): Eligibility and Benefit Amounts in State TANF Cash Assistance Programs." Congressional Research Service. July 22, www.hsdl.org.

Feemster, Ron. 2004. "Economic Rights Are Human Rights." *Shelterforce Online*. Issue #135. National Housing Institute, www.nhi.org.

Ferdman, Roberto A. 2015. "Missouri Republicans Are Trying to Ban Food Stamp Recipients from Buying Steak and Seafood." April 3, www.washingtonpost.com.

Field, Kelly. 2014. "In the Final 'Gainful Employment' Rule, a Key Measure Vanishes." October 30, www.chronicle.com.

Fisher, Gordon M. 1992. "The Development and History of Poverty Thresholds." *Social Security Bulletin* 55 (4): 3–14.

Fletcher, Michael A. 2005. "Two Fronts in the War on Poverty." May 17, www.washingtonpost.com.

Flores-Yeffal, Nadia Yamel. 2013. *Migration-Trust Networks: Social Cohesion in Mexican U.S.-Bound Emigration*. College Station: Texas A&M University Press.

Floyd, Ife, and Liz Schott. 2013. "TANF Cash Benefits Continued to Lose Value in 2013." Center on Budget and Policy Priorities. October 21, www.cbpp.org.

"Food Stamp Usage across the Country—Interactive Map." 2009. November 28, www.nytimes.com.

Fox, Liana, Christopher Wimer, Irwin Garfinkel, Neeraj Kaushal, JaeHyun Nam, and Jane Waldfogel. 2015. "Trends in Deep Poverty from 1968 to 2011: The Influence of Family Structure, Employment Patterns, and the Safety Net." *Russell Sage Foundation Journal* 1 (1):14–34, www.rsfjournal.org.

Franklin, Benjamin. 2005. *Benjamin Franklin: Autobiography, Poor Richard: Autobiography, Poor Richard, and Later Writings*, edited by J. A. Leo Lemay. New York: Library of America.

Friedersdorf, Conor. 2014. "Working Mom Arrested for Letting Her 9-Year-Old Play Alone at Park." July 15, www.theatlantic.com.

Furstenberg, Frank F., Jr. 2001. "The Fading Dream: Prospects for Marriage in the Inner City." Pp. 224–46 in *Problem of the Century: Racial Stratification in the United States*, edited by Elijah Anderson and Douglas S. Massey. New York: Russell Sage Foundation.

Furstenberg, Frank F., Jr., with Alisa Belzer, Colleen Davis, Judith A. Levine, Kristine Morrow, and Mary Washington. 1993. "How Families Manage Risk and Opportunity in Dangerous Neighborhoods." Pp. 231–58 in *Sociology and the Public Agenda*, edited by William Julius Wilson. London, U.K.: Sage Publications.

Furstenberg Frank F., Jr., Thomas D. Cook, Jacquelynne Eccles, Glen H. Elder, Jr., and Arnold Sameroff. 1999. *Managing to Make It: Urban Families and Adolescent Success*. Chicago: University of Chicago Press.

Gans, Herbert J. 1995. *The War against the Poor: The Underclass and Antipoverty Policy*. New York: BasicBooks.

Garin, Geoffrey, Guy Molyneux, and Linda DiVall. 1994. "Public Attitudes toward Welfare Reform." *Social Policy* 25: 44–49.

Gibson, Keegan. 2013. "Defending Jobs Numbers, Corbett Cites Drug Test Failures." April 30, www.politicspa.com.

Gilbert, Dennis L. 2011. *The American Class Structure in an Age of Growing Inequality.* 8th edition. Los Angeles: Pine Forge Press.

Gilens, Martin. 1999. *Why Americans Hate Welfare: Race, Media, and the Politics of Antipoverty Policy.* Chicago: University of Chicago Press.

Goldberg, Michelle. 2004. "Down and Out and on the Move." *Salon.* August 5, www.economichumanrights.org.

Goldfarb, Zachary A., and Michelle Boorstein. 2013. "Pope Francis Denounces 'Trickle-Down' Economic Theories in Sharp Criticism of Inequality." November 26, www.washingtonpost.com.

Goldsmith, Julie D. 1998. "Working the System: Clients' Use and Experience of Social Welfare Institutions in Philadelphia, 1940 to the Present." Ph.D. dissertation, University of Pennsylvania.

Goode, Judith, and Robert T. O'Brien. 2006. "Whose Social Capital? How Economic Development Projects Disrupt Local Social Relations." Pp. 159–176 in *Social Capital in the City: Community and Civic Life in Philadelphia*, edited by Richardson Dilworth. Philadelphia: Temple University Press.

Goodman, Peter S. 2010. "After Training, Still Scrambling for Employment." July 18, www.nytimes.com.

Gould, Elise, and Alyssa Davis. 2015. "Families as They Really Are: Persistent Poverty's Largest Cause Is Inequality, Not Family Structure." August 10, www.thesocietypages.org.

Gould, Elise, Alyssa Davis, and Will Kimball. 2015. "Broad-Based Wage Growth Is a Key Tool in the Fight against Poverty." *Economic Policy Institute*, www.epi.org.

Gouldner, Alvin W. 1960. "The Norm of Reciprocity: A Preliminary Statement." *American Sociological Review* 25(2): 161–178.

Granovetter, Mark. 1973. "The Strength of Weak Ties." *American Journal of Sociology* 78 (6): 1360–1380.

———. [1974] 1995. *Getting a Job: A Study of Contacts and Careers.* Chicago: University of Chicago Press.

Grasgreen, Allie. 2015. "Barack Obama Pushes For-Profit Colleges to the Brink." July 1, www.politico.com.

Gross, Joan, and Nancy Rosenberger. 2010. "The Double Binds of Getting Food among the Poor in Rural Oregon." *Food, Culture, and Society* 13 (1): 47–70.

Gutiérrez, Lorraine Margot, and Edith Anne Lewis. 1999. *Empowering Women of Color.* New York: Columbia University Press.

Hacker, Jacob S. 2004. "Privatizing Risk without Privatizing the Welfare State: The Hidden Politics of Social Policy Retrenchment in the United States." *American Political Science Review* 98 (2): 243–260.

———. 2008. *The Great Risk Shift: The New Economic Insecurity and the Decline of the American Dream.* Revised and expanded edition. New York: Oxford University Press.

Hacker, Jacob S., and Paul Pierson. 2010. *Winner-Take-All Politics: How Washington Made the Rich Richer—and Turned Its Back on the Middle Class*. New York: Simon & Schuster.

Hamblin, James. 2015. "The Paradox of Effort: A Medical Case against Too Much Self-Control." July 16, www.theatlantic.com.

Hamilton, Gayle, and Judith M. Gueron. 2002. "The Role of Education and Training in Welfare Reform." April, www.brookings.edu.

Hamilton, Gayle, and Susan Scrivener. 2012. "Facilitating Postsecondary Education and Training for TANF Recipients." Brief # 07. *Urban Institute*. March, www.urban.org.

Handler, Joel F., and Yeheskel Hasenfeld. 1997. *We the Poor People: Work, Poverty, and Welfare*. New Haven, Conn.: Yale University Press.

Hannerz, Ulf. 1969. *Soulside: Inquiries into Ghetto Culture and Community*. New York: Columbia University Press.

Hansen, Karen V. 2004. "The Asking Rules of Reciprocity in Networks of Care for Children." *Qualitative Sociology* 27 (4): 421–437.

———. 2005. *Not-So-Nuclear Families: Class, Gender, and Networks of Care*. New Brunswick, N.J.: Rutgers University Press.

Harknett, Kristen. 2006. "The Relationship between Private Safety Nets and Economic Outcomes among Single Mothers." *Journal of Marriage and Family* 68 (1): 172–191.

Harris, Deborah A., and Jamilatu Zakari. 2015. "Neo-Liberalism and Private Emergency Food Networks." Pp. 307–315 in *The Routledge Handbook of Poverty in the United States*, edited by Stephen Nathan Haymes, María Vidal de Haymes, and Reuben Jonathan Miller. New York: Routledge.

Harvey, David. 2005. *A Brief History of Neoliberalism*. New York: Oxford University Press.

Haxton, Clarisse L., and Kristen Harknett. 2009. "Racial and Gender Differences in Kin Support." *Journal of Family Issues* 30: 1019–1040.

Hays, Sharon. 2003. *Flat Broke with Children: Women in the Age of Welfare Reform*. New York: Oxford University Press.

Heckman, James J., John Eric Humphries, and Nicholas S. Mader. June 2011. "The GED." *Handbook of the Economics of Education*. Vol. 3 (2). Edited by Erik Hanushek, Stephen Machin, and Ludger Woessmann. Philadelphia: Elsevier.

Henderson, Tim. 2015. "Attacking Homelessness with 'Rapid Rehousing.'" April 21, www.pewtrusts.org.

Henly, Julia R. 2002. "Informal Support Networks and the Maintenance of Low-Wage Jobs." Pp. 179–203 in *Laboring below the Line: The New Ethnography of Poverty, Low-Wage Work, and Survival in the Global Economy*, edited by Frank Munger. New York: Russell Sage Foundation.

Henly, Julia R., Sandra K. Danziger, and Shira Offer. 2005. "The Contribution of Social Support to the Material Well-Being of Low-Income Families." *Journal of Marriage and Family* 67 (1): 122–140.

Hertz, Rosanna, and Faith I. T. Ferguson. 1997. "Kinship Strategies and Self-Sufficiency among Single Mothers by Choice: Post Modern Family Ties." *Qualitative Sociology* 20: 187–209.

Hochschild, Jennifer L. 1995. *Facing Up to the American Dream: Race, Class, and the Soul of the Nation*. Princeton: Princeton University Press.

Hofferth, Sandra L. 1984. "Kin Networks, Race, and Family Structure." *Journal of Marriage and the Family* 46: 791–806.

Hofferth, Sandra L., Johanne Boisjoly, and Greg J. Duncan. 1999. "The Development of Social Capital." *Rationality and Society* 11 (1): 79–110.

Hogan, Dennis P., David J. Eggebeen, and Clifford C. Clogg. 1993. "The Structure of Intergenerational Exchange in American Families." *American Journal of Sociology* 98: 1428–1458.

Hogan, Dennis P., Ling-Xin Hao, and William L. Parish. 1990. "Race, Kin Networks, and Assistance to Mother-Headed Families." *Social Forces* 68: 797–812.

Holeywell, Ryan. 2013. "Which State, Local Grants Got Cut in Obama's 2014 Budget?" *Governing the States and Localities*. April 12, www.governing.com.

Holley, Peter, and Elahe Izadi. 2015. "Kansas Bans Welfare Recipients from Seeing Movies, Going Swimming on Government's Dime." April 6, www.washingtonpost.com.

Honkala, Cheri, Richard Goldstein, Elizabeth Thul, William Baptist, and Patrick Grugan. 1999. "Globalisation and Homelessness in the USA: Building a Social Movement to End Poverty." *Development in Practice* 9 (5): 526–538.

Hotez, Peter J. 2014. "Neglected Infections of Poverty in the United States and Their Effects on the Brain." *Journal of American Medical Association Psychiatry* 71 (10): 1099–1100, www.archpsyc.jamanetwork.com.

"HUD House Occupied." October 1999. *Progressive* 63 (10): 16.

Hulse, Carl. 2009. "Bill Changing Credit Card Rules Is Sent to Obama with Gun Measure Included." May 20, www.nytimes.com.

Institute for College Access & Success. 2014. *Quick Facts about Student Debt*. ticas.org.

Jacobs, Jane. 1961. *The Death and Life of Great American Cities*. New York: Random House.

Jacoby, Tamar. 2014. "The Euro-Apprentice." Weekly Wonk. October 16, weeklywonk. newamerica.net.

Jencks, Christopher. 1992. *Rethinking Social Policy: Race, Poverty, and the Underclass*. New York: Harper Perennial.

Jeroslow, Phyllis. 2015. "Creating a Sustainable Society: Human Rights in the U.S. Welfare State." Pp. 559–566 in *The Routledge Handbook of Poverty in the United States*, edited by Stephen Nathan Haymes, María Vidal de Haymes, and Reuben Jonathan Miller. New York: Routledge.

Jewell, Jennifer R. 2015. "Too Legit to Quit: Gaining legitimacy through Human Rights Organizing." Pp. 522–530 in *The Routledge Handbook of Poverty in the United States*, edited by Stephen Nathan Haymes, María Vidal de Haymes, and Reuben Jonathan Miller. New York: Routledge.

Kahne, Hilda, and Zachary Mabel. 2010. "Single Mothers and Other Low Earners: Policy Routes to Adequate Wages." *Poverty and Public Policy* 2 (3): article 7.

Kamenetz, Anya. 2015. "The Forces behind the Decline of For-Profit Colleges." *NPRed: How Learning Happens*. June 8, www.npr.org.

Katz, Michael B. 1983. *Poverty and Policy in American History.* New York: Academic Press.

———. 1986. *In the Shadow of the Poorhouse: A Social History of Welfare in America.* New York: Basic Books.

———. 1989. *The Undeserving Poor: From the War on Poverty to the War on Welfare.* New York: Pantheon Books.

Kennedy, Bruce. 2015. "America's 11 Poorest Cities." *MoneyWatch.* February 18, www.cbsnews.com.

King, Martin Luther, Jr. 1968. "Remaining Awake through a Great Revolution." Delivered at the National Cathedral, Washington, D.C., on 31 March 1968. *Congressional Record.* April 9, 1968. Martin Luther King, Jr. Research and Education Institute, www.mlkkpp01.stanford.edu.

Klinenberg, Eric. 2002. *Heat Wave: A Social Autopsy of Disaster in Chicago.* Chicago: University of Chicago Press.

Kluegel, James R., and Eliot R. Smith. 1986. *Beliefs about Inequality: Americans' Views of What Is and What Ought to Be.* New York: Aldine de Gruyter.

Kornbluh, Felicia. 2007. *The Battle for Welfare Rights: Politics and Poverty in Modern America.* Philadelphia: University of Pennsylvania Press.

Kristof, Nicholas. 2015. "It's Not Just about Bad Choices." June 13, www.nytimes.com.

Krueger, Alan B. 2005. "Inequality, Too Much of a Good Thing." Pp 1–75 in *Inequality in America: What Role for Human Capital Policies?* edited by James J. Heckman and Alan B. Krueger. Cambridge, Mass.: MIT Press.

Labaton, Stephen. 2009. "Obama Pressures Credit Card Issuers on Rates." April 23, www.nytimes.com.

Lachman, Samantha. 2014. "GOP Senate Candidate Likens Food Stamp Recipients to Wild Animals." May 1, www.huffingtonpost.com.

Lambert, Susan J., Peter J. Fugiel, and Julia R. Henly. 2014. "Precarious Work Schedules among Early-Career Employees in the U.S.: A National Snapshot." *Employment Instability, Family Well-Being, and Social Policy Network.* University of Chicago, www.ssascholars.uchicago.edu.

Lamont, Michèle. 1992. *Money, Morals, and Manners: The Culture of the French and American Upper-Middle Class.* Chicago: University of Chicago Press.

———. 2000. *The Dignity of Working Men: Morality and the Boundaries of Race, Class, and Immigration.* New York: Russell Sage Foundation.

Lamont, Michèle, and Marcel Fournier, eds. 1992. *Cultivating Differences: Symbolic Boundaries and the Making of Inequality.* Chicago: University of Chicago Press.

Lareau, Annette. 2003. *Unequal Childhoods: Class, Race, and Family Life.* Berkeley: University of California Press.

Lavee, Einat, and Shira Offer. 2012. "'If You Sit and Cry No One Will Help You': Understanding Perceptions of Worthiness and Social Support Relations among Low-Income Women under a Neoliberal Discourse." *Sociological Quarterly* 53 (3): 374–393.

Lee, Yean-Ju, and Isik A. Aytac. 1998. "Intergenerational Financial Support among Whites, African Americans, and Latinos." *Journal of Marriage and the Family* 60 (2): 426–441.

Lemann, Nicholas. 2015. "Unhappy Days for America." May 21, www.nybooks.com.

Leonhardt, David. 2005. "The College Dropout Boom," in Class Matters. *New York Times*. May 24, www.nytimes.com.

Lepore, Jill. 2015. "Richer and Poorer: Accounting for inequality." March 16, www.newyorker.com.

Levin, Josh. 2013. "The Real Story of Linda Taylor, America's Original Welfare Queen." December 19, www.slate.com.

Levine, Judith. 2013. *Ain't No Trust: How Bosses, Boyfriends, and Bureaucrats Fail Low-Income Mothers and Why It Matters*. Berkeley: University of California Press.

Levi-Strauss, Claude. 1969. *The Elementary Structures of Kinship*, translated by J. Bell von Sturmer and R. Needham. Boston: Beacon Press.

Levitan, Sar A. 1969. "The Community Action Program: A Strategy to Fight Poverty." *Annals of the American Academy of Political and Social Science* 385 (1): 63–75.

Lew, Jacob. 2011. "The Easy Cuts Are Behind Us." February 5, www.nytimes.com.

Liebow, Elliot. 1967. *Tally's Corner: A Study of Negro Streetcorner Men*. Boston: Little, Brown.

Lifson, Thomas. 2011. "Community Service Block Grants Spared Much Pain in 2011 Budget Deal." April 13, www.americanthinker.com.

Lin, Nan. 1999. "Building a Network Theory of Social Capital." *Connections* 22 (1): 28–51.

———. 2001a. "Building a Network Theory of Social Capital." Pp. 3–30 in *Social Capital Theory and Research*, edited by Nan Lin, Karen Cook, and Ronald S. Burt. New York: Aldine de Gruyter.

———. 2001b. *Social Capital: A Theory of Structure and Action*. Cambridge: Cambridge University Press.

Lubrano, Alfred. 2014. "Phila. Rates Highest among Top 10 Cities for Deep Poverty." September 26, www.articles.philly.com.

Luxton, Meg. 2010. "Doing Neoliberalism: Perverse Individualism in Personal Life." Pp. 163–183 in *Neoliberalism and Everyday Life*, edited by Susan Braedley and Meg Luxton. Montreal, Quebec: McGill-Queen's University Press.

Macleod, Jay. 2008. *Ain't No Makin' It: Aspirations and Attainment in a Low-Income Neighborhood*. 3rd edition. Boulder, Colo.: Westview Press.

Marcus, Seth R. 2006. "Community Development Block Grants." In *Encyclopedia of American Urban History*, edited by David R. Goldfield. New York: Russell Sage Foundation.

Marwell, Nicole P. 2007. *Bargaining for Brooklyn: Community Organizations in the Entrepreneurial City*. Chicago: University of Chicago Press.

Marwell, Nicole P., and Michael McQuarrie. 2013. "People, Place, and System: Organizations and the Renewal of Urban Social Theory." *ANNALS of the American Academy of Political and Social Science* 647 (1): 126–143.

Massey, Douglas S. 2007. *Categorically Unequal: The American Stratification System.* New York: Russell Sage Foundation.

Massey, Douglas S., and Nancy A. Denton. 1993. *American Apartheid: Segregation and the Making of the Underclass.* Cambridge, Mass: Harvard University Press.

Mazelis, Joan Maya. 2015. "'I Got to Try to Give Back': How Reciprocity Norms in a Poor People's Organization Influence Members' Social Capital." *Journal of Poverty* 19 (1): 109–131.

Mazelis, Joan Maya, and Brendan M. Gaughan. 2015. "*We Are the 99 Percent*: The Rise of Poverty and the Decline of Poverty Stigma." Pp. 161–169 in *Handbook of Poverty in the United States*, edited by Stephen Nathan Haymes, María Vidal de Haymes, and Reuben Jonathan Miller. New York: Routledge.

Mazelis, Joan Maya, and Laryssa Mykyta. 2011. "Relationship Status and Activated Kin Support: The Role of Need and Norms." *Journal of Marriage and Family* 73 (2): 430–445.

McCall, Leslie. 2013. *The Undeserving Rich: American Beliefs about Inequality, Opportunity, and Redistribution.* Cambridge, U.K.: Cambridge University Press.

McCoy, Sean. 2015. "The American Dream Is Suffering, but Americans Are Satisfied: 15 Charts." July 1, www.theatlantic.com.

McDonald, Katrina Bell, and Elizabeth M. Armstrong. 2001. "De-Romanticizing Black Intergenerational Support: The Questionable Expectations of Welfare Reform." *Journal of Marriage and Family* 63 (1): 213–223.

McDonald, Soraya Nadia. 2014. "Shanesha Taylor, Arrested for Leaving Children in Car during Job Interview, Speaks." June 23, www.washingtonpost.com.

Media Matters Staff. 2013. "Hannity Compares Individuals on Government Programs to Animals That Become Dependent on People for Food." January 3, www.media-matters.org.

Mendenhall, Ruby, Kathryn Edin, Susan Crowley, Jennifer Sykes, Laura Tach, Katrin Kriz, and Jeffrey R. Kling. 2012. "The Role of Earned Income Tax Credit in the Budgets of Low-Income Households." *Social Service Review* 86 (3): 367–400.

Menjívar, Cecilia. 2000. *Fragmented Ties: Salvadoran Immigrant Networks in America.* Berkeley: University of California Press.

Mishel, Lawrence. 2013. "Declining Value of the Federal Minimum Wage Is a Major Factor Driving Inequality." Economic Policy Institute: Research and Ideas for Shared Prosperity. February 21, www.epi.org.

Molm, Linda D. 2010. "The Structure of Reciprocity." *Social Psychology Quarterly* 73 (2): 119–131.

Molm, Linda D., Nobuyuki Takahashi, and Gretchen Peterson. 2000. "Risk and Trust in Social Exchange: An Experiment of a Classical Proposition." *American Journal of Sociology* 105 (5): 1396–1427.

Mullainathan, Sendhil, and Eldar Shafir. 2013. *Scarcity: Why Having Too Little Means So Much.* New York: Times Books.

National Alliance to End Homelessness. 2014. "Cost of Homelessness," www.endhome-lessness.org.

———. 2015. "FY 2016 Appropriations: HUD Homeless Assistance Grants." February 3, www.endhomelessness.org.

National Conference of State Legislatures. 2016. "State Minimum Wages: 2016 Minimum Wage by State." April 14, http://www.ncsl.org.

Nelson, Margaret K. 2000. "Single Mothers and Social Support: The Commitment to, and Retreat from, Reciprocity." *Qualitative Sociology* 23 (3): 291–317.

———. 2002. "The Challenge of Self-Sufficiency. Women on Welfare Redefining Independence." *Journal of Contemporary Ethnography* 31 (5): 582–614.

———. 2005. *The Social Economy of Single Motherhood: Raising Children in Rural America*. New York: Routledge.

Newman, Katherine S. 1999. *No Shame in My Game: The Working Poor in the Inner City*. New York: Vintage Books.

New York Times. 2005. *Class Matters*. New York: Times Books. Also available online at www.nytimes.com.

———. 2012. "Affluent Students Have an Advantage and the Gap Is Widening." December 22, www.nytimes.com.

Nixon, Richard. 1969. "Special Message to the Congress on Reform of the Nation's Welfare System." *American Presidency Project*. August 11, www.presidency.ucsb.edu.

Offer, Shira. 2010. "Agency-Based Support: A 'Last-Resort' Strategy for Low-Income Families?" *Social Science Quarterly* 91 (1): 284–300.

———. 2012a. "Barriers to Social Support among Low-Income Mothers." *International Journal of Sociology and Social Policy* 32 (3): 120–133.

———. 2012b. "The Burden of Reciprocity: Processes of Exclusion and Withdrawal from Personal Networks among Low-Income Families." *Current Sociology* 60 (6): 788–805.

Offer, Shira, Sarit Sambol, and Orly Benjamin. 2010. "Learning to Negotiate Network Relations: Social Support among Working Mothers Living in Poverty." *Community, Work & Family* 13 (4): 467–482.

Page, Benjamin I., and Lawrence R. Jacobs. 2009. *Class War? What Americans Really Think about Economic Inequality*. Chicago: University of Chicago Press.

Perriello, Pat. 2013. "Pope Francis on Capitalism." December 11, www.ncronline.org.

Phan Mai B., Nadine Blumer, and Erin I. Demaiter. 2009. "Helping Hands: Neighborhood Diversity, Deprivation, and Reciprocity of Support in Non-Kin Networks." *Journal of Social and Personal Relationships* 26 (6–7): 899–918.

Philadelphia City Planning Commission. 2013. "City of Philadelphia Planning Districts and Geographic Assignments for Planning Division Staff," www.phila.gov.

Piven, Frances Fox, and Richard A. Cloward. 1993. *Regulating the Poor: The Functions of Public Welfare*. New York: Vintage.

Portes, Alejandro. 1998. "Social Capital: Its Origins and Applications in Modern Sociology." *Annual Review of Sociology* 24: 1–24.

"Program Integrity: Gainful Employment-Debt Measures." 2011. *Federal Register: The Daily Journal of the United States Government*. June 13, www.federalregister.gov.

Putnam, Robert D. 2000. *Bowling Alone: The Collapse and Revival of American Community*. New York: Simon & Schuster.

———. 2015. *Our Kids: The American Dream in Crisis.* New York: Simon & Schuster.

Rainwater, Lee. 1970. *Behind Ghetto Walls: Black Families in a Federal Slum.* Chicago: Aldine.

Ralph, Laurence. 2014. *Renegade Dreams: Living through Injury in Gangland Chicago.* Chicago: University of Chicago Press.

Reese, Ellen. 2005. *Backlash against Welfare Mothers: Past and Present.* Berkeley: University of California Press.

Rehmann, Jan. 2015. "Hypercarceration: A Neoliberal Response to 'Surplus Population.'" *Rethinking Marxism* 27 (2): 303–311.

Robles, Frances. 2013. "Florida Law on Drug Tests for Welfare Is Struck Down." December 31, www.nytimes.com.

Roll, Susan, and Sue Steiner. 2015. "Returning to the Collective: New Approaches to Alleviating Poverty." Pp. 567–575 in *The Routledge Handbook of Poverty in the United States,* edited by Stephen Nathan Haymes, María Vidal de Haymes, and Reuben Jonathan Miller. New York: Routledge.

Roschelle, Anne R. 1997. *No More Kin: Exploring Race, Class, and Gender in Family Networks.* Thousand Oaks, Calif.: Sage.

Ross, Catherine E., John Mirowsky, and Shana Pribesh, S. 2001. "Powerlessness and the Amplification of Threat: Neighborhood Disadvantage." *American Sociological Review* 66: 568–591.

Rumberger, Russell. 2011. *Dropping Out: Why Students Drop Out of High School and What Can Be Done About It.* Cambridge, Mass.: Harvard University Press.

Sadeghi, Akbar. 2008. "The Births and Deaths of Business Establishments in the United States." *Monthly Labor Review* (December): 3–18, www.bls.gov.

Sahlins, Marshall D. 1972. *Stone Age Economics.* Hawthorne, N.Y.: Aldine de Gruyter.

Sampson, Robert J. 2000. "The Neighborhood Context of Investing in Children: Facilitating Mechanisms and Undermining Risks." Pp. 205–227 in *Securing the Future: Investing in Children from Birth to College,* edited by Sheldon Danziger and Jane Waldfogel. New York: Russell Sage Foundation.

———. 2012. *Great American City: Chicago and the Enduring Neighborhood Effect.* Chicago: University of Chicago Press.

Sampson, Robert J., Jeffrey D. Morenoff, and Felton Earls. 1999. "Beyond Social Capital: Spatial Dynamics of Collective Efficacy for Children." *American Sociological Review* 64: 633–660.

Sanchez, Claudio. 2012. "In Today's Economy, How Far Can a GED Take You?" February 18, www.npr.org.

Sarkisian, Natalia, Mariana Gerena, and Naomi Gerstel. 2007. "Extended Family Integration among Euro and Mexican Americans: Ethnicity, Gender, and Class." *Journal of Marriage & Family* 69 (1): 40–54.

Sarkisian, Natalia, and Naomi Gerstel. 2004. "Kin Support among Blacks and Whites: Race and Family Organization." *American Sociological Review* 69: 812–837.

Schnurer, Eric. 2013. "Just How Wrong Is Conventional Wisdom about Government Fraud?" August 15, www.theatlantic.com.

Schott, Liz. 2015. "Policy Basics: An Introduction to TANF." Center on Budget and Policy Priorities. June 15, www.cbpp.org.

Schulte, Brigid. 2013. "Rapid Rehousing: A New Way to Head Off Homelessness." August 18, www.washingtonpost.com.

Seccombe, Karen. 1999. *So You Think I Drive a Cadillac? Welfare Recipients' Perspectives on the System and Its Reform.* Boston, Mass.: Allyn and Bacon.

Seefeldt, Kristin S., and Heather Sandstrom. 2015. "When There Is No Welfare: The Income Packaging Strategies of Mothers without Earnings or Cash Assistance Following an Economic Downturn." *Russell Sage Foundation Journal of the Social Sciences* 1 (1): 139–158, www.rsfjournal.org.

Seinen, Ingrid, and Arthur Schram. 2006. "Social Status and Group Norms: Indirect Reciprocity in a Repeated Helping Experiment." *European Economic Review* 50: 581–602.

Sennett, Richard, and Jonathan Cobb. 1972. *The Hidden Injuries of Class.* New York: W. W. Norton.

Shaefer, H. Luke, and Kathryn Edin. 2013. "Rising Extreme Poverty in the United States and the Response of Federal Means-Tested Transfer Programs." *Social Service Review* 87 (2): 250–268.

Shaefer, H. Luke, Kathryn Edin, and Elizabeth Talbert. 2015. "Understanding the Dynamics of $2-a-Day Poverty in the United States." *Russell Sage Foundation Journal of the Social Sciences* 1 (1):120–138, www.rsfjournal.org.

Shea, Sandra. 2014. "Tapped Out: An Intimate Look at Hardship in Philly." May 12, www.philly.com.

Sherman, Jennifer. 2009. *Those Who Work, Those Who Don't: Poverty, Morality, and Family in Rural America.* Minneapolis: University of Minnesota Press.

———. 2013. "Surviving the Great Recession: Growing Need and the Stigamatized Safety Net." *Social Problems* 60 (4) 409–32.

Silva, Jennifer M. 2013. *Coming Up Short: Working-Class Adulthood in an Age of Uncertainty.* New York: Oxford University Press.

Skobba, Kimberly, Deirdre Oakley, and Dwanda Farmer. 2015. "Privatizing the Housing Safety Net: HOPE VI and the Transformation of Public Housing in the United States." Pp. 285–295 in *The Routledge Handbook of Poverty in the United States,* edited by Stephen Nathan Haymes, María Vidal de Haymes and Reuben Jonathan Miller. New York: Routledge.

Skocpol, Theda. 1992. *Protecting Soldiers and Mothers: The Political Origins of Social Policy in the United States.* Cambridge, Mass.: Belknap Press of Harvard University Press.

Small, Mario Luis. 2004. *Villa Victoria: The Transformation of Social Capital in a Boston Barrio.* Chicago and London: University of Chicago Press.

———. 2006. "Neighborhood Institutions as Resource Brokers: Childcare Centers, Interorganizational Ties, and Resource Access among the Poor." *Social Problems* 5 (2): 274–292.

———. 2008. "Lost in Translation: How Not to Make Qualitative Research More Scientific." Pp. 165–71 in *Workshop on Interdisciplinary Standards for Systematic Qualitative Research,* edited by Michèle Lamont and Patricia White. Washington, D.C.: National Science Foundation.

———. 2009a. "'How Many Cases Do I Need?' On Science and the Logic of Case Selection in Field Based Research." *Ethnography*. 10 (1): 5–38.

———. 2009b. *Unanticipated Gains: Origins of Network Inequality in Everyday Life.* New York: Oxford University Press.

Small, Mario Luis, and Scott W. Allard. 2013. "Reconsidering the Urban Disadvantaged: The Role of Systems, Institutions, and Organizations." *ANNALS of the American Academy of Political and Social Science* 647 (1): 6–20.

Small Business Administration. n.d. "What Are the Major Reasons for Small Business Failure?" www.sba.gov.

Smith, Sandra Susan. 2005. "'Don't Put My Name on It': Social Capital Activation and Job-Finding Assistance among the Black Urban Poor." *American Journal of Sociology* 111 (1): 1–57.

———. 2007. *Lone Pursuit: Distrust and Defensive Individualism among the Black Poor.* New York: Russell Sage Foundation.

Snow, David A., and Leon Anderson. 1993. *Down on Their Luck: A Study of Homeless People.* Berkeley: University of California Press.

Social Security Administration. n.d. "Supplemental Security Income (SSI) Benefits," www.ssa.gov.

Stack, Carol B. 1974. *All Our Kin: Strategies for Survival in a Black Community.* New York: Harper & Row.

"State Minimum Wages: 2015 Minimum Wage by State." 2015. *National Conference of State Legislatures.* June 30, www.ncsl.org.

Stern Smallacombe, Patricia. 2006. "Rootedness, Isolation, and Social Capital in an Inner-City White Neighborhood." Pp. 177–195 in *Social Capital in the City: Community and Civic Life in Philadelphia*, edited by Richardson Dilworth. Philadelphia: Temple University Press.

Stiglitz, Joseph E. 2012. *The Price of Inequality.* New York: W. W. Norton.

———. 2013. "The Great Divide: Inequality Is Holding Back the Recovery." January 19, www.opinionator.blogs.nytimes.com.

Strauss, Anselm, and Juliet Corbin. 1998. *Basics of Qualitative Research: Techniques and Procedures for Developing Grounded Theory.* 2nd edition. Thousand Oaks, Calif.: Sage.

Sum, Andrew, Ishwar Khatiwada, Mykhaylo Trubskyy, and Sheila Palma. 2012. "The Impacts of the GED Credential and Regular High School Diploma on the Employment, Unemployment, Weekly and Annual Earnings, and Income Experiences of Native-Born Adults (16–74) in the U.S. in 2000, 2009, and 2010." Center for Labor Market Studies, Northeastern University. June, www.lincs. ed.gov.

Tach, Laura, and Sarah Halpern-Meekin. 2014. "Tax Code Knowledge and Behavioral Responses among EITC Recipients: Policy Insights from Qualitative Data." *Journal of Policy Analysis and Management* 33 (2): 413–439.

"Tapped Out: A Timeline of Philadelphia Poverty through the 21st Century." n.d. www.philly.com.

Udesky, Laurie. 1991. "'Looks Like I Got Mad': Welfare Rights Activist Annie Smart Talks about Going on Welfare under Truman—and Fighting for Reform under Bush." *Southern Exposure* 19: 27–30.

Uehara. Edwina S. 1990. "Dual Exchange Theory, Social Networks, and Informal Social Support." *American Journal of Sociology* 96: 521–557.

———. 1995. "Reciprocity Reconsidered: Gouldner's 'Moral Norm of Reciprocity' and Social Support." *Journal of Social and Personal Relationships* 12 (4): 483–502.

U.S. Census Bureau. n.d. "Philadelphia County Quick Facts from the U.S. Census Bureau," www.quickfacts.census.gov.

U.S. Department of Agriculture. 2016a. "Supplemental Nutrition Assistance Program Participation and Costs (Data as of May 6, 2016)." Food and Nutrition Service, www.fns.usda.gov.

———. 2016b. "Women, Infants, and Children (WIC)." www.fns.usda.gov.

U.S. Department of Education. 2011. "Obama Administration Announces New Steps to Protect Students from Ineffective Career College Programs." June 2, www.ed.gov.

U.S. Department of Health and Human Services. n.d.a. "The 2005 HHS Poverty Guidelines: One Version of the [U.S.] Federal Poverty Measure," www.aspe.hhs.gov.

———. n.d.b. "The 2013 Poverty Guidelines: One Version of the [U.S.] Federal Poverty Measure," www.aspe.hhs.gov.

———. n.d.c. "The 2014 Poverty Guidelines: One Version of the [U.S.] Federal Poverty Measure," www.aspe.hhs.gov.

———. n.d.d. "About Community Services Block Grants." *Office of Community Services. An Office of the Administration for Children and Families*, www.acf.hhs.gov.

U.S. Department of Justice. 2005. Federal Bureau of Investigation. Uniform Crime Reporting Program. Crime in the United States: 2005. "Crime in the United States by Volume and Rate per 100,000 Inhabitants, 1986–2005," www2.fbi.gov.

———. n.d. Federal Bureau of Investigation. Uniform Crime Reporting Statistics, www.ucrdatatool.gov.

U.S. Department of Labor. 2013. "Changes in Basic Minimum Wages in Non-Farm Employment under State Law: Selected Years 1968 to 2013." Wage and Hour Division (WHD), www.dol.gov.

———. 2015. "Momentum Is Building to #RaisetheWage," www.dol.gov.

U.S. Social Forum. "What Is the U.S. Social Forum?" accessed November 5, 2014, www.ussocialforum.net.

Volsky, Igor. 2014. "Paul Ryan Blames Poverty on Lazy 'Inner City' Men." March 12, www.thinkprogress.org.

Walker, Darren. 2015. "What's Next for the Ford Foundation?" June 11, www.fordfoundation.org.

Warren, Mark R., J. Phillip Thompson, and Susan Saegert. 2001. "The Role of Social Capital in Combating Poverty." Pp. 1–28 in *Social Capital and Poor Communities*, edited by Susan Saegert, J. Phillip Thompson, and Mark R. Warren. New York: Russell Sage Foundation.

Watkins-Hayes, Celeste. 2009. *The New Welfare Bureaucrats: Entanglements of Race, Class, and Policy Reform*. Chicago: University of Chicago Press.

————. 2013. "The Micro Dynamics of Support Seeking: The Social and Economic Utility of Institutional Ties for HIV-Positive Women." *ANNALS of the American Academy of Political and Social Science* 647 (1): 83–101.

Weber, Max. 1905. *The Protestant Ethic and the Spirit of Capitalism.* Translated by Talcott Parsons, 1930 [1992, 2001]. New York: Routledge.

Weise, Karen. 2014a. "New Rules Put More For-Profit Colleges in a Warning 'Zone.'" October 31, www.bloomberg.com.

————. 2014b. "The Renewed Pushback against For-Profit College Rules." November 12, www.bloomberg.com.

Weissmann, Jordan. 2013. "This Chart Blows Up the Myth of the Welfare Queen." December 17, www.theatlantic.com.

————. 2015. "Forget Steak and Seafood: Here's How Welfare Recipients Actually Spend Their Money." April 15, www.slate.com.

Wellman, Barry. 1979. "The Community Question: The Intimate Networks of East Yorkers." *American Journal of Sociology* 84 (5): 1201–1231.

————. 1999. "From Little Boxes to Loosely Bounded Networks: The Privatization and Domestication of Community." Pp. 94–114 in *Sociology for the Twenty-First Century: Continuities and Cutting Edges*, edited by Janet L. Abu-Lughod. Chicago: University of Chicago Press.

White House. Office of the Press Secretary. 2013. "Remarks by the President on Economic Mobility." December 4, www.whitehouse.gov.

————. 2014a. "FACT SHEET: The Economic Case for Increasing the Minimum Wage: State by State Impact." March 19, www.whitehouse.gov.

————. 2014b. "Statement by the President on the 50th Anniversary of the War on Poverty." January 08, www.whitehouse.gov.

Willis, Paul. 1977. *Learning to Labor: How Working Class Kids Get Working Class Jobs.* New York: Columbia University Press.

Wilson, William Julius. 1987. *The Truly Disadvantaged: The Inner City, the Underclass, and Public Policy.* Chicago: University of Chicago Press.

————. 1991. "Studying Inner-City Social Dislocations: The Challenge of Public Agenda Research." *American Sociological Review* 56: 1–14.

————.1996.*WhenWorkDisappears:TheWorldoftheNewUrbanPoor*.NewYork:VintageBooks.

————. 2000. "Welfare, Children and Families: The Impact of Welfare Reform in the New Economy." Beth and Richard Sackler Lecture, University of Pennsylvania. October 6, Philadelphia, Pa.

————. 2001. "Jobless Poverty: A New Form of Social Dislocation in the Inner-City Ghetto." Pp. 651–660 in *Social Stratification: Class, Race, and Gender in Sociological Perspective*, edited by David B. Grusky. 2nd edition. Boulder, Colo.: Westview Press.

Yamagishi, Toshio, and Karen S. Cook. 1993. "Generalized Exchange and Social Dilemmas." *Social Psychological Quarterly* 56: 235–248.

Yellen, Janet. 2006. "Economic Inequality in the United States." *Federal Reserve Bank of San Francisco (FRBSF) Economic Letter, 2006-33-34*, December 1.

Zucchino, David. 1997. *Myth of the Welfare Queen.* New York: Touchstone.

INDEX

achievement ideology: advantages of believing in, 32–33, 52–53, 224n24; in American tradition, 20, 22, 180; compatible with reliance on kin ties, 10, 63–65; definition, 23; as a driver of policy, 7; health effects, 33; hindering social ties, 9, 23, 67, 89, 173; persistence among KWRU members, 21, 24, 90, 112; among poor people generally, 35; rejection by KWRU members, 10, 48–49, 92, 173, 224n34; rejection to protect sense of self, 33, 112, 224n24; among religious participants, 32; strengthened by a weakened private safety net, 4, 6

agency of individuals: belief that it has more power than structure, 21, 23, 32, 43, 46–54, 61–62, 63, 134, 140; belief in its power leading to avoiding asking for help, 61; belief in its power compatible with dependence on the state, 229n14; belief in its power leading to belief in the power of education, 57; definition, 29; power of as an aspect of the American Dream, 29; understanding that it exists within limited choices, 12, 18–19, 108, 110, 140, 172–73, 190, 243–4n30, 246n25. *See also* achievement ideology

Aid to Families with Dependent Children (AFDC). *See* welfare

alcoholism, of participants' parents, 3

Alice (KWRU member), 70, 82, 103, 108, 119, 134–35, 215

Alyssa, 55, 67, 82, 86, 98, 184, 192, 214, 241n2

Amanda (KWRU member), 134, 146, 167, 168, 215, 237n2

American Dream, the: belief among participants, 28, 29, 47; definition, 29, 30–31; disappointment in, 54, 183, 224n34; waning, 170; widespread belief among Americans, 30, 32, 35, 170–71, 180, 224n4

Anderson, Elijah, 80

Anderson, Leon, 35, 80

April, 71, 75, 79–80, 82–83, 88, 214

Armstrong, Elizabeth M., 241n3

Barro, John, 247n44

Bebe, 31, 37, 40, 41, 67, 86, 214, 224–25n18, 226n37

Beck, Ulrich, 171

Becky (KWRU member), 55, 95–96, 100, 115, 141, 157–58, 168, 215

Beezat, Robert, 189, 251–52n69

Betty, 1–3, 10–11, 16–17, 82, 86, 192, 214

Bianca, 38, 56, 187, 214, 253n10

Bourgois, Philippe, 35

brokerage: definition, 242–43n22; by KWRU, 24, 92, 100, 102, 103–4, 106, 118, 119, 157, 177–78, 242–43nn22, 23

Broughton, Chad, 81

Carmen (KWRU member), 72–3, 106–7, 111, 112, 115–16, 128, 134, 161–62, 168, 215, 236n20

Carole, 41, 47, 66, 99, 214, 253n10

ABOUT THE AUTHOR

Joan Maya Mazelis is Assistant Professor of Sociology in the Department of Sociology, Anthropology and Criminal Justice at Rutgers, the State University of New Jersey in Camden, New Jersey, and an affiliated scholar at Rutgers-Camden's Center for Urban Research and Education.